BONES OF TEXAS

BONES OF TEXAS

Photos and Stories from Bygone Places

MORGAN PAGE AND DUSTIN RICE

University of Texas Press *Austin*

Publication of this work was made possible in part by support from Clifton and Shirley Caldwell and a challenge grant from the National Endowment for the Humanities.

Printed in China.
First edition, 2026

♾ The paper used in this book meets the minimum requirements of ANSI/NISO Z39.48-1992 (R1997) (Permanence of Paper).

Cataloging-in-Publication Data is available from the Library of Congress

ISBN 978-1-4773-3446-1 (hardcover)
ISBN 978-1-4773-3447-8 (PDF)
ISBN 978-1-4773-3448-5 (ePub)

doi:10.7560/334461

The University of Texas Press gratefully acknowledges the Clifton and Shirley Caldwell Texas Heritage Endowment for its support of this publication.

This book is dedicated to our son, August.

CONTENTS

BONES OF TEXAS

INTRODUCTION

DUSTIN RICE

We had no grand plan for writing this book. The idea arose from a date, something to share between ourselves. We are a couple with different backgrounds and common interests. Morgan has a wealth of knowledge in, and a love for, photography and the arts. I have always loved Texas history and would visit historical sites and towns as opportunities arose. I am also interested in abandoned and forgotten places, always curious about who left them and why. So one day I asked Morgan if she wanted to go see a ghost town. Luckily for both of us, she said yes.

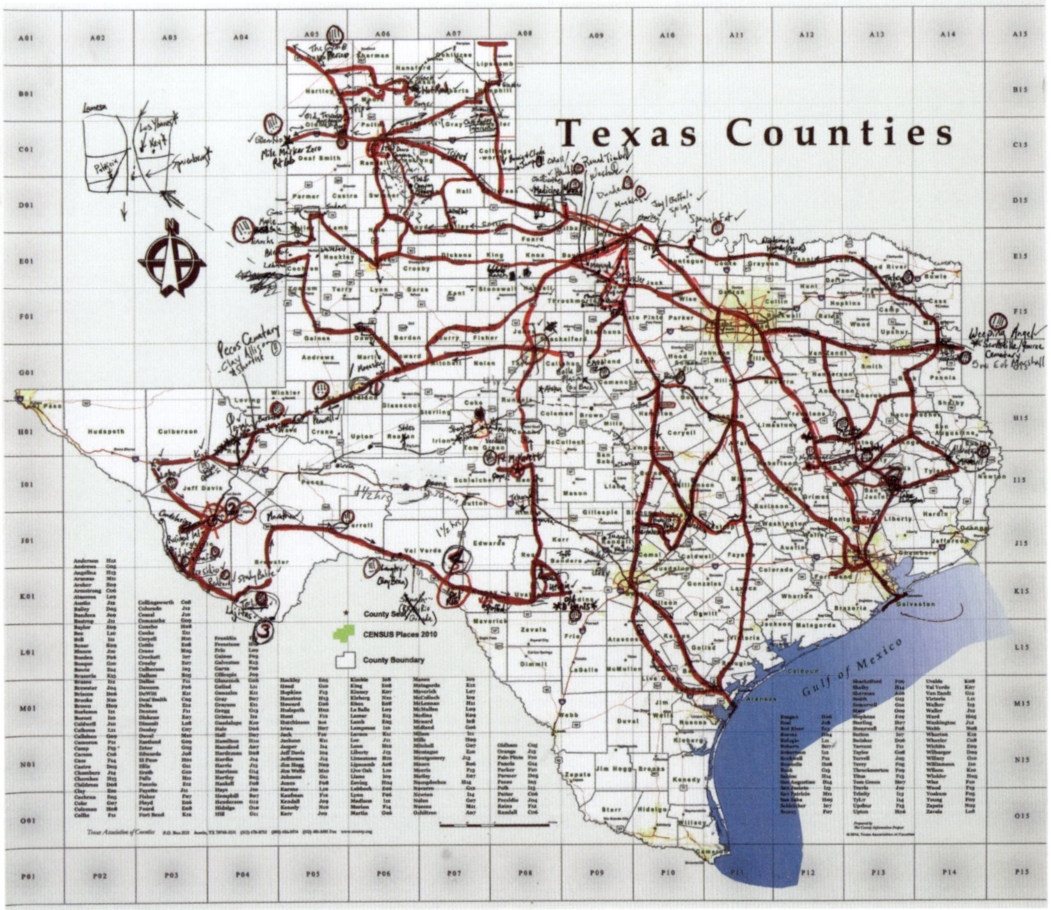

Map of our travels through the course of the project.

Spanish Fort is within an hour of Wichita Falls, where we lived at the time. My research revealed that the town was originally a Native American site where the area's Taovaya Indians traded with the French. Later, it became an important trading post for settlers of the Red River Valley. As a photographer, Morgan suggested we bring a couple of DSLRs on the trip. When we arrived, we found an old general store and schoolhouse still standing, just begging to be photographed. We were hooked, and I began researching other day trips we could take, always bringing our cameras along. One hour-long drive turned into another. Then we started going farther. I began to string towns together for day trips. We did overnight trips, then weekend-long trips, and it became a project that neither of us could help but be excited about.

Morgan became the driving force, pushing us further than I ever would have gone on my own. We started looking at our favorite photographs and realized we had a great subject that might have an audience. We sought to record the abandonment of these towns, to document places as they are and to leave them as unaffected by us as possible. In this way, we hoped to celebrate history by capturing what is left of it in our photographs. In reflecting on the work of Walker Evans, American photography critic Vicki Goldberg wrote in her book *Light Matters*, "Evans was exceptionally fine-tuned to the cruel radiance of what is." Cruel radiance abounds in these towns.

We have also been inspired by the photographers Dorothea Lange and Russell Lee, who were commissioned to compile a comprehensive record of American life from the 1930s to the 1940s as part of a Farm Security Administration (FSA) undertaking. That project had more than one focus, but the second phase concentrated on the lives of sharecroppers in the South as well as on migratory agricultural workers. We visited some of the same places as Lange and Lee, but attempted to capture the natural textures and patterns in each scene, now more visible without people in the frame, often creating a stark contrast between the dilapidation left behind and the still-thriving landscape around it.

Still, no matter how big the landscape, traces of humanity persist. It may be my love of history, or an innate need to animate these human-made places, but as our photos accumulated, we began writing people back into the project. It began in Fort McKavett, where a helpful guide told us how the former officers' quarters had burned down. It made me think about how certain stories don't qualify as history with a capital H, but are relegated to local lore. Some are even purposely swept under the rug in order to protect the overarching mythos of Texas. Those are the stories that interested us.

Seven years and thousands of miles into this endeavor, what we found is similar to much of Texas history: an immense and complicated combination of legend, fact, and myth. While we have invested hours upon hours in researching the stories that accompany some of the photos, neither of us has a background in historical research. Sometimes there is conflicting information, or information from only one side, making for a biased or even blatantly racist version of events. We've done the best we can, including sources for each story at the back of the book.

For a story to work in our project, though, we had to have more than a few solid facts. A person or event had to be traced to a place we visited. This may sound obvious, but I found out it wasn't. A place we've photographed may not have a colorful history or one that's traceable at all. That's why there aren't stories for every photo. The opposite was also true: Research provided a great story, but when we got to the area, there was nothing to photograph. This led to innumerable frustrations and lots of rewriting, but it also opened our eyes to things we never intended to explore. We have prioritized histories that were new to us, that surprised us and changed how we thought about Texas.

In the end, we decided to organize the stories chronologically. Where photos are directly related to a story, the photographs are in, or adjacent to, the story. Photos not directly tied to a story are placed where we felt they might have the most impact. (Geography buffs may notice that some photos were taken between sites of stories, as if we stopped along the way and snapped a photo—which, in some cases, we did.) All this is to say, the images are not as systematically placed as the stories are. Thank you for joining us in this very particular exploration of Texas.

We have met the entire spectrum of personalities that Texas offers. Often, there have been quizzical looks about what we are doing, usually followed by questions. Some of our best leads started with crazy looks. We've met self-appointed security guards that protect these abandoned places. They start off gruff, then soften when they understand why we came. The people have been one of the best surprises in a project about places without people.

Bones of Texas has been our dream come true. It has been a life-changing experience for the both of us. Joyous at times, scary at others, daunting and enlightening, frustrating and fascinating. We got married about halfway through it. Like our marriage, this project doesn't have an end in sight. We hope that our son shares our curiosity for the abandoned and joins the project he's grown up with.

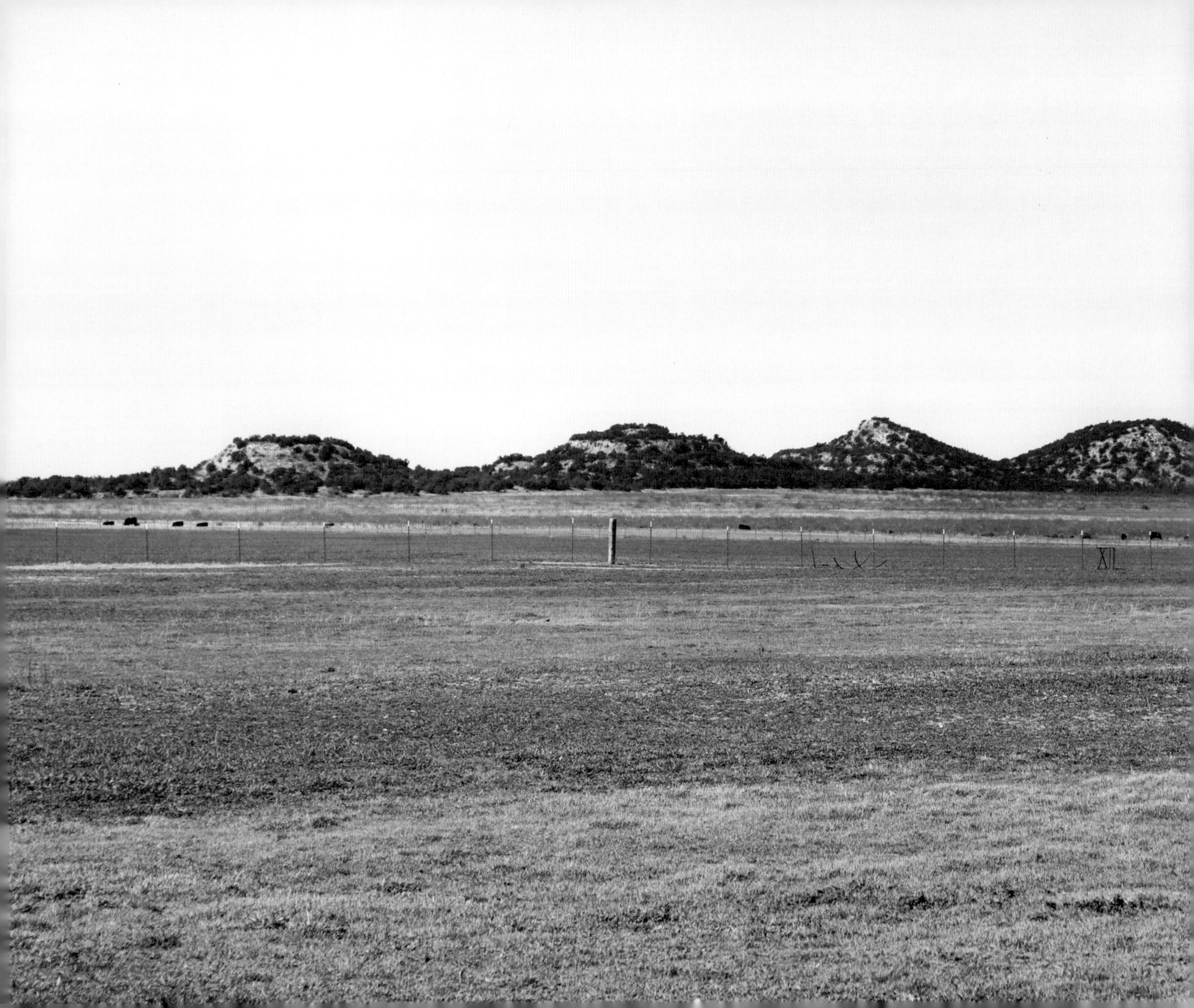

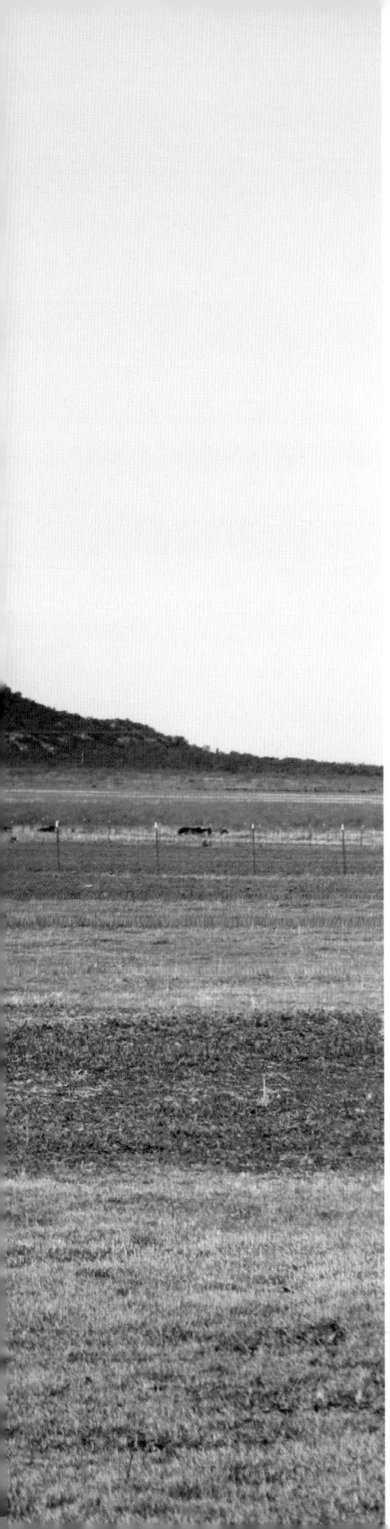

THE MOUNDS (PRECIVILIZATION)

DUSTIN RICE, WITH THE HELP OF LANCE TAHMAHKERA

One of the first places we visited as we started our project was a town called Medicine Mound. Not much remains: a store and a gas station sit at an intersection, and the red-brick walls of a school stand in the distance. About a mile to the west, though, are four rock outcroppings, each one larger than the one be side it. These are what the town was named for, though in the singular, Medicine Mound. They have remained unchanged for millennia and are sacred places for the Comanche people. Respected as a source of powerful medicine, they were used as a meeting spot and place of worship, as well as the gateway to the Comanche's winter fortress.

All four mounds. PHOTO BY DUSTIN RICE

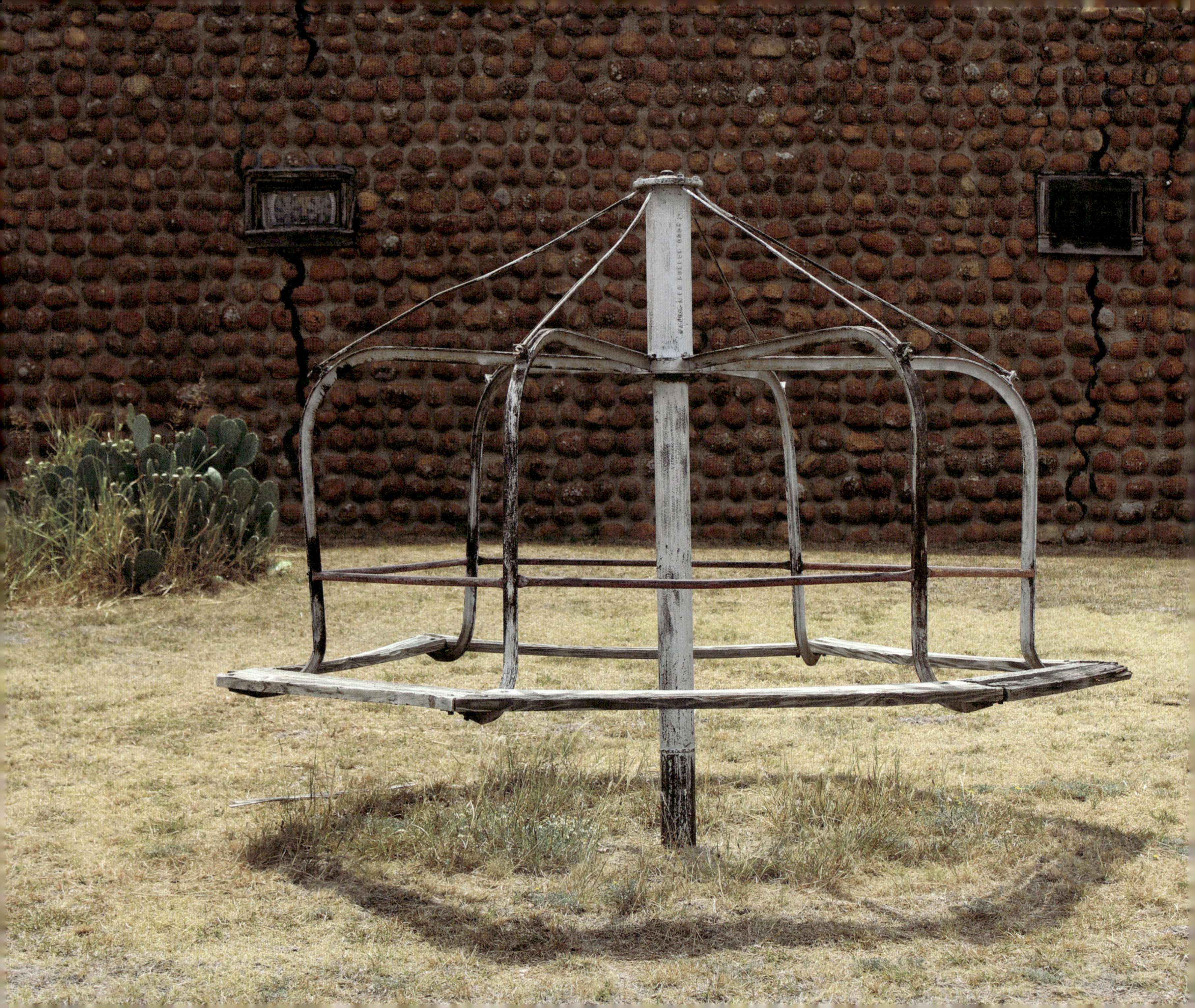

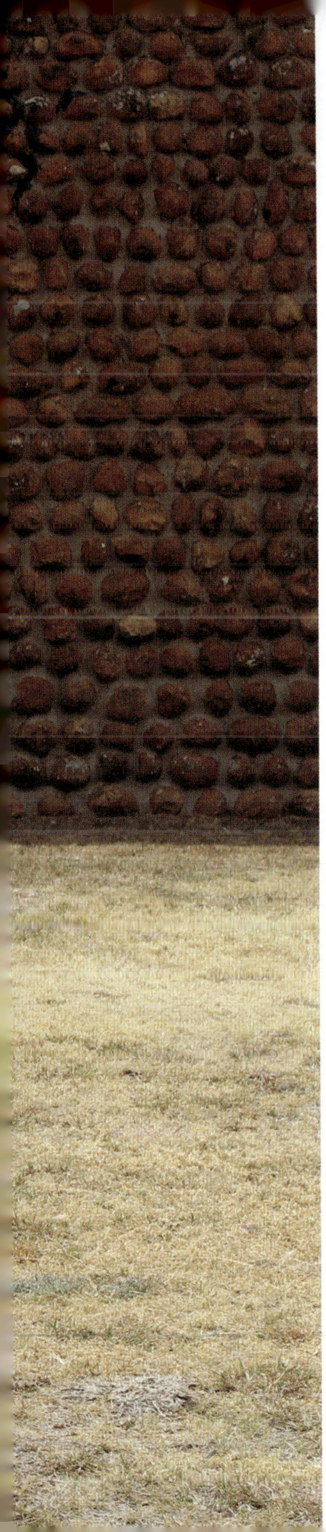

As we've presented our project at museums, conferences, cultural centers, and galleries, we've been fortunate to develop relationships with all kinds of Texas historians. Lance Tahmahkera is a great-great-grandson of Quanah Parker, the last chief of the Comanche. He is his family's historian and storyteller. We are proud to call him a friend, and over the years he has shared with us some of his people's experiences at the mounds.

Gypsum, a fine white powder, can be found at the base of the Big Mound, the tallest of the Medicine Mounds. Comanche warriors used to come to the mounds to collect the powder and make a paste that, when applied to their faces, reflected the moonlight on their nighttime raids. It lent a ghostly appearance that made an already menacing warrior look utterly terrifying. This was just one of the many reasons for the Comanche to visit the mounds. White sage, used by Plains tribes for thousands of years in purification ceremonies, grows in abundance there. Redberry juniper, which also grows there, is highly revered and is still used in modern-day rituals and blessings. Even the water was medicinal. Mineral springs used to bubble from the ground, and water taken from them was used to heal the sick. The water has since been diverted, and is used to fill cattle ponds.

According to Lance, the mounds were also part of the founding of the Native American Church. As the Comanche moved to reservations in the late 1800s, their leaders, Quanah, Isa-Tai, and Lone Wolf, began adapting Comanche religion to the Christianity they had been introduced to. This was a delicate process, as many Comanche had no desire to adopt the practices forced on them by Anglo settlers.

Lance explained that his family's oral traditions tell of a ceremony that was arranged atop the Big Mound, the tallest of the Medicine Mounds. The three leaders met there to discuss their beliefs. Peyote and the powerful visions it produces would have been used in combination with the scriptures of a typical Christian service. Lance noted that it was a warm day, and as details were agreed upon and the ceremony on the mound was ending, a cold wind blew from above, directly down on the three men. This was taken as a very good sign, and with that the ceremony was concluded.

The mounds and the land surrounding them have been sold several times; they are now part of a private ranch. The Comanche must seek permission to worship at their own sacred grounds, but the owner of the ranch is committed to protecting the mounds. The elders of the tribe all have his phone number, and he allows all tribal members access at any time. There is a celebration of the mounds every summer, and non-Comanche are welcome. Lance placed an arrow at the top of the Big Mound in 2021, and, while he couldn't attend in 2022, he was told that it still lay there, just as it had when the ceremony took place.

We never spoke to another soul the entire day on our first visit to Medicine Mound, but we have met some special people because we stopped there. It has provided professional relationships that have

Merry-go-round at Medicine Mound. PHOTO BY MORGAN PAGE

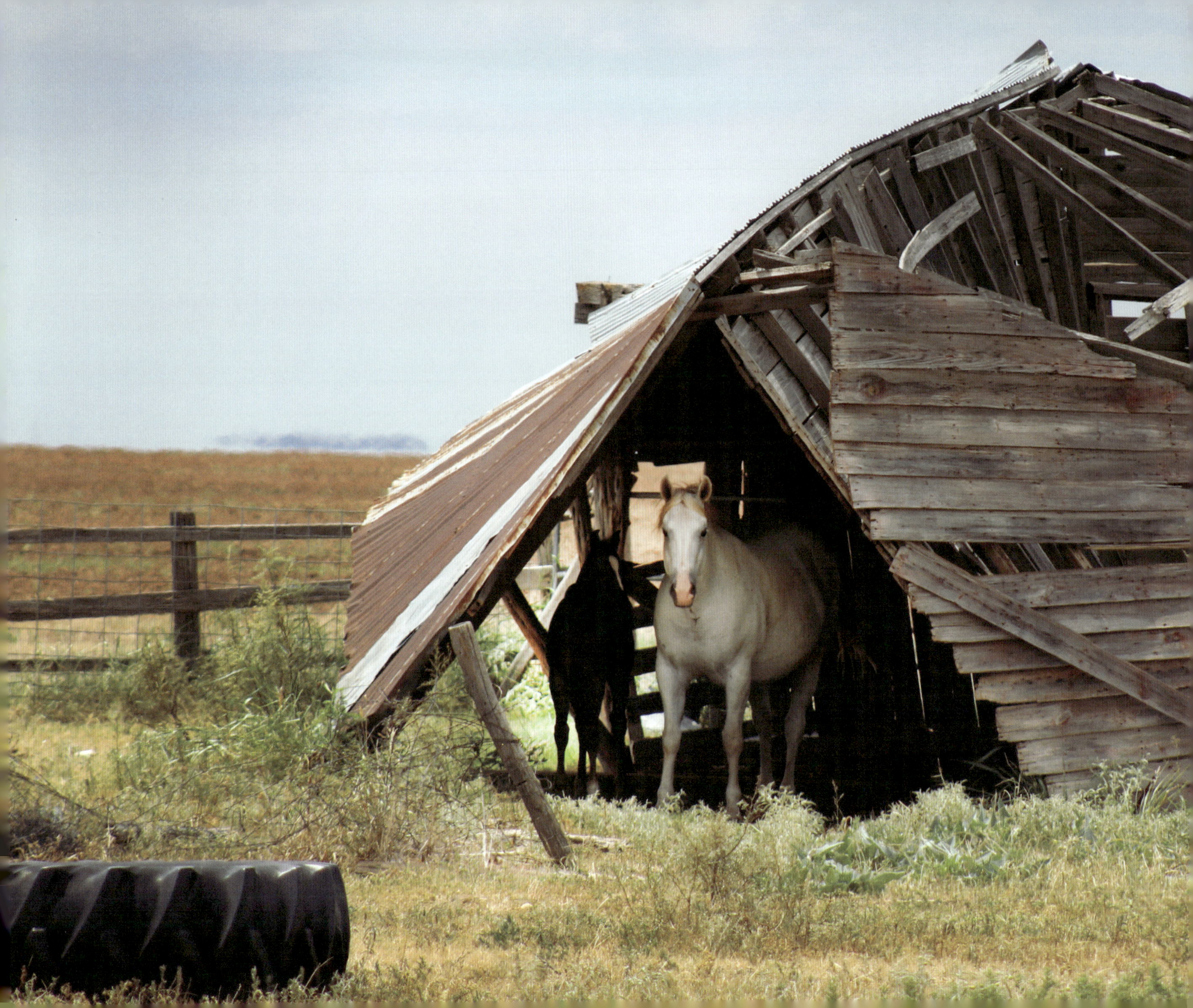

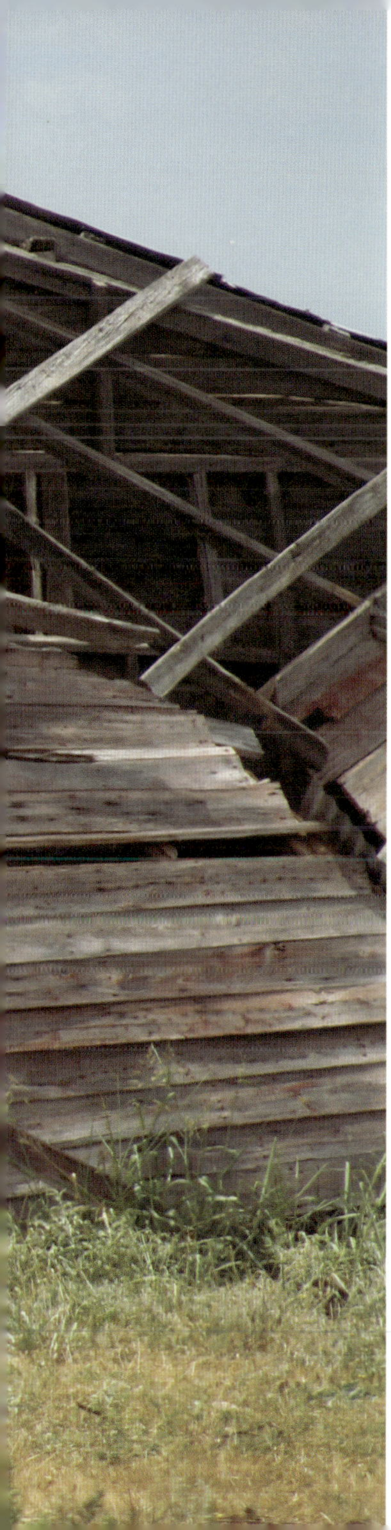

turned into friendships, helping us understand Comanche culture. That first day, though, I admit we didn't know as much about the Comanche as we do now. What we did know was that horses were essential to their lives. And we found some horses as we were leaving town that day. A mare and her foal were in their broken-down stable, which is now gone. Though it provided some shade on a hot day, it was a poignant sight.

Horses in barn at Medicine Mound. The barn is no longer standing. PHOTO BY MORGAN PAGE

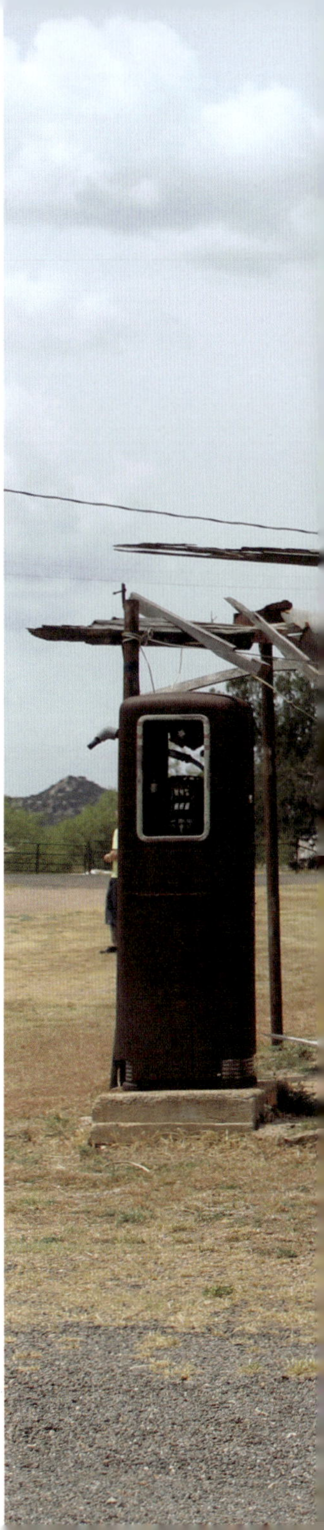

Abandoned gas station at Medicine Mound. PHOTO BY MORGAN PAGE

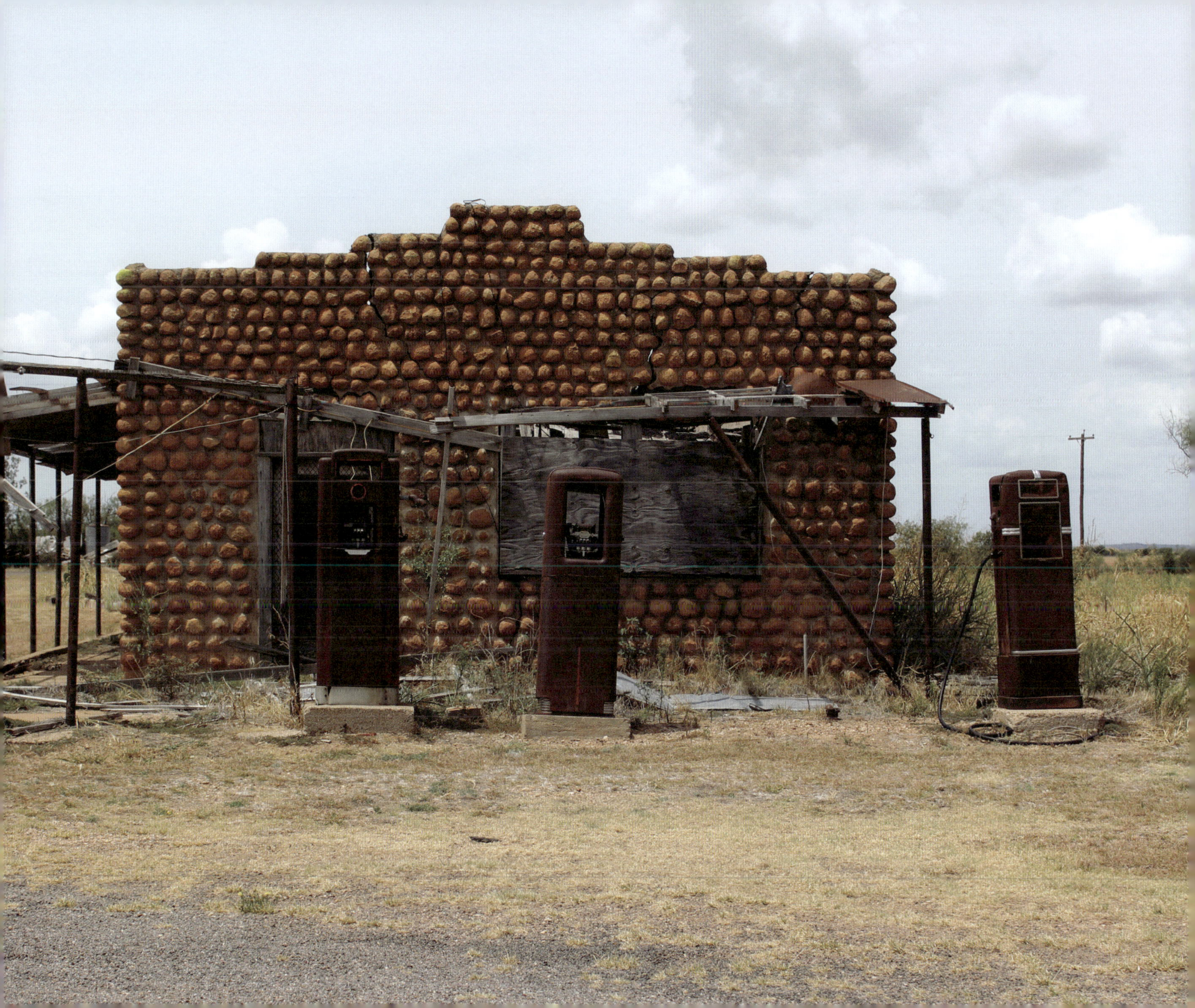

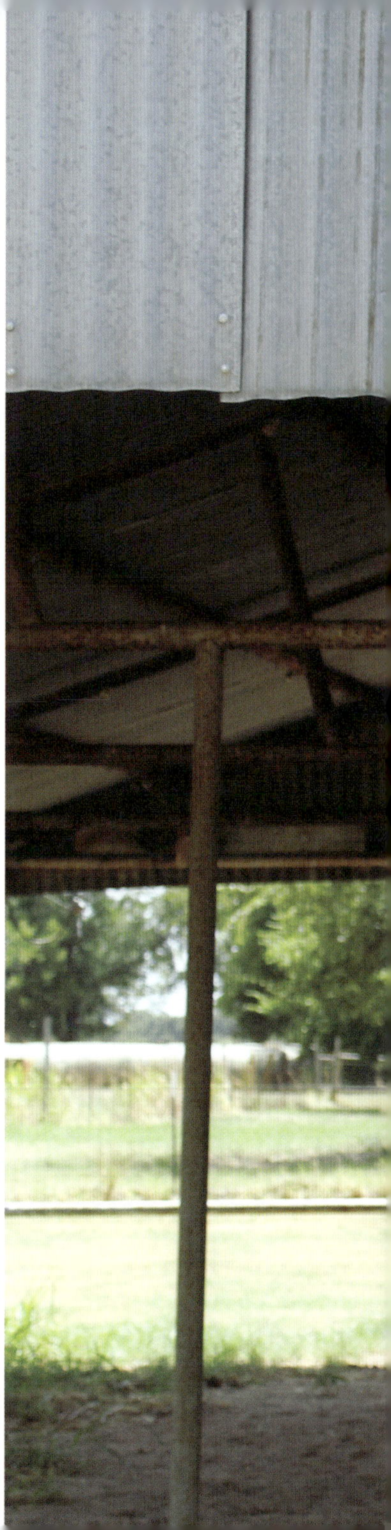

Spanish Fort Tabernacle. PHOTO BY MORGAN PAGE

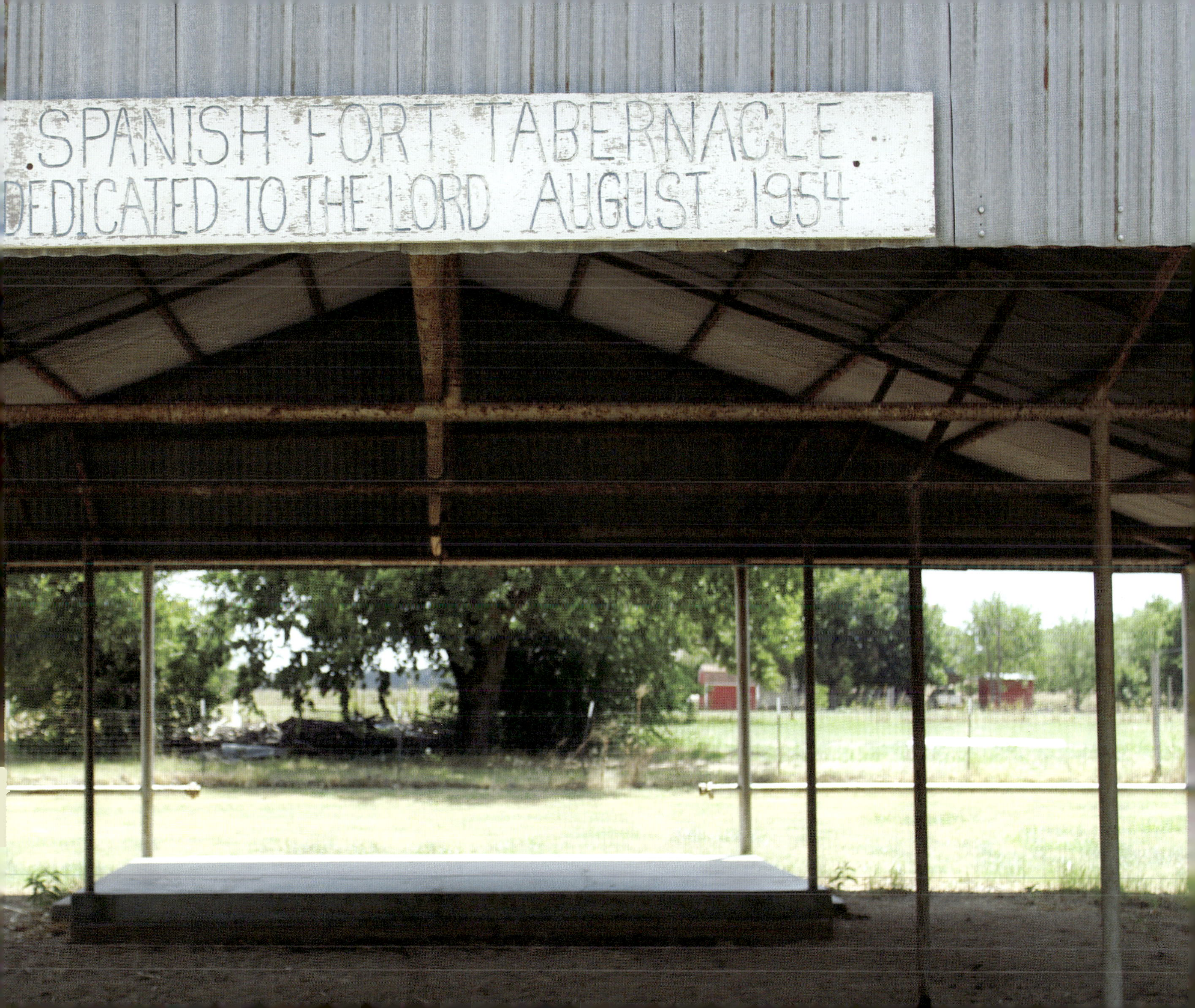
SPANISH FORT TABERNACLE
DEDICATED TO THE LORD AUGUST 1954

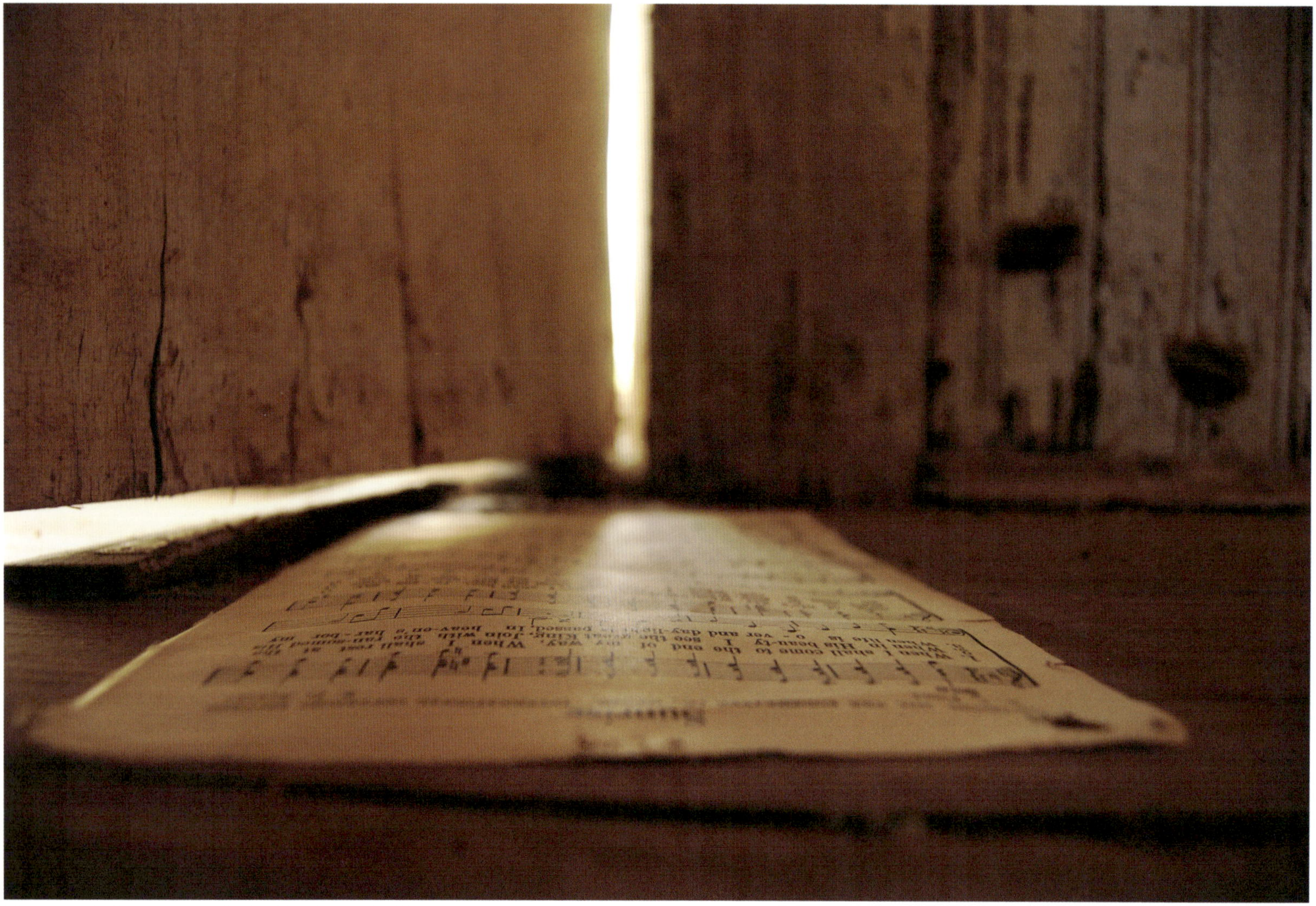

Hymn on the floor. First Methodist Church, est. 1909, Jermyn. PHOTO BY DUSTIN RICE

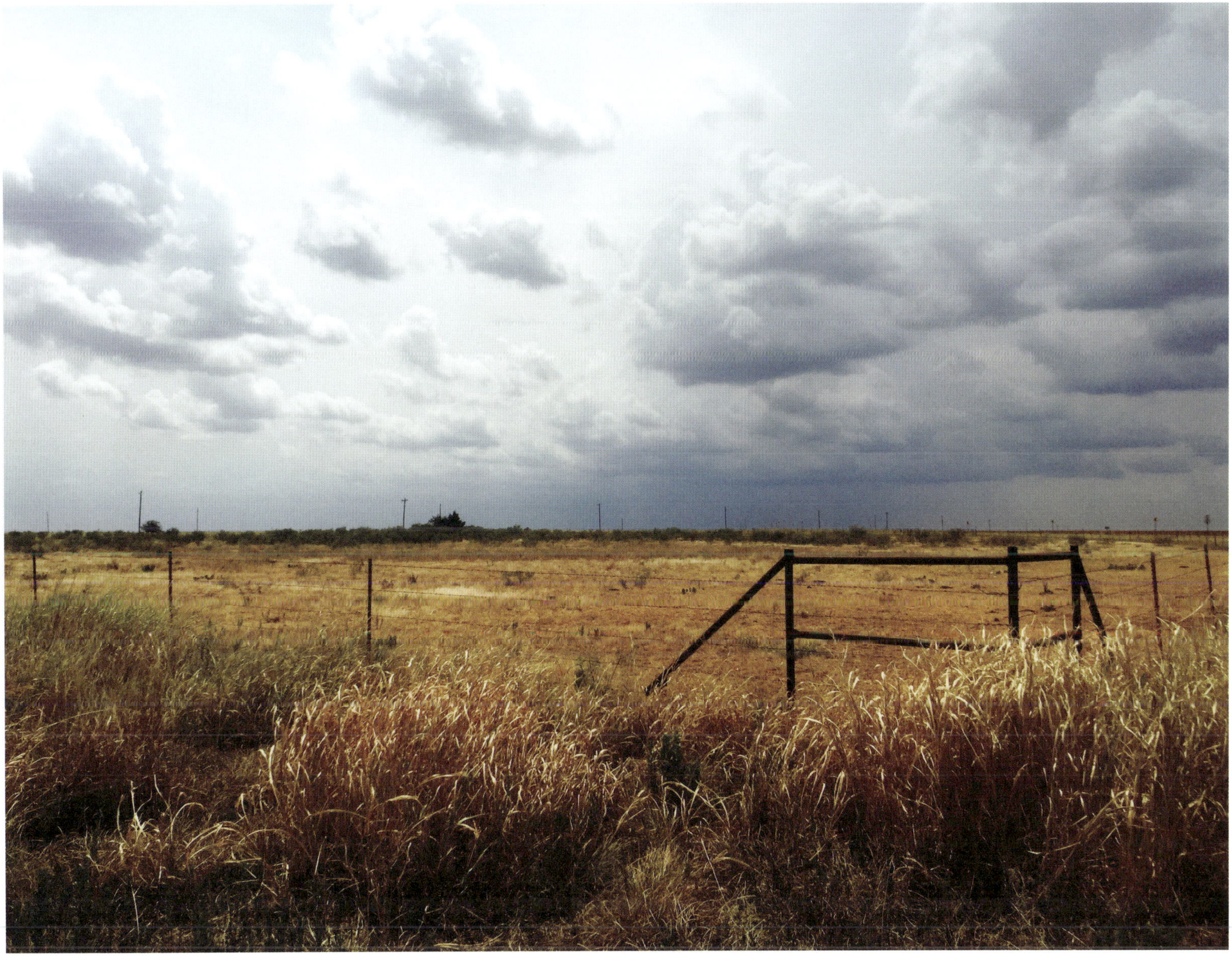

The Pasture's Corner in Spanish Fort. PHOTO BY DUSTIN RICE

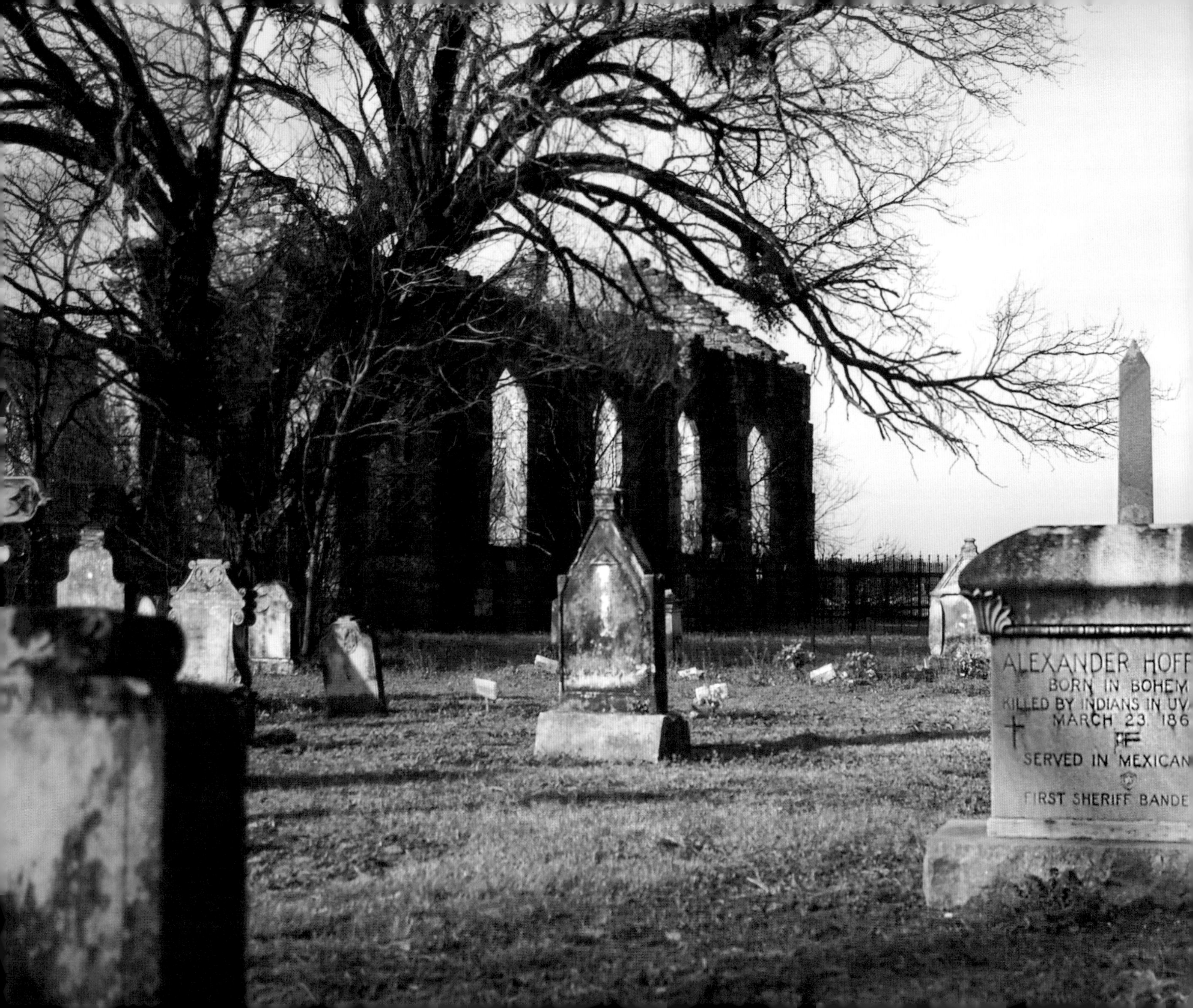
ALEXANDER HOFF
BORN IN BOHEM
KILLED BY INDIANS IN UV
MARCH 23. 186
SERVED IN MEXICAN
FIRST SHERIFF BANDE

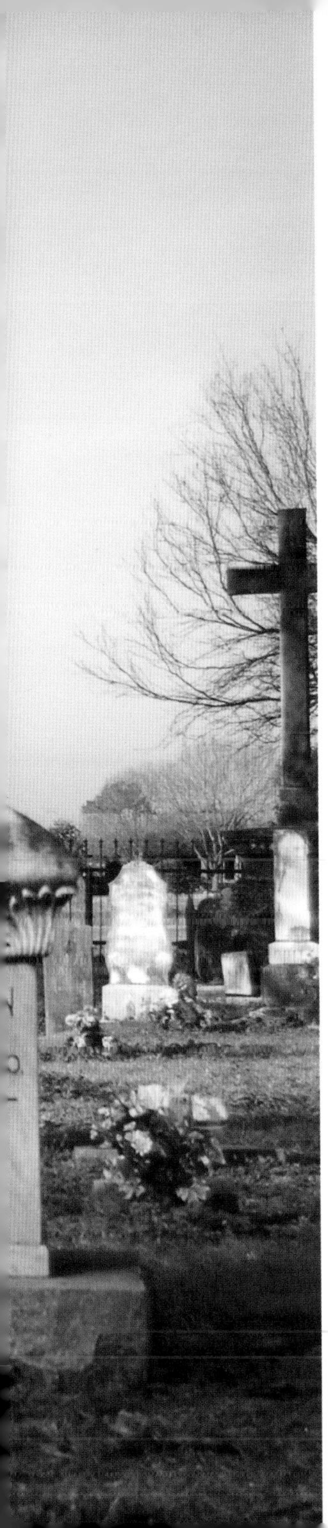

FIRST SHERIFF OF BANDERA COUNTY (1860)

DUSTIN RICE

We were on a back road south of US-90, looking for St. Dominic's Catholic Church. We had made some wrong turns, but eventually found all that remains of old D'Hanis, Texas, one of the original colonies of Henri Castro. There were once some five hundred families here, and many family members were buried in the graveyard beside St. Dominic's, one of the most beautiful cemeteries in Texas. We walked through rows of wrought-iron crosses and hand-cut headstones until one grave stopped me.

Sheriff Hoffman's final resting place, old D'Hanis. PHOTO BY DUSTIN RICE

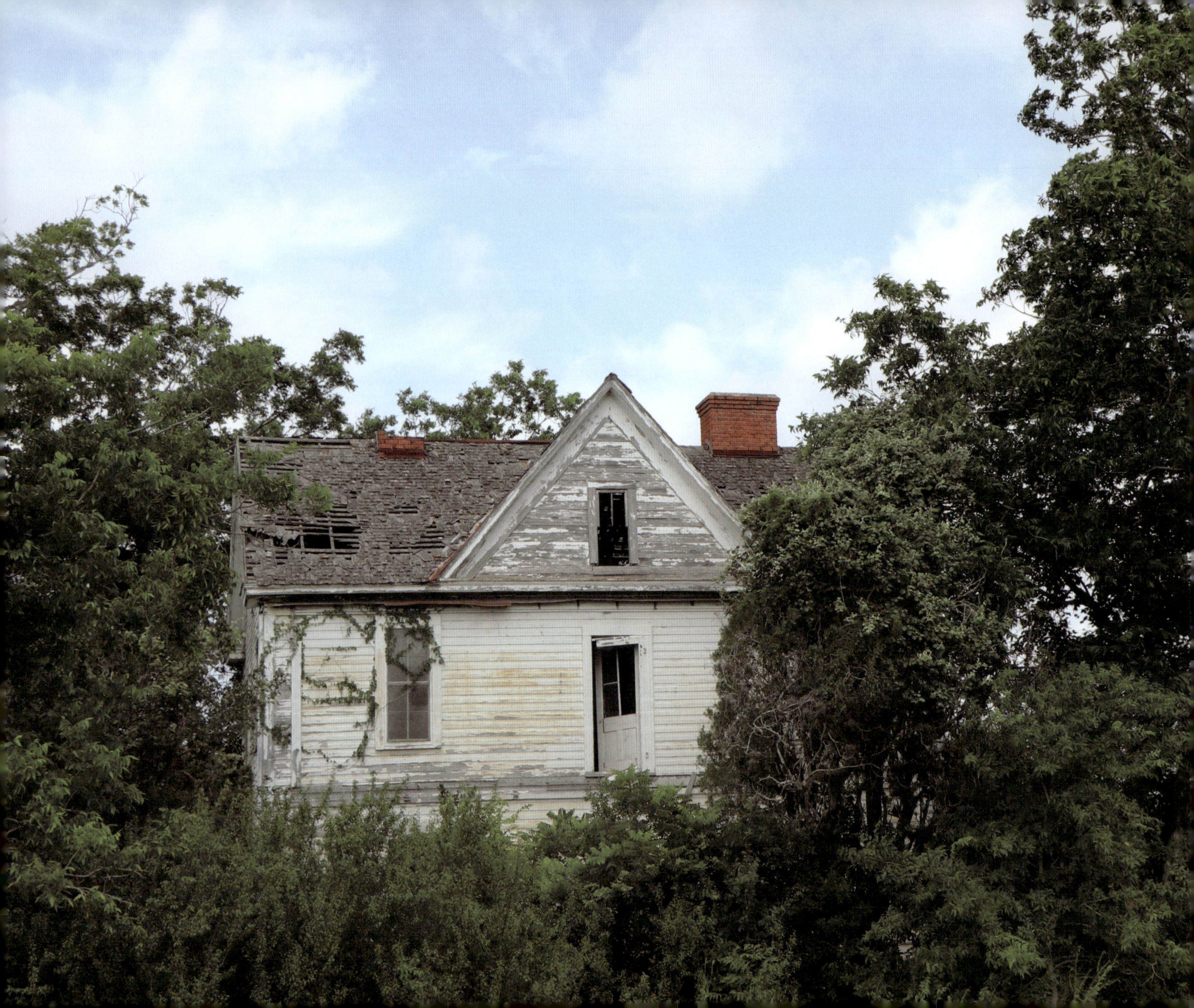

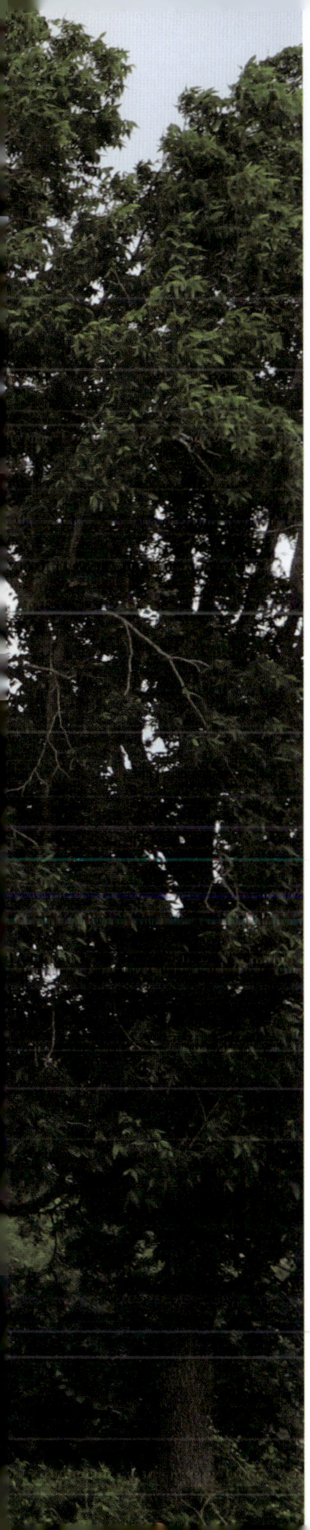

Alexander Hoffmann
Born in Bohemia
Killed by Indians in Uvalde Co.
March 23, 1860
Served in Mexican War
First Sheriff Bandera Co.

From the six short lines of description on his headstone, we learned that Alexander Hoffmann was a traveler, a fighter, a lawman, and ultimately a mystery.

Almost no records remain about the life of Alexander Hoffmann, but if he was born in Bohemia, now in the Czech Republic, and fought in the Mexican-American War (1846–1848), he was likely one of the earliest of Castro's colonists. Over the span of a few years, he had left Bohemia and traveled across Germany to either Alsace or Paris, France. He then gained passage to Texas as a colonist and sailed across the Atlantic to either Indianola or Galveston, though it's possible he may have come from as far as New Orleans. In exchange for all the hard work getting there, Castro's colonist families received 640 acres and individual men received 320 acres. It is not clear whether Alexander had a family, but he likely received a colony grant.

After his service in the war, Hoffmann may have returned to the colony to develop his land, but something had shifted by 1856, when Bandera County was established. If he was the first sheriff of the county, as his headstone says, he would have been elected or appointed then. But what happened during the next four years? What led to the events of March 23, 1860?

Uvalde County includes some of the roughest country in Texas, so it must have been important business that took Hoffmann beyond his jurisdiction. Whether rescuing a kidnapped woman or child, pursuing a rustler or horse thief, or tracking down a raiding party that doubled back on him, he was attacked and killed by Native Americans that day. He was buried at St. Dominic's, perhaps halfway between where he held office and where he was killed, possibly because of that rough country that stood between D'Hanis and Bandera.

When we drove to D'Hanis, we were expecting to shoot some pictures of a church in ruins, and we did. A beautiful, solitary little church surrounded by mist, and goats, it seemed to be full of sad stories that have long since been forgotten. We have seen graveyards and cemeteries all over the state. I thought I knew what to expect. I wasn't expecting to meet Sheriff Hoffmann, long forgotten in his home of over one hundred and fifty years, on that day.

Tuleta. PHOTO BY DUSTIN RICE

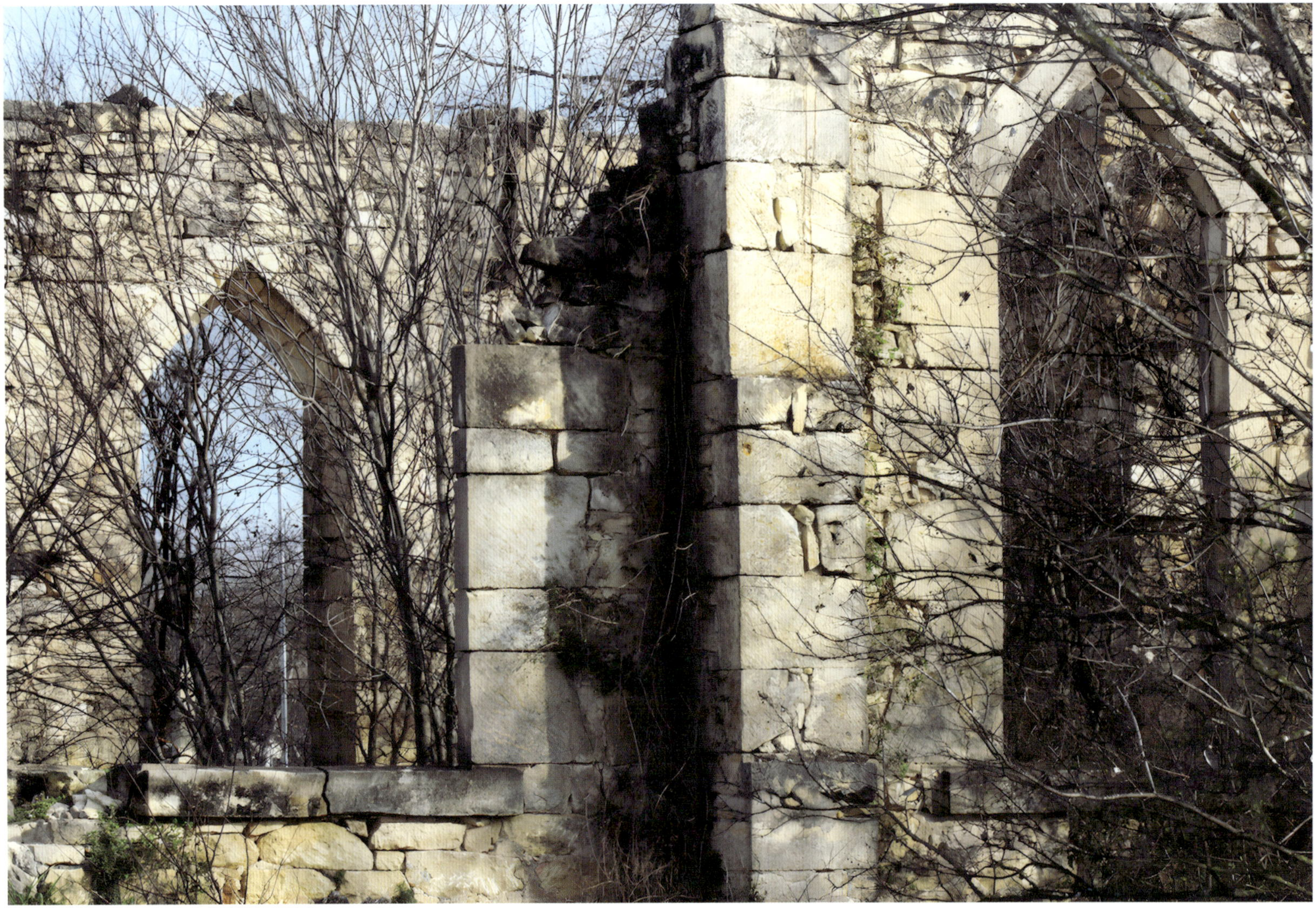

Saint Dominic Catholic Church ruins at old D'Hanis. PHOTO BY MORGAN PAGE

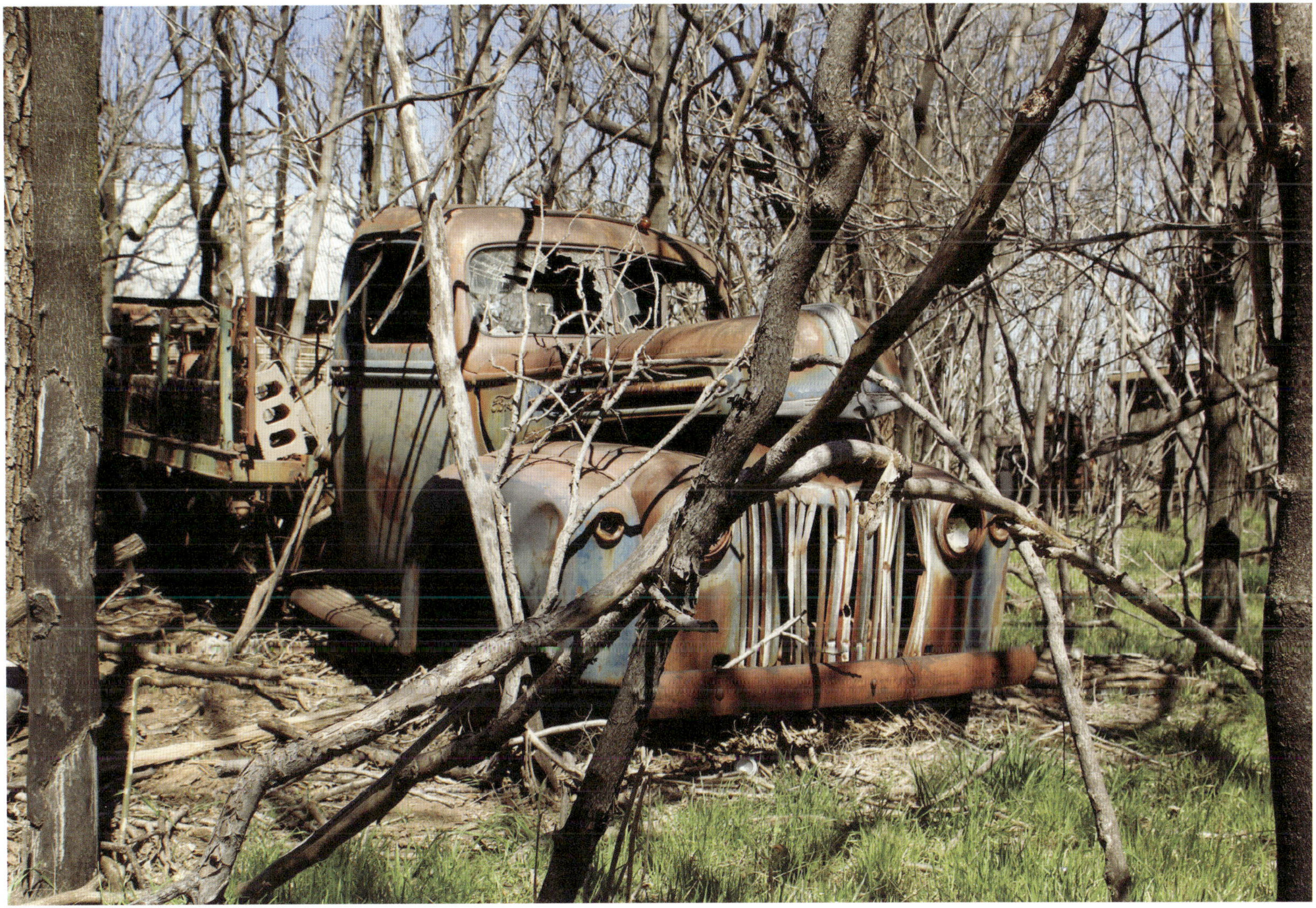

Haulk isn't a town, just the former collector's name. Dozens of vehicles and buildings are now preserved in time on private land north of Quanah. PHOTO BY DUSTIN RICE

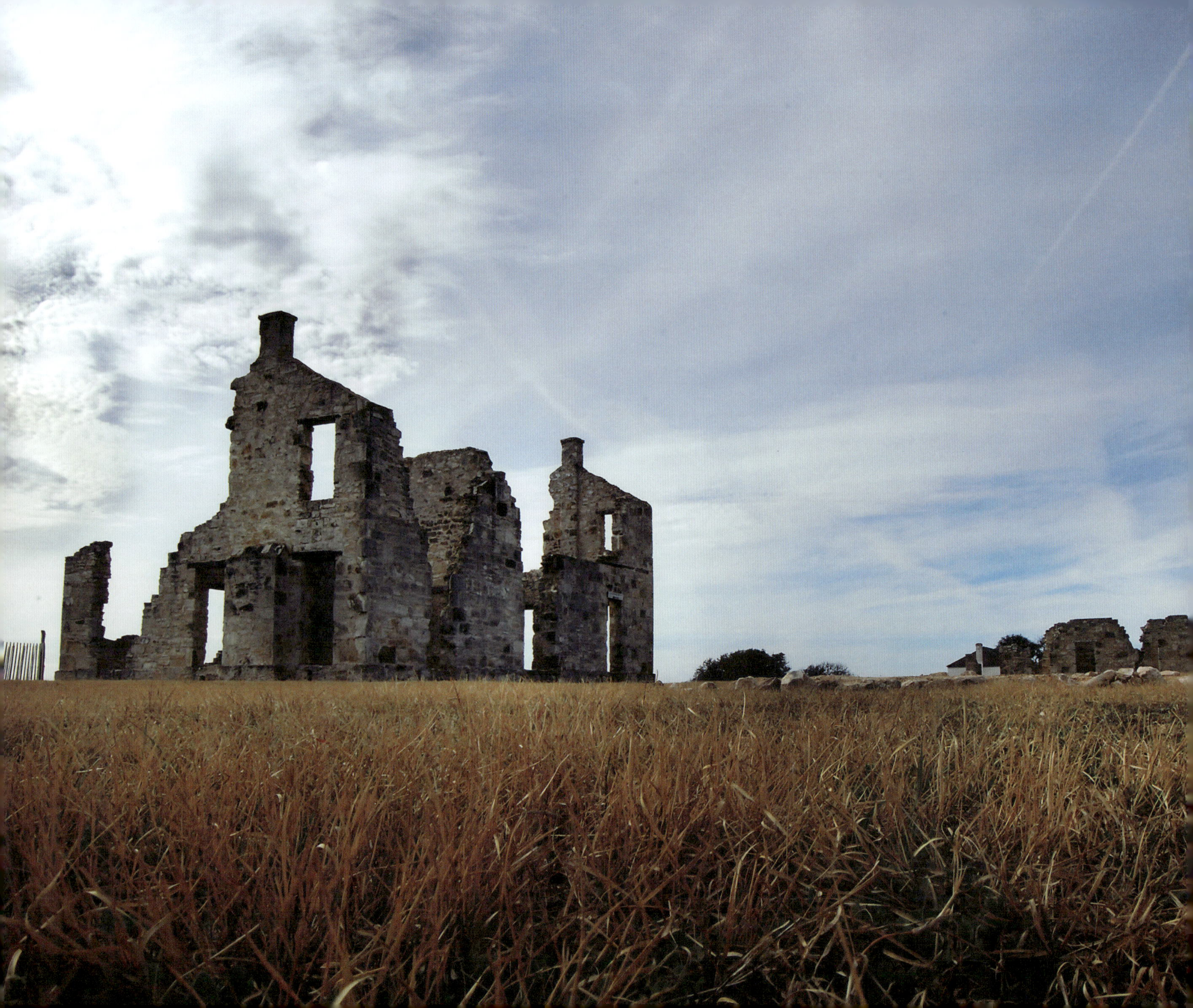

THE SPARK (POST–CIVIL WAR TO WORLD WAR II)

DUSTIN RICE

We were on our way home. The date that started us down this road was one year earlier. This was our longest road trip: four days, dozens of stops planned meticulously along the way, and we were nearing the end. After covering nearly two thousand miles across West and Central Texas, we were really worn out. We had no idea that this last stop on the last day of our first marathon trip would send us down a different path.

The officer's quarters, where the fire began on December 7, 1941, Fort McKavett. PHOTO BY DUSTIN RICE

We had started out with the intention of making a photographic documentary of the decline of small-town Texas. That was why we went to Fort McKavett. Once part of a chain of forts guarding the frontier, it became a town after outliving its military purpose. We were there to shoot a few photos and get back on the road as soon as possible, so we decided to split up and meet back at the gift shop in an hour.

The fort is spread over many acres and the views are stunning. It sits on top of a hill, with limestone buildings framing the former parade ground. The former barracks once made up the longest building west of the Mississippi. As you take in the stone against the sky and the sprawling ruins, the history of the fort just grabs you and pulls you in. This kind of site was what our project was made for. I was particularly drawn to the tallest building, which reminded me of a crumbling castle. How could this be Texas? How had I never seen this before? I sprawled in the grass and shot from the perspective of an animal, low to the ground. Before I could blink, it seemed, it was time to wrap up. So I made my way to the gift shop, figuring I would get a T-shirt and we would start for home. It was there, however, that our project changed.

A tour guide was passing time in the shop. He was curious about why we were at the fort. We explained our project and he said he had a story that we might find interesting. The building I was so enraptured with, the tall one with the great chimneys rising like castle spires? According to the guide, the building, a former officers' quarters, had alternately served as a hotel, a boardinghouse, and a private residence in the years after Fort McKavett became a town in the 1870s. Its lifespan as a hotel lasted seventy years, until it ended one fateful day in a story that has been passed down through oral history:

On that day, a commotion roused the sleepy town and everyone, including hotel staff and guests alike, took off for the source of the disturbance—the former mess hall. Converted to a town meeting hall, it housed the best radio in the county. That afternoon, a newsman broke into the broadcast to tell of a bombing halfway around the world.

It was just at that moment that someone noticed smoke coming from the hotel. In their haste to leave, someone had left a fire unattended. The old quarters were still heated by fireplaces, and sparks had landed on the ancient spruce flooring. It didn't take long for the fire to spread; it was already out of control before anyone noticed. There was no hope of saving the hotel. The date was December 7, 1941, and the event broadcast on the radio was the bombing of Pearl Harbor.

While the actual date of the fire cannot be confirmed, we loved the story. And we wondered: How many other potential coincidences are there in Texas history that are little known? What other stories lay among the ruins that we were photographing? That was when we resolved to capture not just photos of the past, but also the stories that could bring these places back to life. Uncovering the coincidental, the marginalized, and the forgotten histories of Texas became our new objective. Suddenly, we couldn't wait to get back on the road.

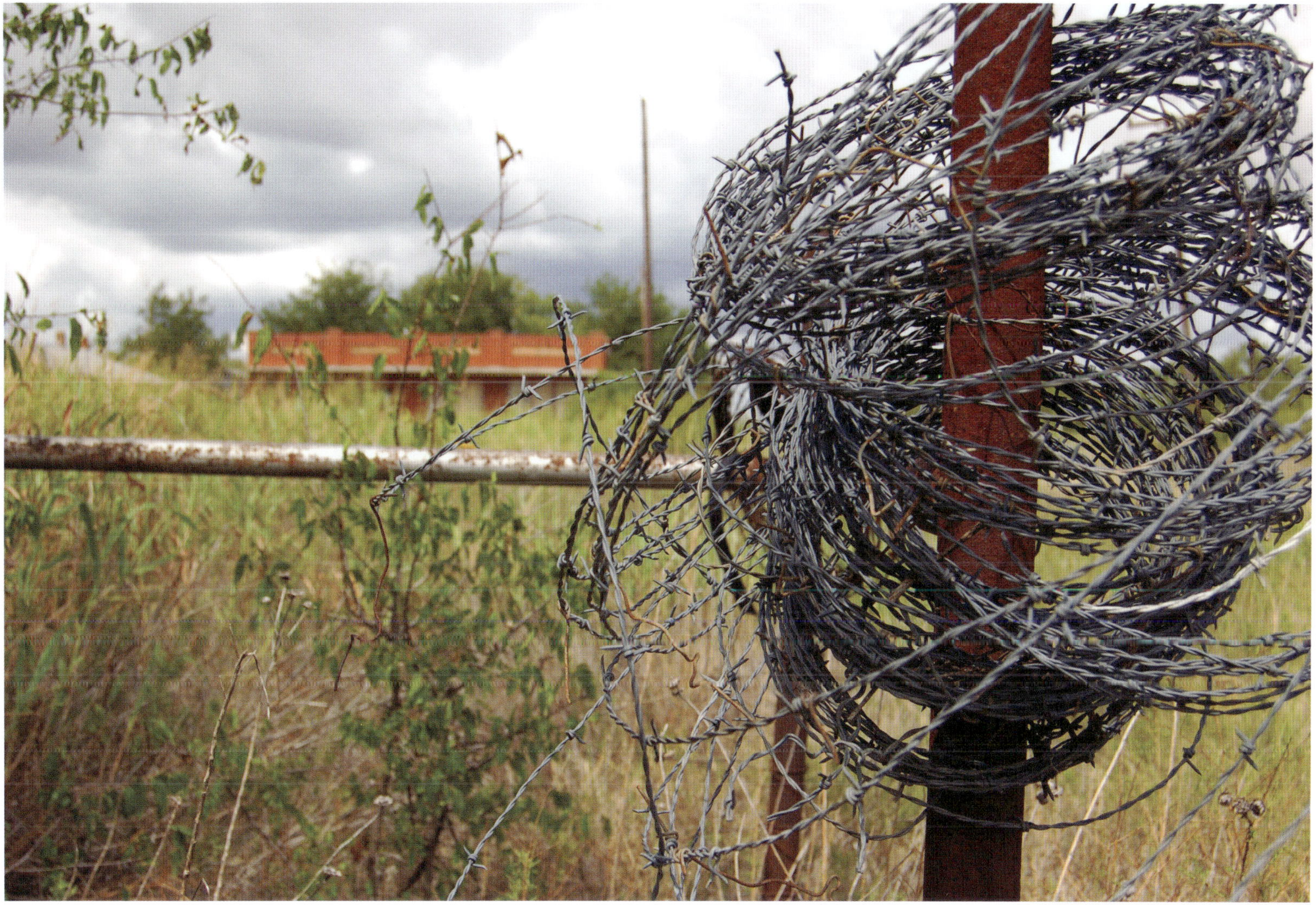

Dundee. PHOTO BY DUSTIN RICE

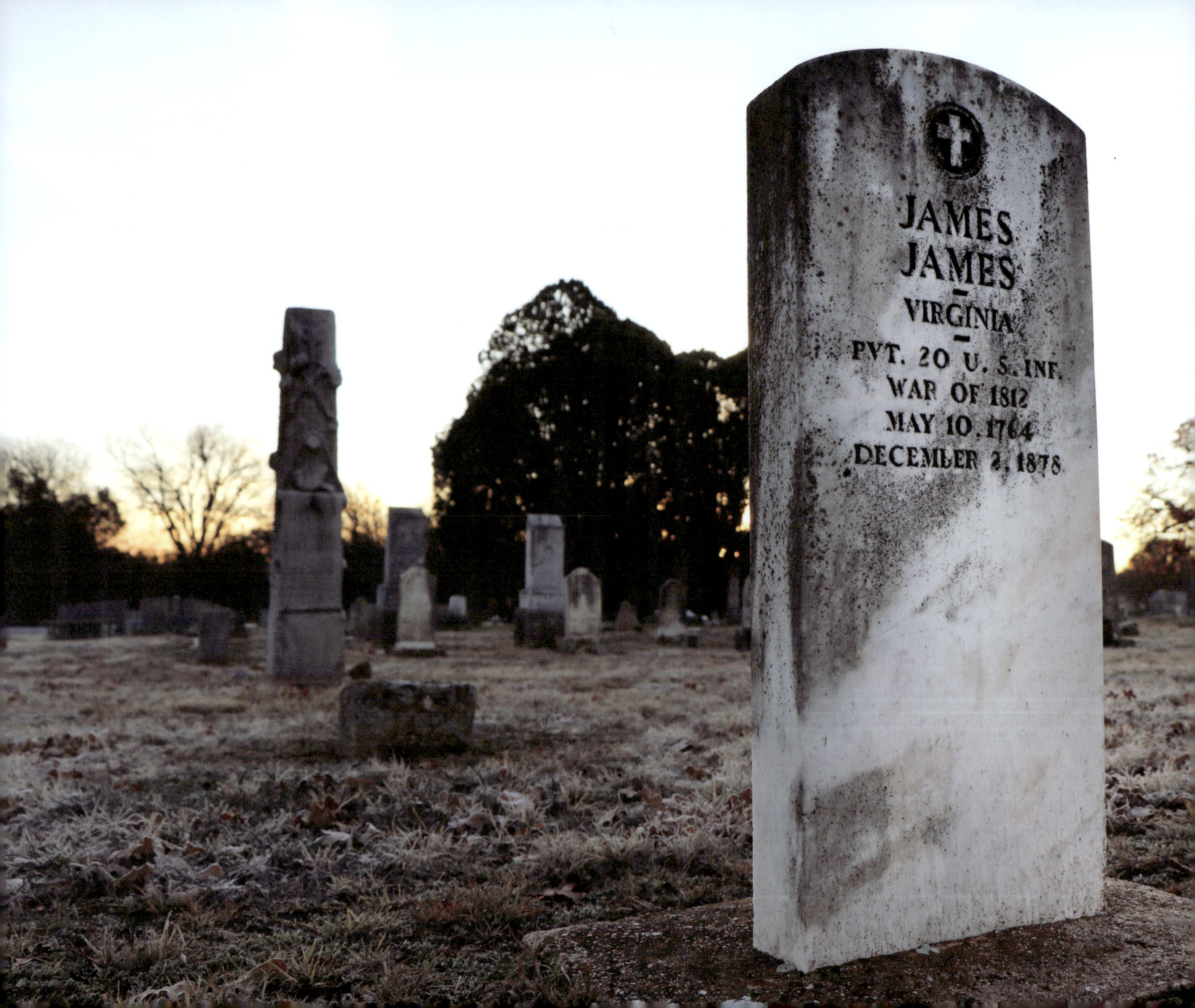
JAMES
JAMES
VIRGINIA
PVT. 20 U. S. INF.
WAR OF 1812
MAY 10. 1764
DECEMBER 2, 1878

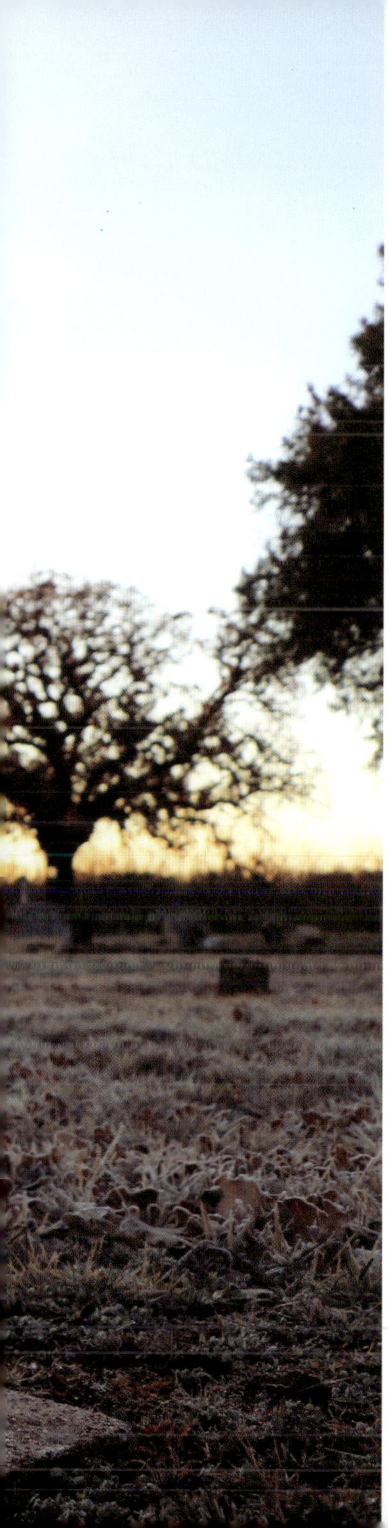

DOUBLE JIMMY (1860s)

DUSTIN RICE

Moving to Texas from Virginia in the early 1860s meant leaving an established society in the midst of the upheaval of the Civil War and entering a far wilder, wide-open frontier. This move was an incredible gamble that would require months of hard travel. Even a very young person would have had a hard time, but moving at nearly one hundred years of age? Not possible. But in 1864 it happened.

Double Jimmy's gravesite in Gooseneck Cemetery in Graham. PHOTO BY DUSTIN RICE

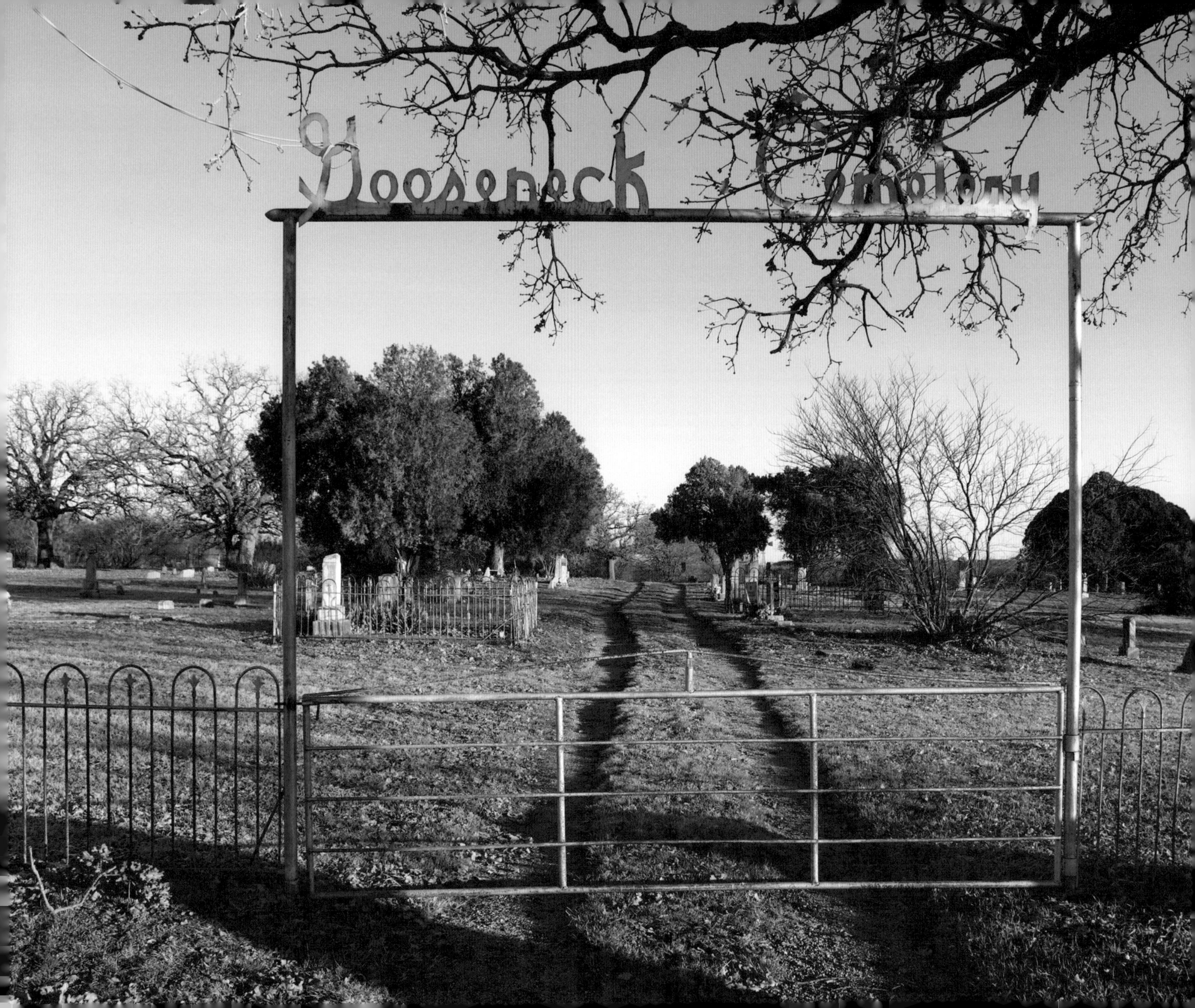
Gooseneck Cemetery

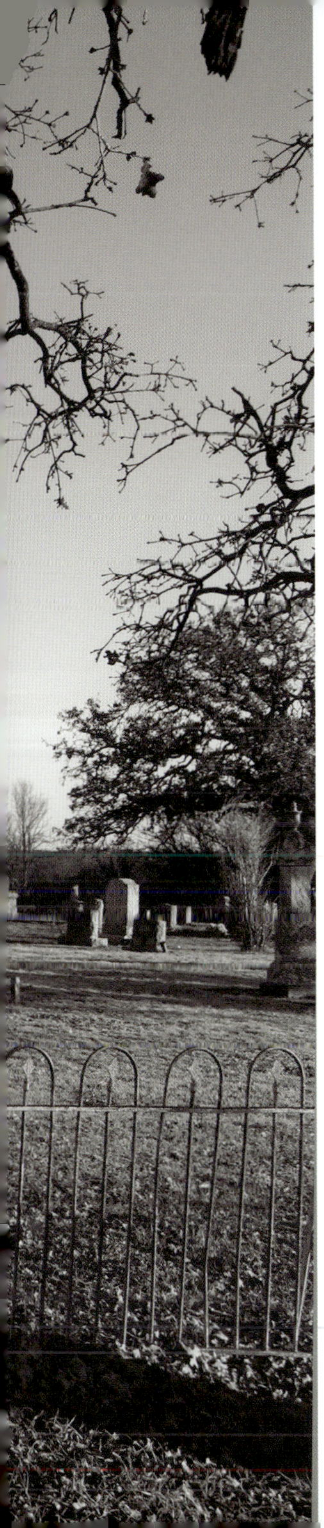

James James grew up on a plantation in Prince William County, Virginia, a neighbor to Lawrence Washington, a half-brother of George. He was just a few years too young to fight in the Revolutionary War, and the next few decades of his life are lost to history. Records reappear from the War of 1812, in which he is documented as a private. That's right, a private at the age of forty-eight. He was serving next to men well under half his age. Yet at the end of the war, he was personally recognized for his service by George Washington, according to documents still held by the family; James was also given a knife by the former president. He would be paid $8 a month for the rest of his days, and his grave would be marked with a modern military headstone upon his passing.

What brought "Double Jimmy," as we came to call James James, to Texas in 1864 is lost to time. He came with his widowed daughter, Nancy, herself sixty-three at the time, and they rented land in Parker County. James tended watermelons, a centenarian working the soil with a one-row plow. He tended his melons in Parker County for over a decade.

By 1874 the James family had settled in the Gooseneck Community of Young County, near Graham. Why they decided on a barely settled, wide-open, formerly Native-controlled parcel of land is, again, lost to history. Availability and price would have factored into the decision, to be sure, since the cheapest land was the most dangerous. Double Jimmy was a regular in local news coverage at the time; everyone wanted to know how the old man was doing. He finally stopped coming to town and stopped tending his rows. His daughter took care of him in the end, and he passed on in the winter of 1878, at the age of 114, according to local lore. Sources marveled that he was easily the oldest man in America, and perhaps the oldest man in the world.

Gooseneck Cemetery in Graham. PHOTO BY DUSTIN RICE

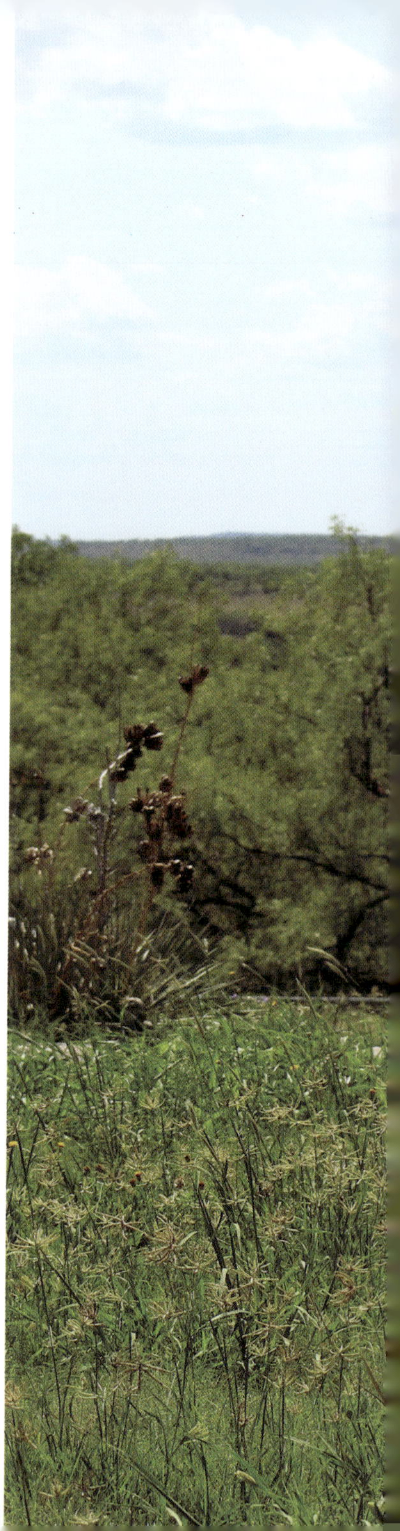

The Damrons' resting place (1840s) at Round Timber Cemetery in Baylor County. PHOTO BY MORGAN PAGE

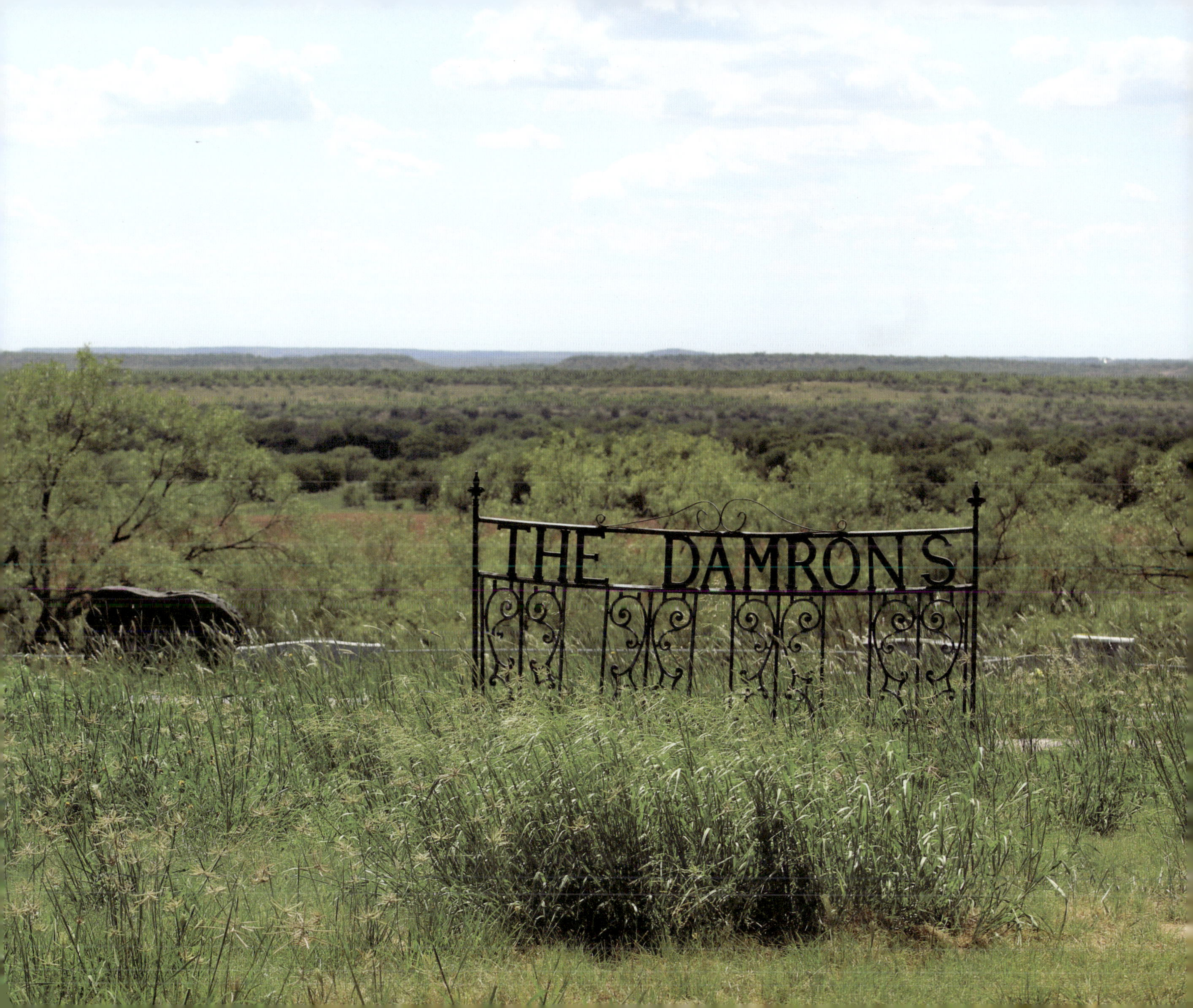
THE DAMRONS

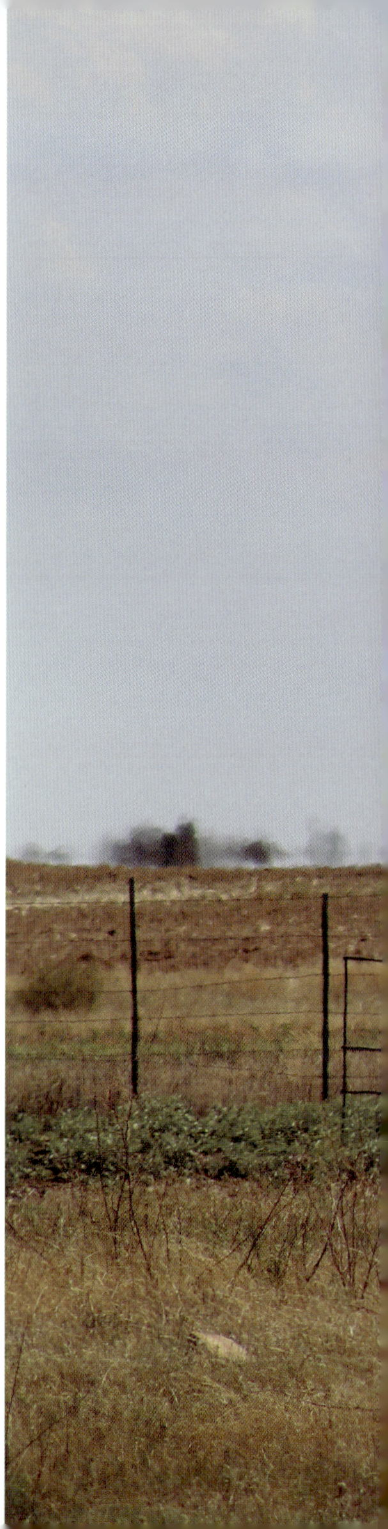

'64 Pontiac, Round Timber. PHOTO BY MORGAN PAGE

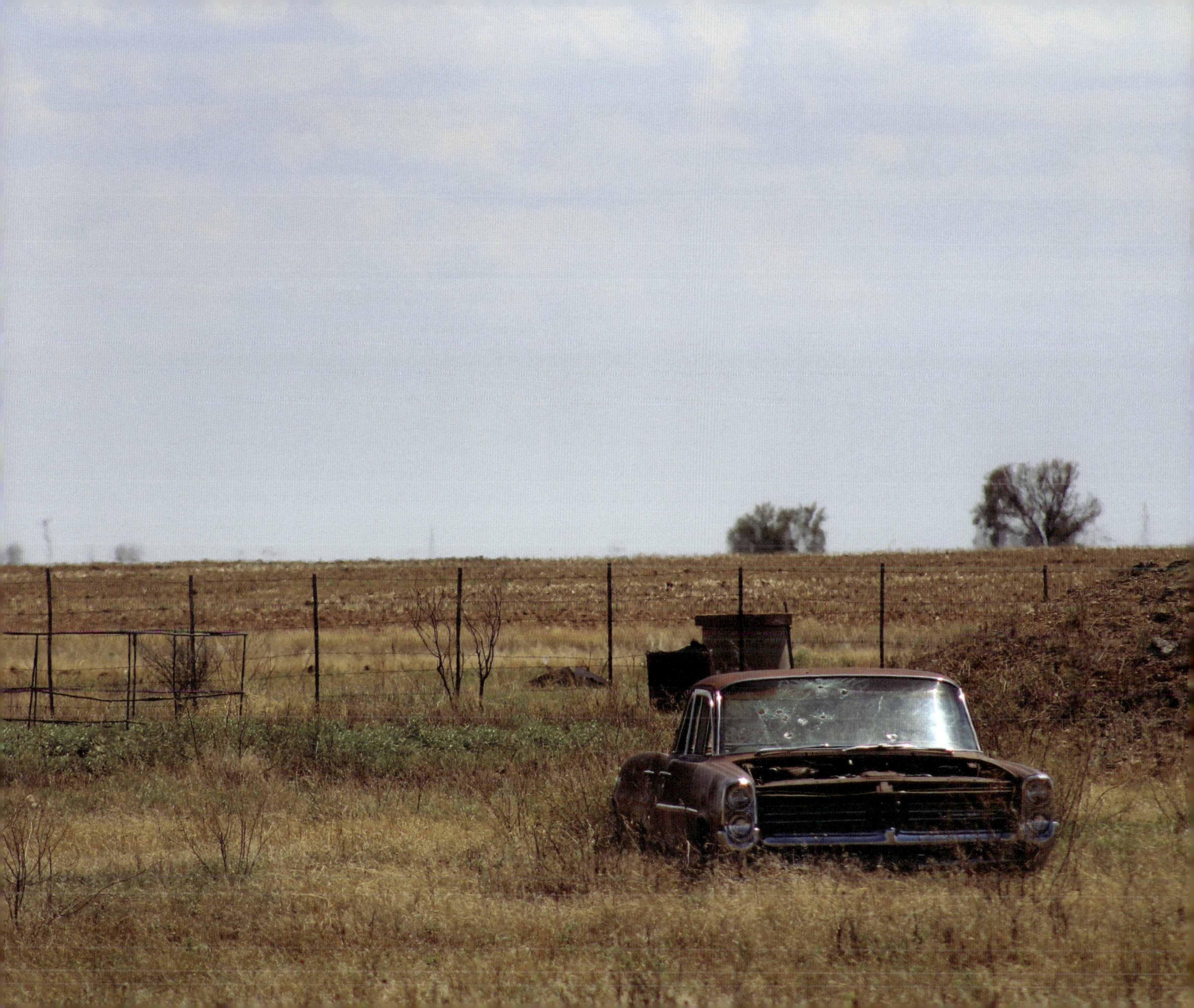

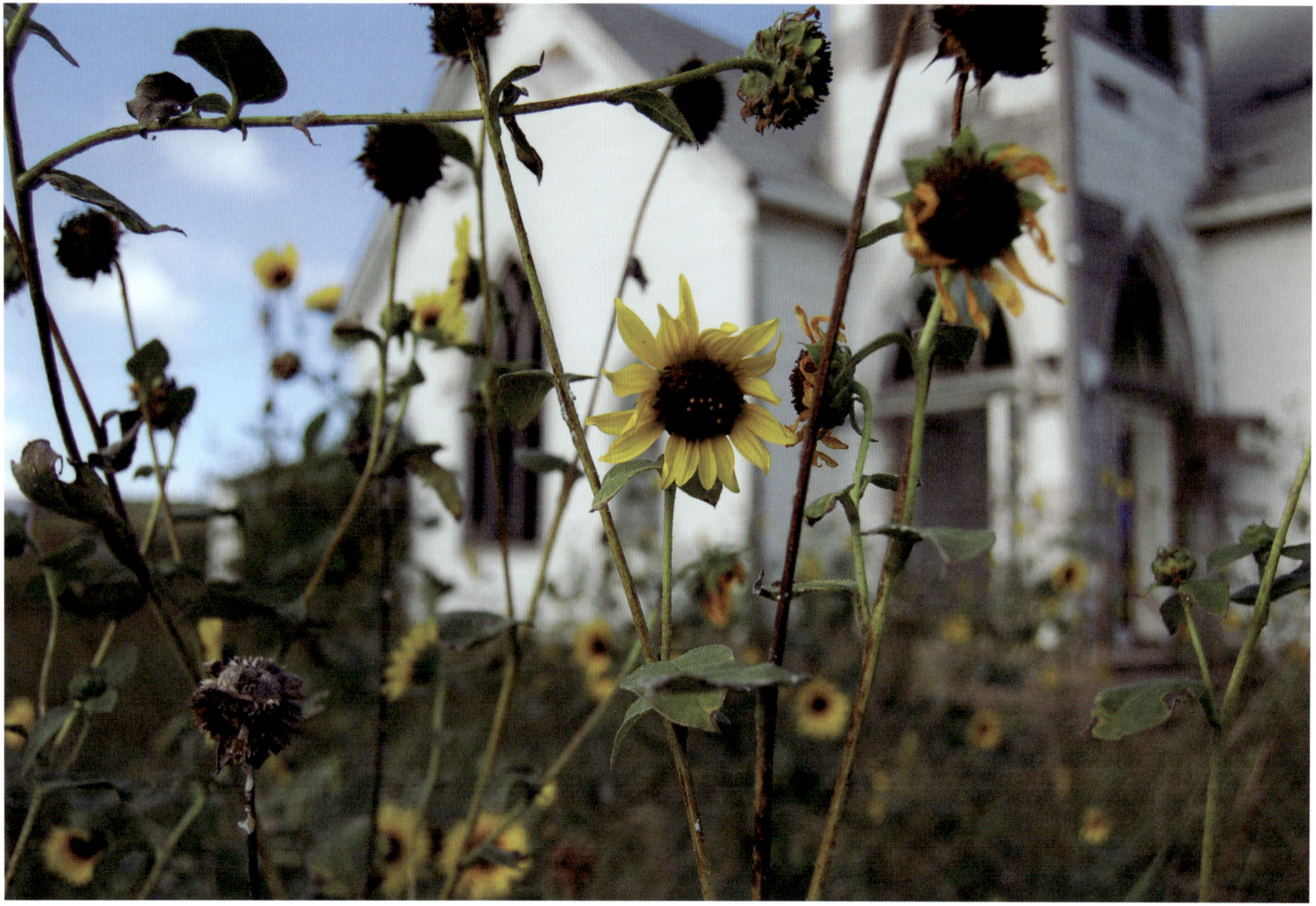

First Methodist Church (exterior), est. 1909, Jermyn. PHOTO BY DUSTIN RICE

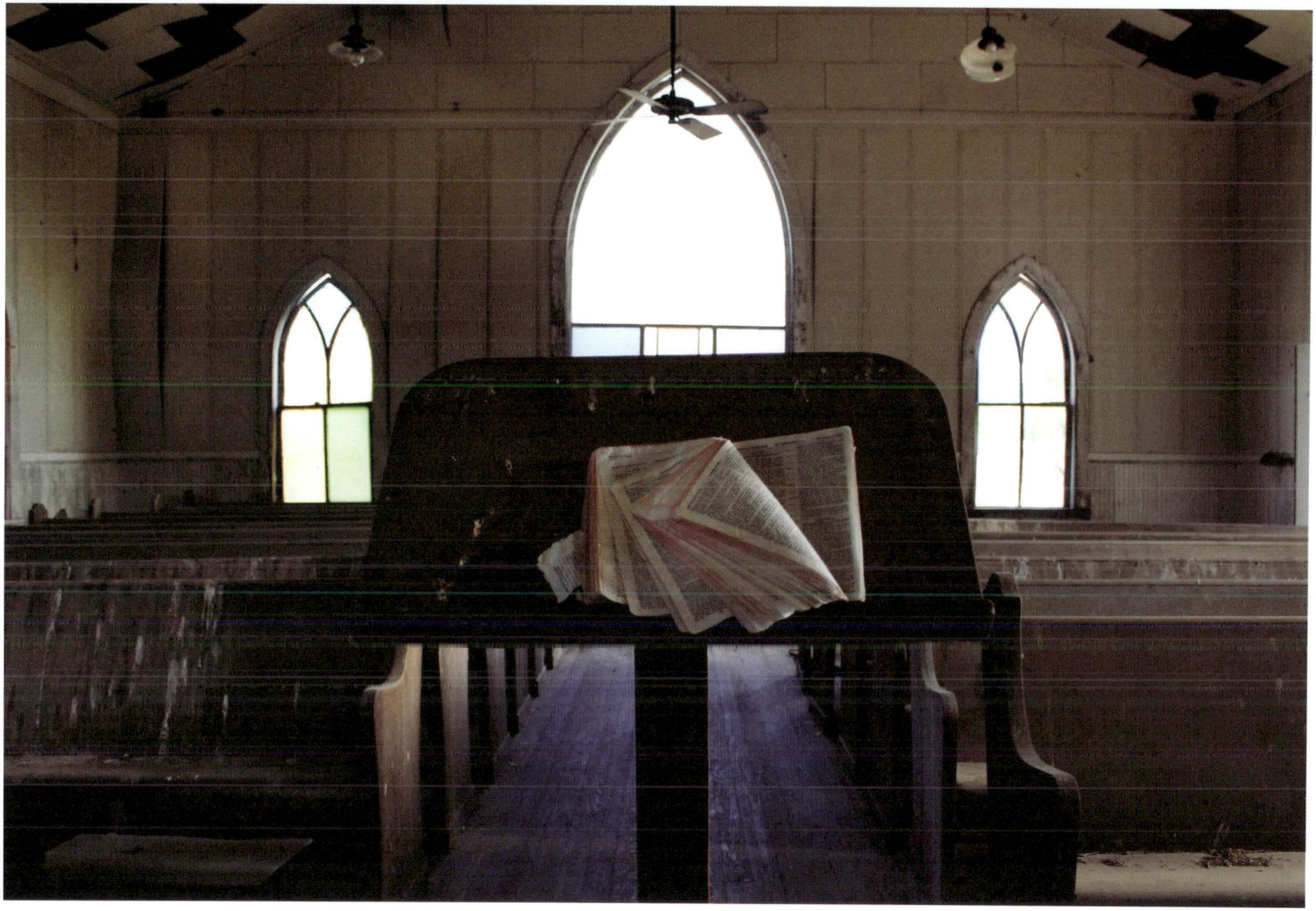

First Methodist Church (interior), est. 1909, Jermyn. PHOTO BY MORGAN PAGE

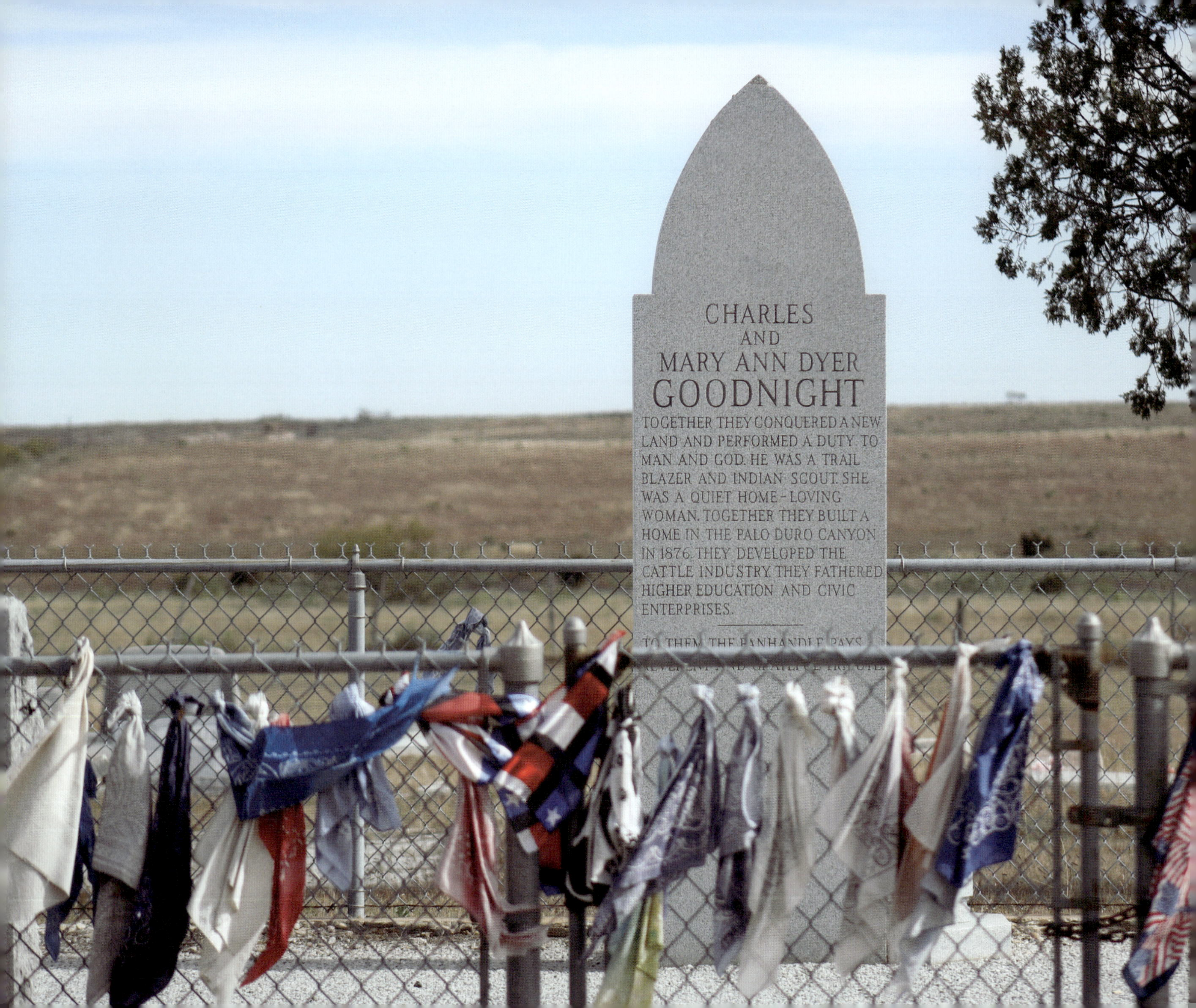
CHARLES
AND
MARY ANN DYER
GOODNIGHT
TOGETHER THEY CONQUERED A NEW LAND AND PERFORMED A DUTY TO MAN AND GOD. HE WAS A TRAIL BLAZER AND INDIAN SCOUT. SHE WAS A QUIET HOME-LOVING WOMAN. TOGETHER THEY BUILT A HOME IN THE PALO DURO CANYON IN 1876. THEY DEVELOPED THE CATTLE INDUSTRY. THEY FATHERED HIGHER EDUCATION AND CIVIC ENTERPRISES.

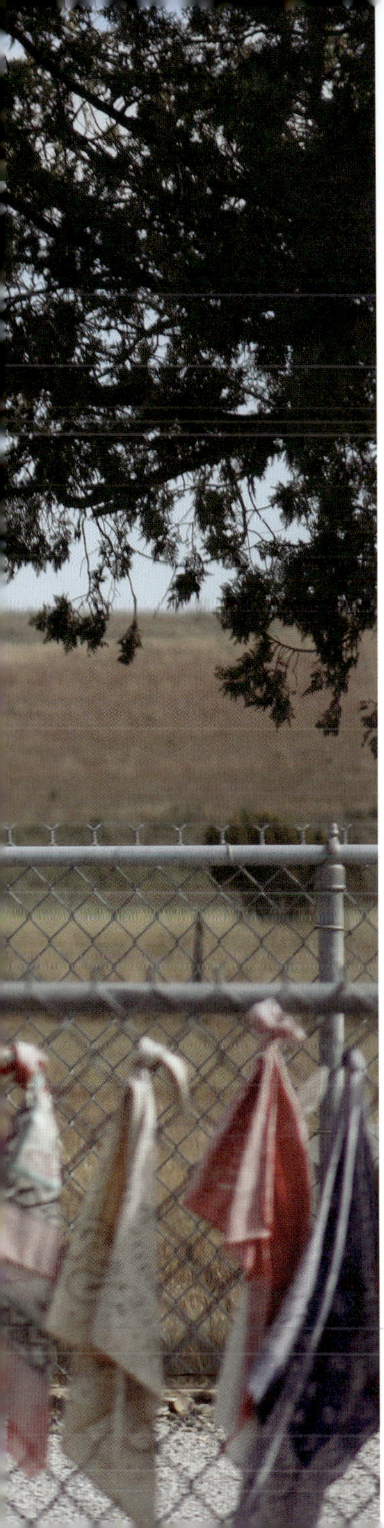

MOTHER OF THE PANHANDLE (1870s)

MORGAN PAGE AND DUSTIN RICE

> One who spent her whole life in the service of others.
>
> Epitaph of Molly Goodnight

Charles Goodnight is a legendary figure in Texas. He was a partner in the first large permanent cattle ranch in the Panhandle and owned a significant portion of what is now Palo Duro Canyon. The most lasting legacy of the Goodnight ranch, however, might be attributable to his wife, Mary Ann Dyer Goodnight, better known as Molly.

Resting place of Charles and Molly Goodnight. PHOTO BY MORGAN PAGE

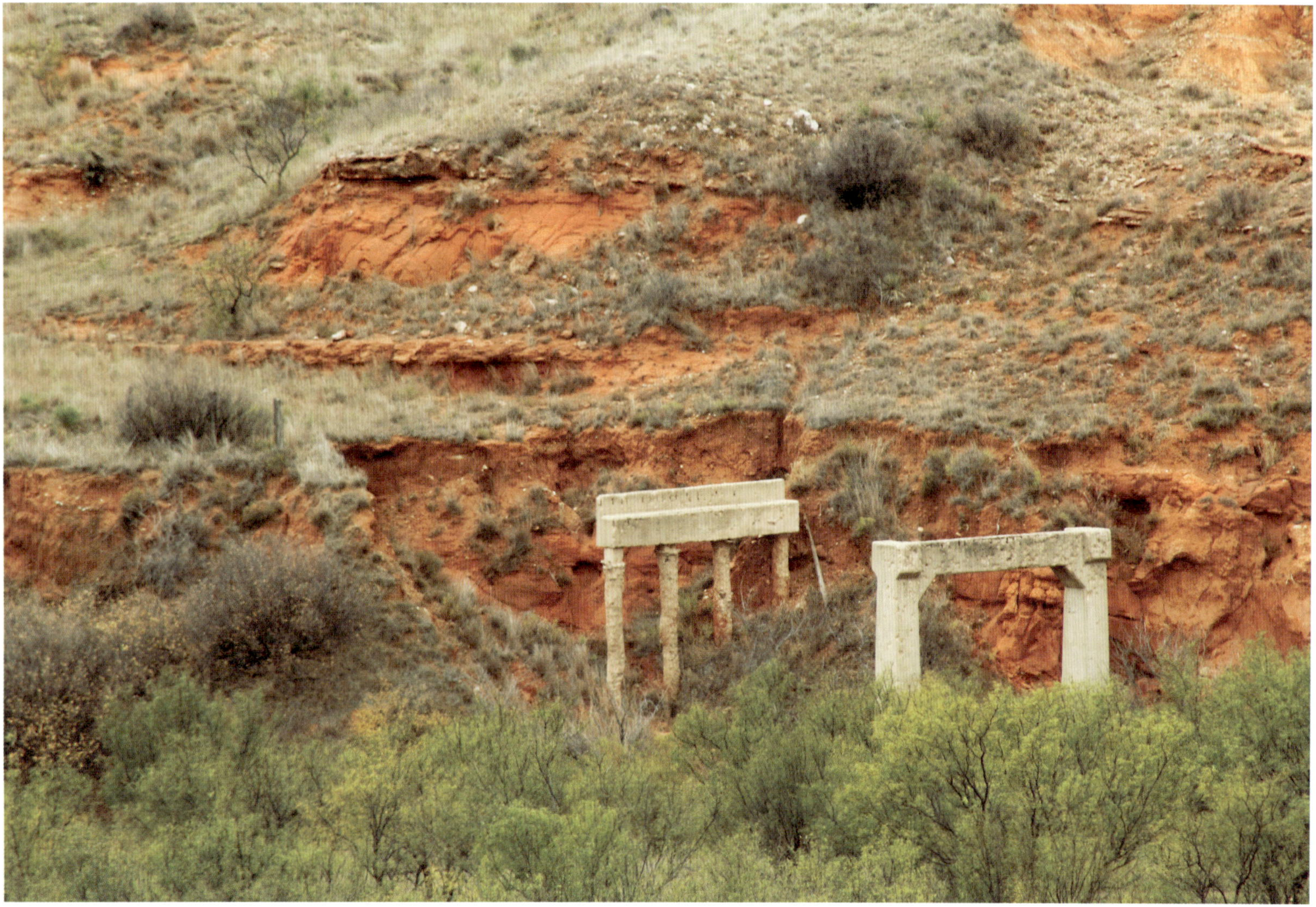

Somewhere in the Panhandle along 385. PHOTO BY MORGAN PAGE

The Goodnights set up a homestead in Palo Duro Canyon in 1877, a few years after the Comanche had been driven out of the area. For months at a time, Molly was the only woman in the canyon. Having no children, "Aunt Molly" became a mother figure to many, many cowhands. A natural caretaker, Molly did not limit her nurturing to those who worked the ranch, but also made friends with travelers and some Native Americans, too. She devised her own catalogue of remedies for common ailments in the Panhandle, a list found in David McComb's *Texas, a Modern History*: "Coal-oil for lice, prickly pear for wounds, salt and buffalo tallow for piles, mud for inflammation and fevers, and buffalo meat broth for a general tonic." She was also known to bring cobblers, pies, and cakes to the men working in distant cow camps in the canyon. In a show of their appreciation, the men ordered a silver tea service from New York for Mrs. Goodnight.

Molly's empathy for lonely souls was not restricted to humankind, either. The Goodnights set up in the Panhandle as the once-prolific bison herds of the southern plains were being hunted nearly to extinction (part of a strategy to force the Native Americans who depended on those herds to move to reservations). In her diary, Molly wrote about how, on windless nights, the agonizing screams of orphaned calves calling for their mothers would carry for miles. Sensing that it was only a matter of time until the bison were gone forever, Molly decided to do something. She had a section of the canyon fenced off and raised a few orphaned calves that her husband captured for her, bottle-feeding them when necessary. At the time, this was absolutely unheard of. In an interview with *Ladies' Home Journal* in 1901, Molly recounted the calves' insatiable appetites, noting that they could take three gallons of milk per day.

Molly passed away in 1926, but her little bison herd eventually grew to more than two hundred head. By then, there were very few true bison left in North America, as most of those that managed to survive the hide hunters had bred with cattle. The JA herd, named for the JA Ranch that Goodnight partnered in, had some of the purest North American bison blood left on the planet, unadulterated by the blood of the "beefalo," the hybrid offspring being raised on many neighboring and rival ranches. Stock from the ranch was essential to conservationists, who worked to rebuild herds across the American West, including the herd in Yellowstone National Park.

In 1996, the estate of Charles Goodnight's former partner in the ranch, John Adair, donated the herd to the Texas Parks and Wildlife Department, and the bison were eventually given a home in Caprock Canyon State Park. There, the Texas State Bison Herd, as it is officially known, still thrives and expands, thanks to Molly Goodnight, a true pioneer who is sometimes referred to, aptly, as the "Mother of the Panhandle."

Molly's generous spirit and good deeds in the early days of the Goodnight ranch at Palo Duro Canyon were commemorated on a quote engraved on a plaque accompanying a grandfather clock her husband gifted her:

> In Honor of Mrs. Mary Dyer Goodnight, Pioneer of the Texas Panhandle. For many months in 1876–1877, she saw few men and no women, her nearest neighbor being seventy-five miles distant and the nearest settlement two hundred miles. She met isolation and hardship with a cheerful smile, and danger with undaunted courage. With unfailing optimism, she took life's varied gifts, and made her home a house of joy.

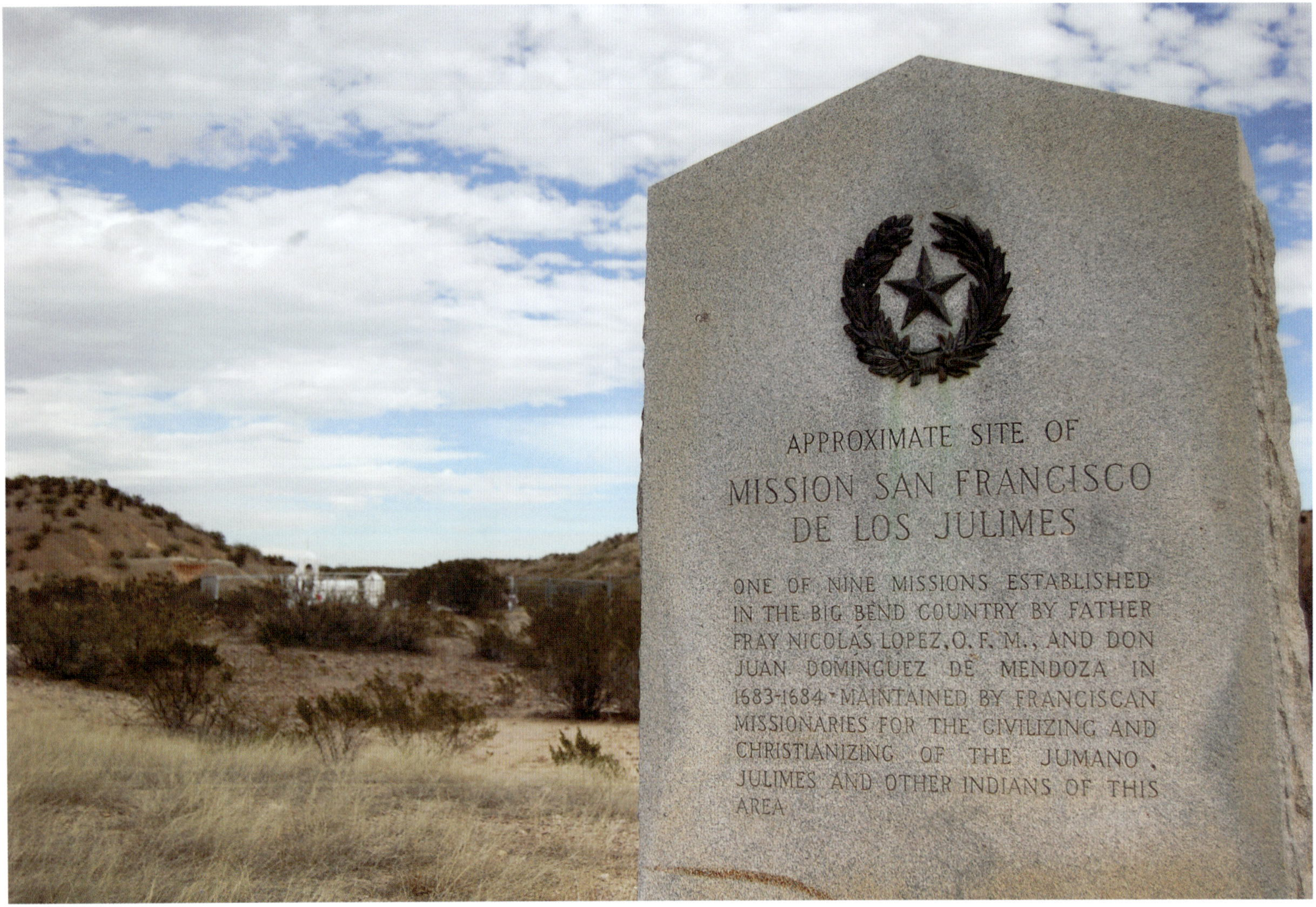

Site of Mission San Francisco De Los Julimes, est. 1683. PHOTO BY DUSTIN RICE

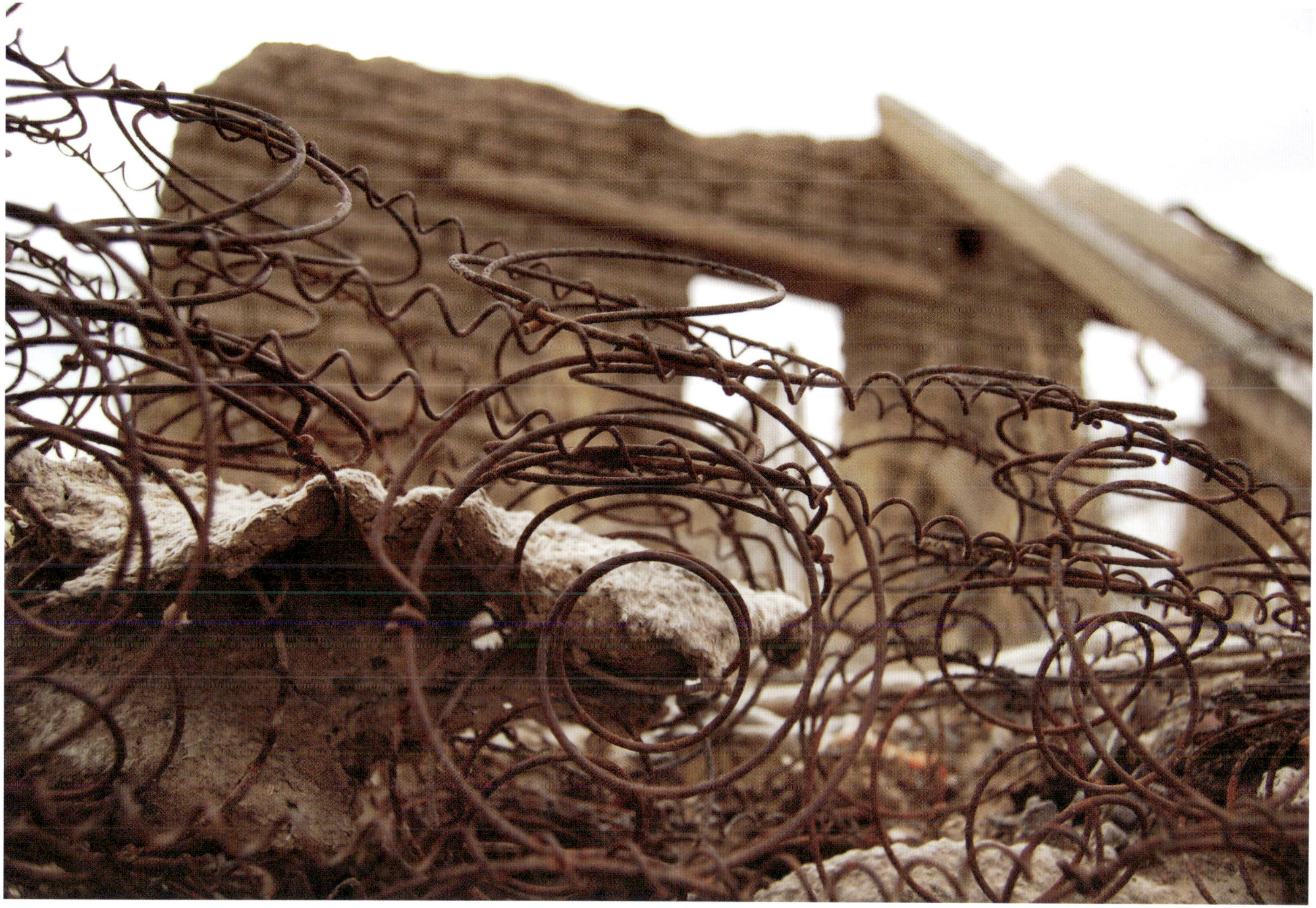

Rusted springs in Redford. PHOTO BY DUSTIN RICE

Wall in Barstow. PHOTO BY MORGAN PAGE

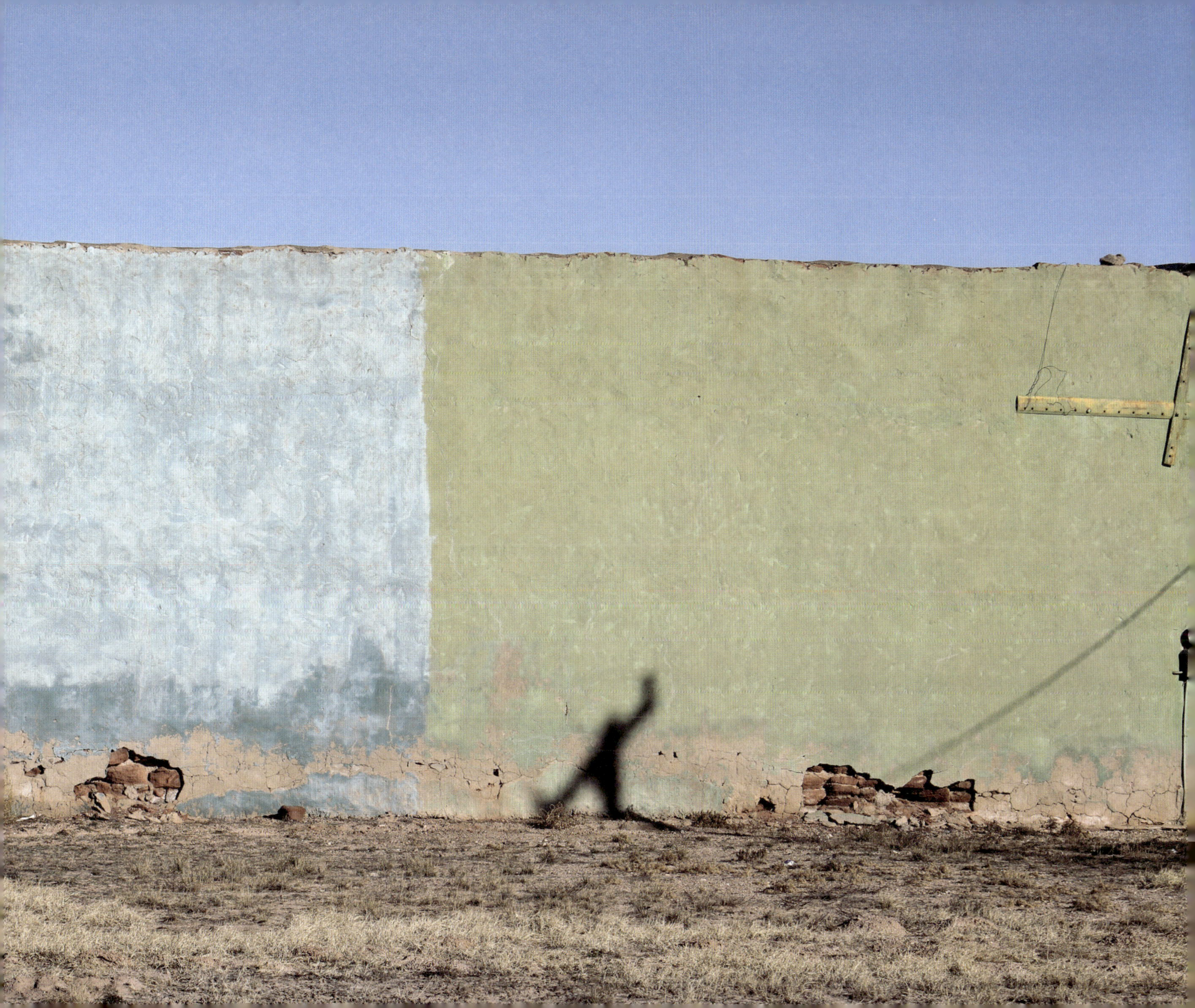

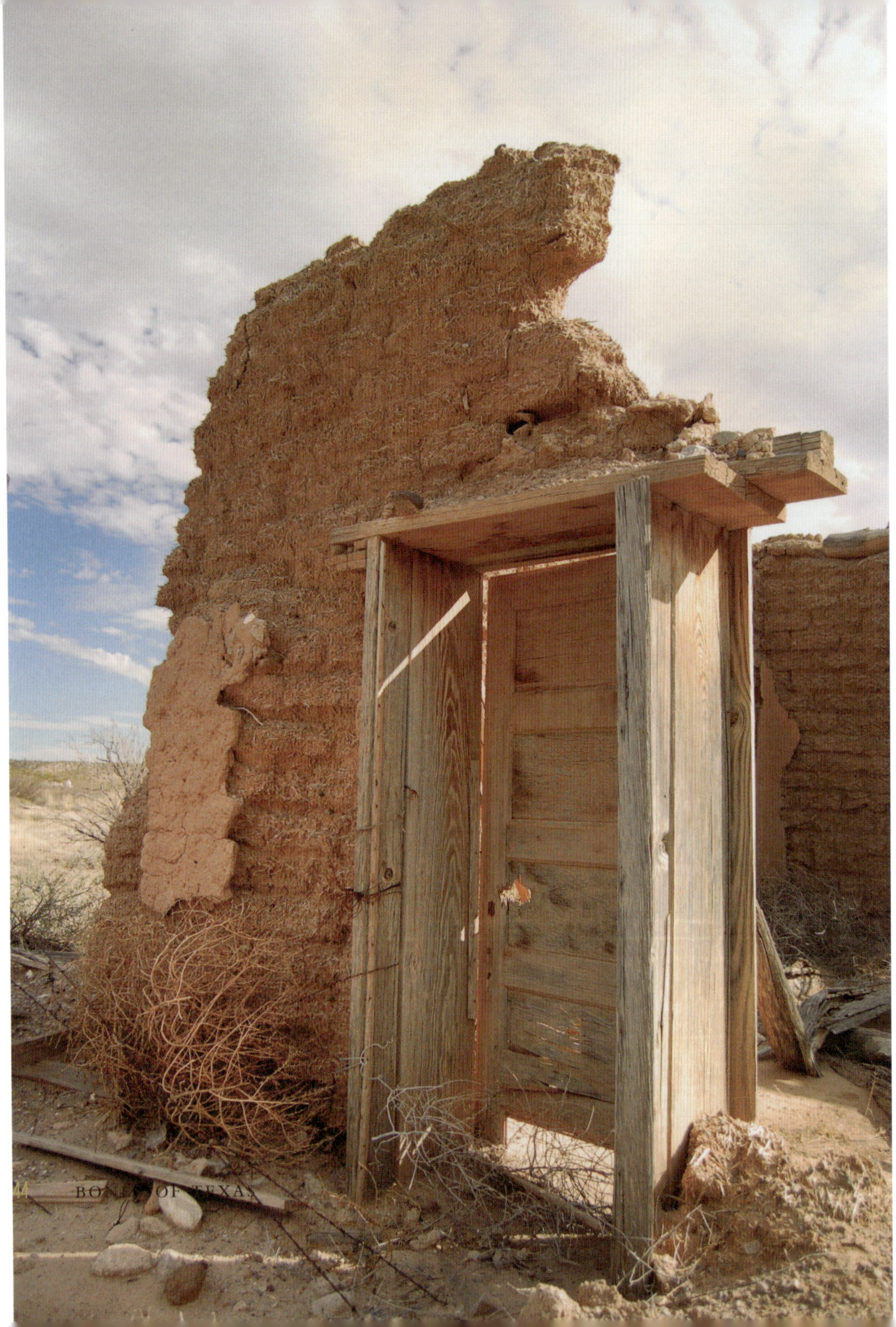

Doorway at Adobes. PHOTO BY DUSTIN RICE

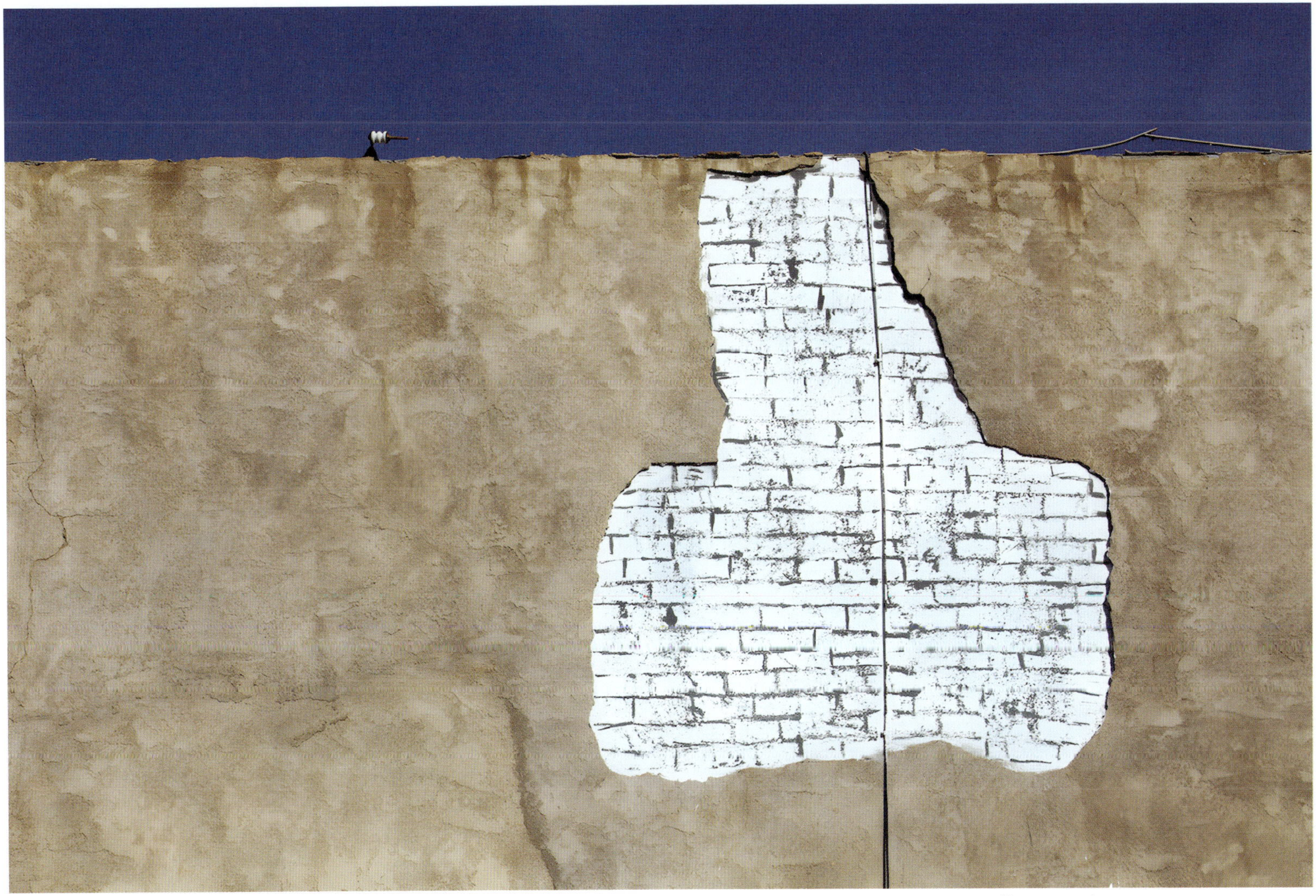

Wall in Seminole. PHOTO BY MORGAN PAGE

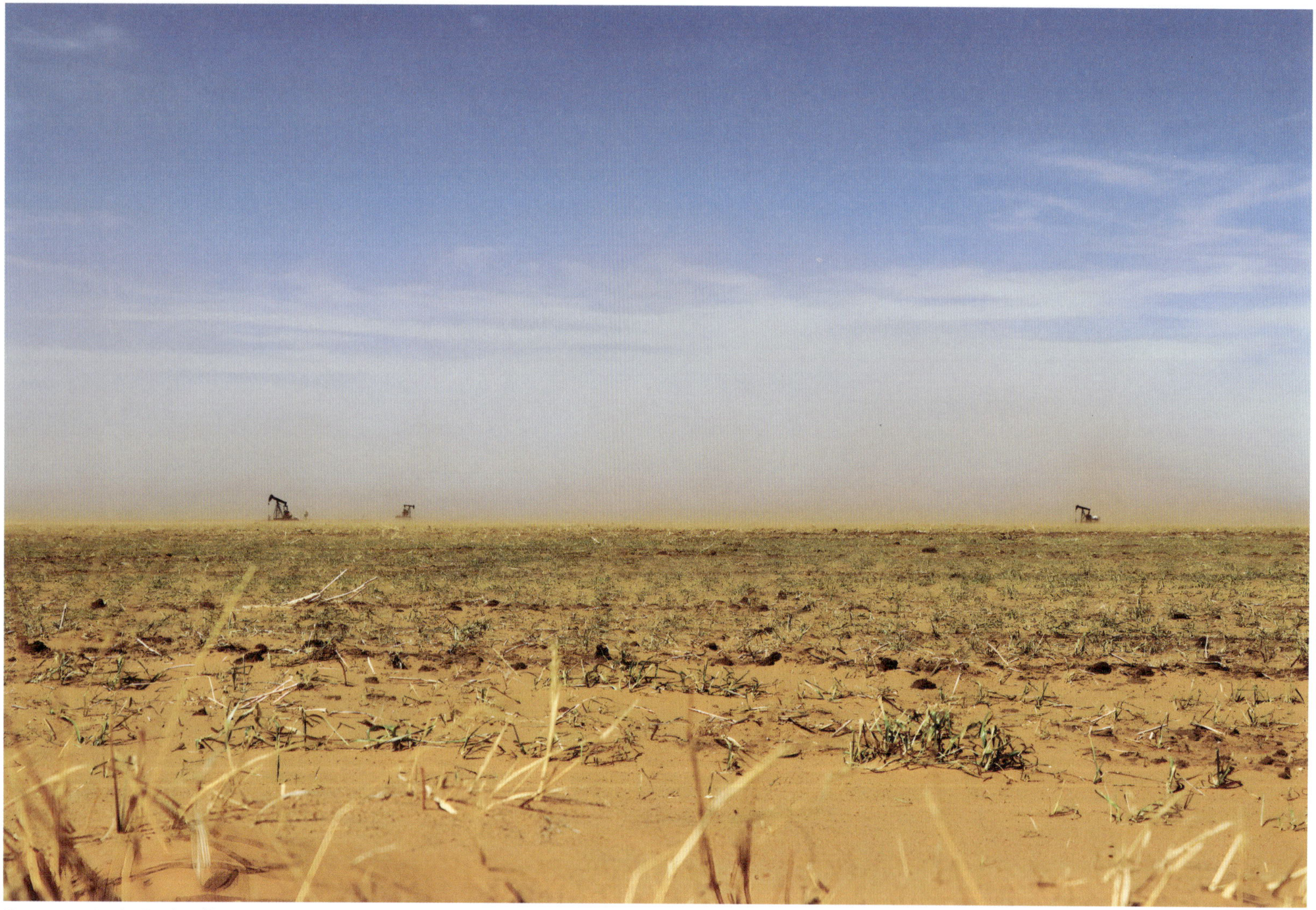

Dust storm in the Panhandle. PHOTO BY DUSTIN RICE

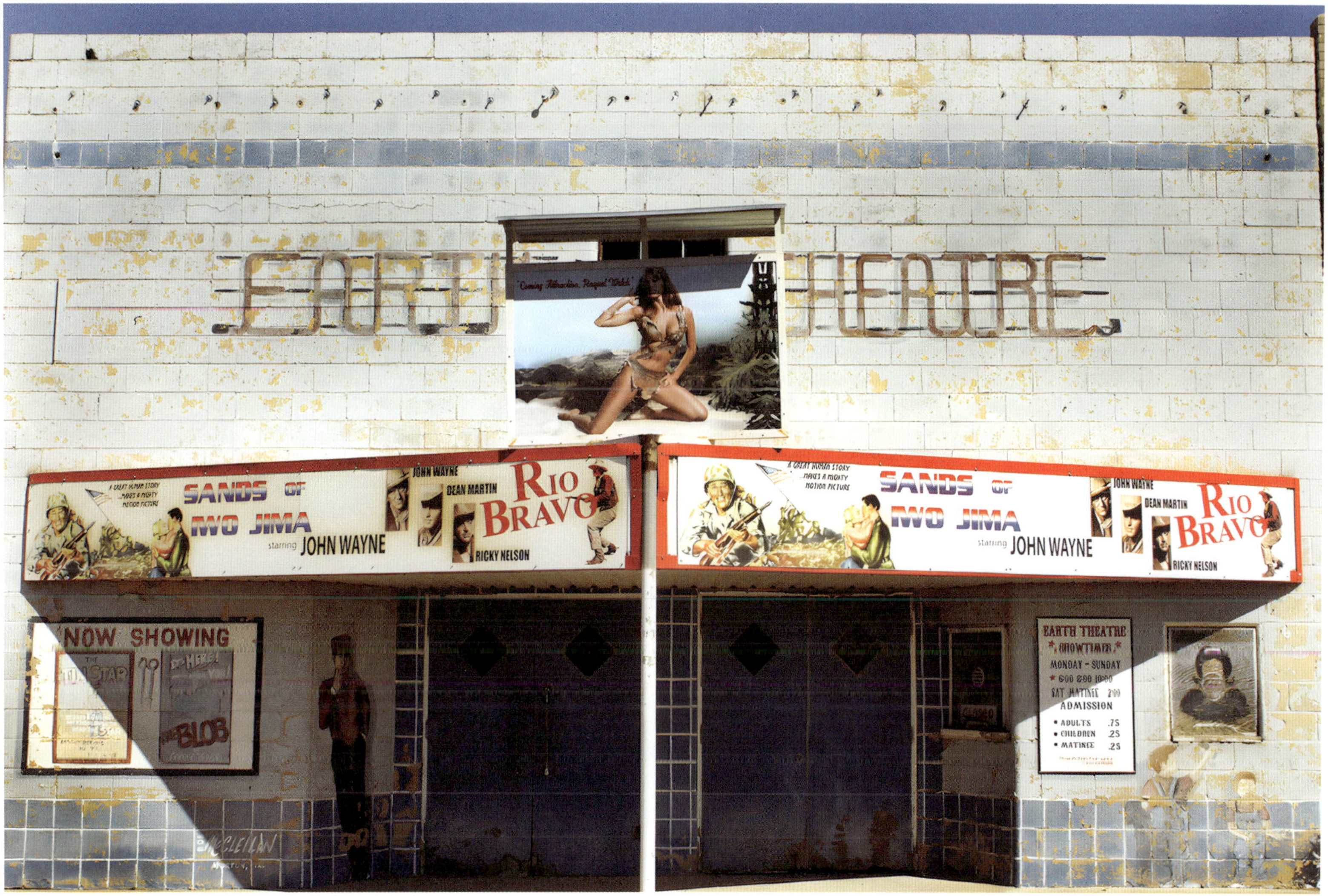

Earth Theatre. PHOTO BY MORGAN PAGE

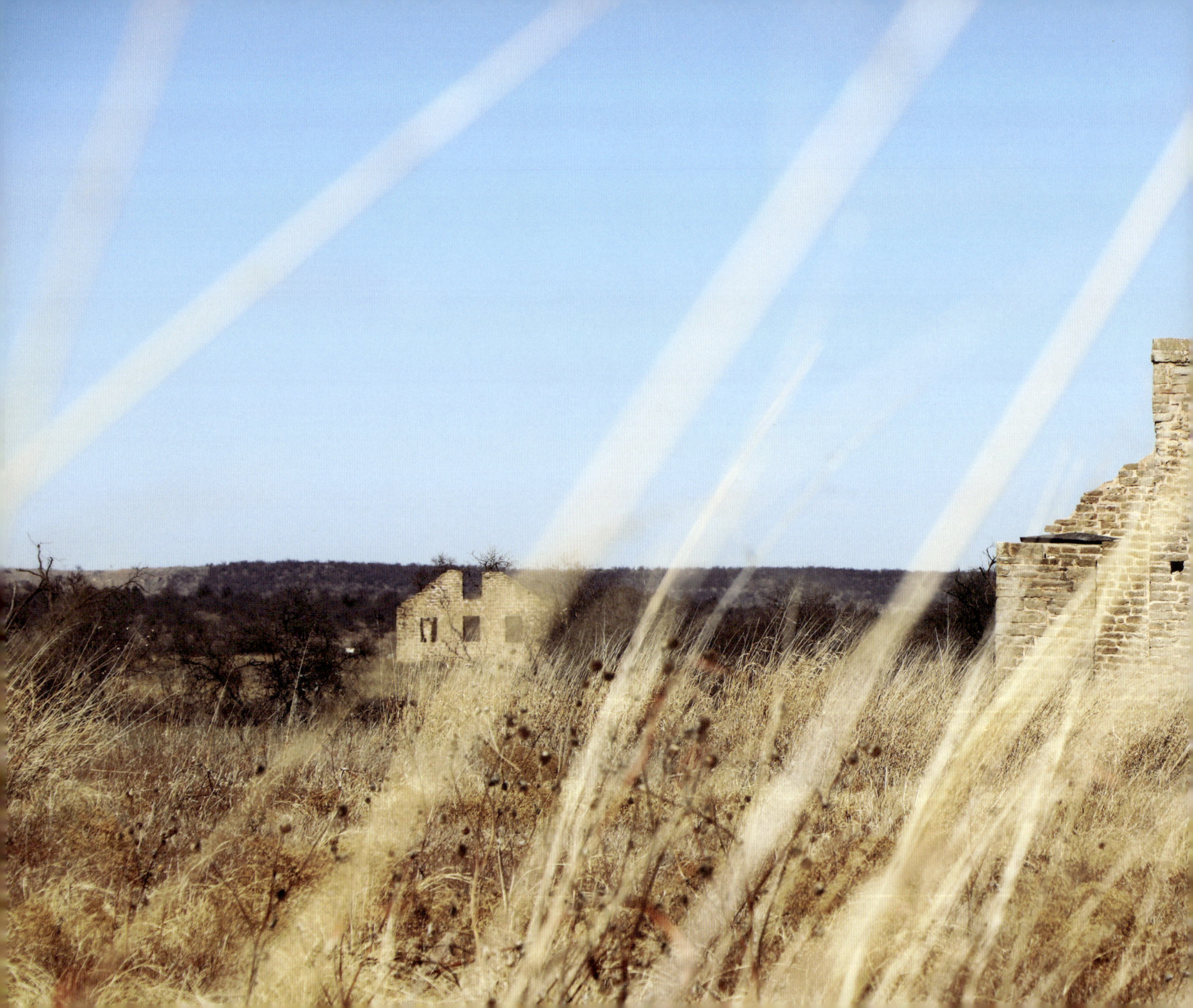

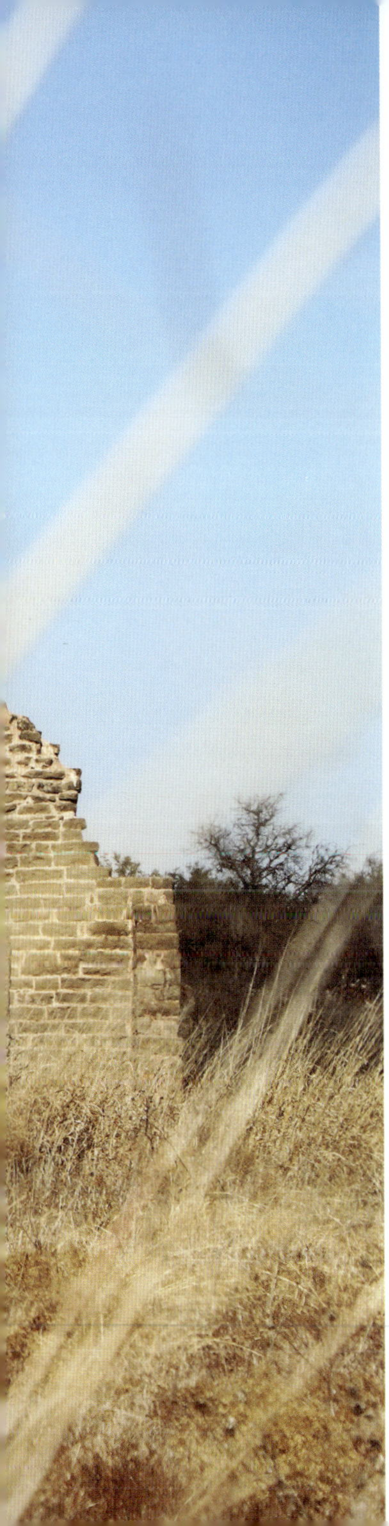

QUEEN OF THE FLATS (1874)

DUSTIN RICE

When the stagecoach lumbered with its four-horse team onto the mesa and into the streets of Fort Griffin, the driver was waiting for a gasp from the woman seated next to him. He had thought it was odd for her to ask to move up top with him for the last leg of the journey. She had said she wanted to see the town when they arrived. He thought it would be a laugh; he had been there many times and knew it was no place for a lady of her stature, and he expected to enjoy seeing the look of regret on her face as they pulled in. But there was no gasp; there was no look of regret. When he turned his head to look at her, his smile faded as he saw hers. When he asked her what she found so funny, she said, "They've not seen the likes of me."

Lottie's playground, ruins of the old fort that was at one time the most dangerous place in North America, Fort Griffin. PHOTO BY DUSTIN RICE

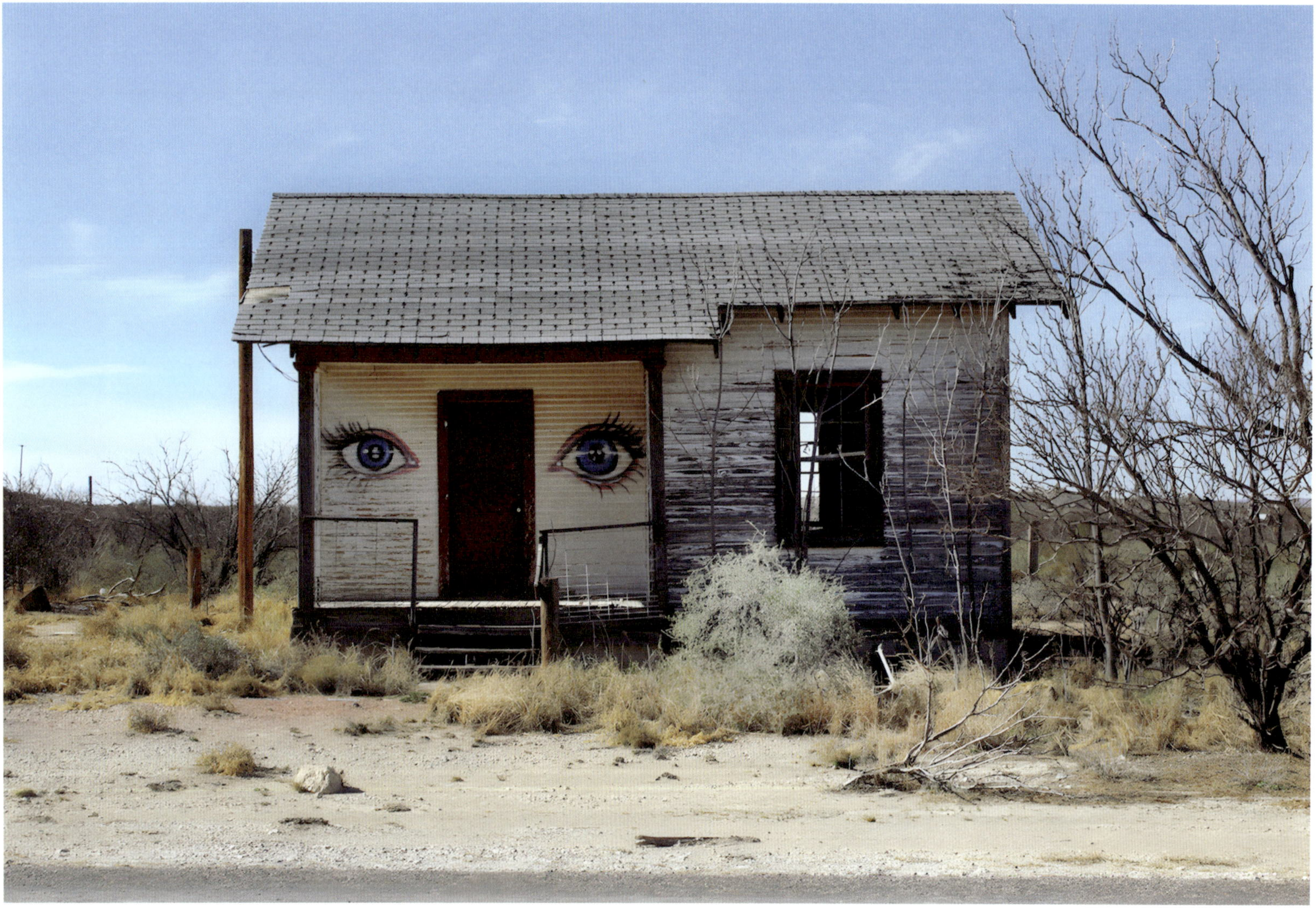

House in Kent, no longer standing as of fall 2021. PHOTO BY MORGAN PAGE

It is difficult to separate the facts from the legends that Texans have written Carlotta Thompkins into. The real person is probably lost to history, as her legend has been told and retold like a game of telephone, and characters based on her in books and television have served to make her larger than life. (For example, she is thought to have been the inspiration for the character Miss Kitty Russell in the TV series *Gunsmoke*.)

What is known is that she arrived at "the Flat," as Fort Griffin was known in 1876, as a combination of qualities not often seen in her time. She wore the latest in Parisian fashions, had a quick wit, and enjoyed engaging conversation. She didn't pass judgment, and she didn't bat an eye at a gunfight. That was a good thing, because the Flat was widely known as one of the wildest towns in the West, with an abundance of brothels and saloons serving buffalo hunters, former Civil War soldiers, outlaws, bounty hunters, con men, cowboys, pimps, prostitutes—and gamblers. Thompkins was possibly the best five-card draw player in the world. She'd been traveling throughout Texas, "playing out" town after town (draining the gamblers of funds and moving on quickly before getting in trouble for cheating) in marathon games that would draw crowds to the saloons at night. She had earned nicknames in her travels, such as "The Angel of San Antonio" and "Mystic Maude" in West Texas, but the sobriquet that stuck was "Lottie Deno," thought to be a play on "lotta dinero."

Lottie was as successful at gambling in Fort Griffin as she was everywhere else. She soon bought lots in town and became co-owner of The Gus, a saloon and brothel. She ran gaming and girls, and her place was popular. Legend has it that she took a sizable amount of money from Doc Holliday. Another legend has it that one night, after a long game with a large pot on the table, "Smokey Joe" and "Monte Bill" both accused each other of cheating. Both were probably right. Both stood and drew on each other. Both were fine shots, and both were dead on the floor in seconds. The whole saloon cleared out in a panic, but when the sheriff arrived, Lottie was still in her seat, counting her chips. When he asked her why she hadn't left, she quietly said, "You've never been a desperate woman, Sheriff."

Lottie is thought to have spent a little more than two years in the Flat. Court records show that she was accused of running an unclean house, among other charges, at which point she decided it was a good time to leave town. She and the love of her life, Frank Thurmond, another gambler, made their way to New Mexico.

They married and settled in the town of Deming, setting out on a new path. Lottie played bridge with ladies of a more respectable nature. They invested in mining, and eventually Frank became vice president of a bank. Frank passed on in his late sixties, a respected man. Lottie lived on for nearly thirty more years and, having no children, eventually became the mother of the town. "Ma" Thurmond, as Lottie came to be known, was buried in 1934. Her funeral was a community event not seen since.

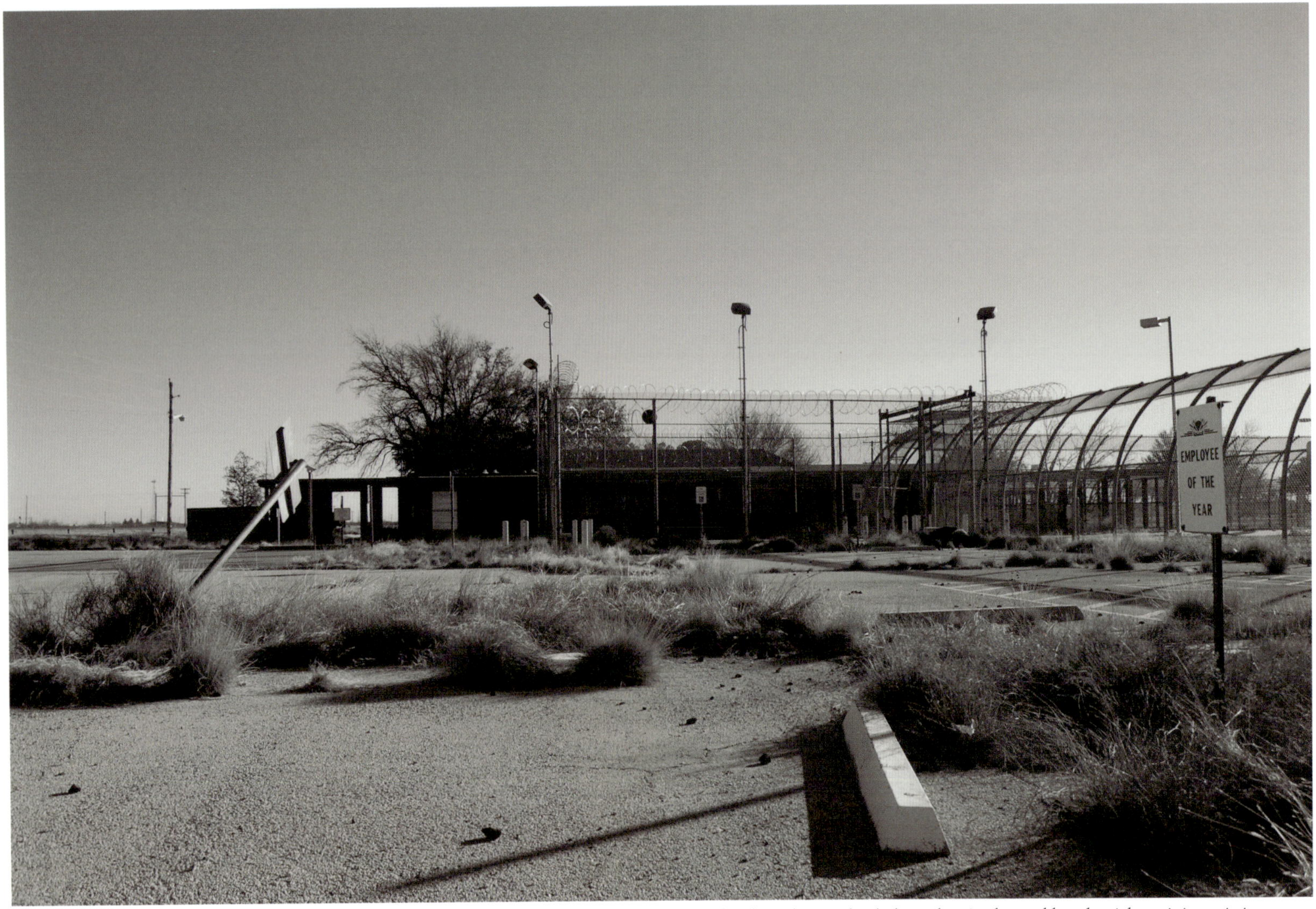

Rattlesnake Air Force Base, Pyote. This World War II bomber training base was remembered by bomber pilots as the darkest place in the world to do night training missions.
PHOTO BY DUSTIN RICE

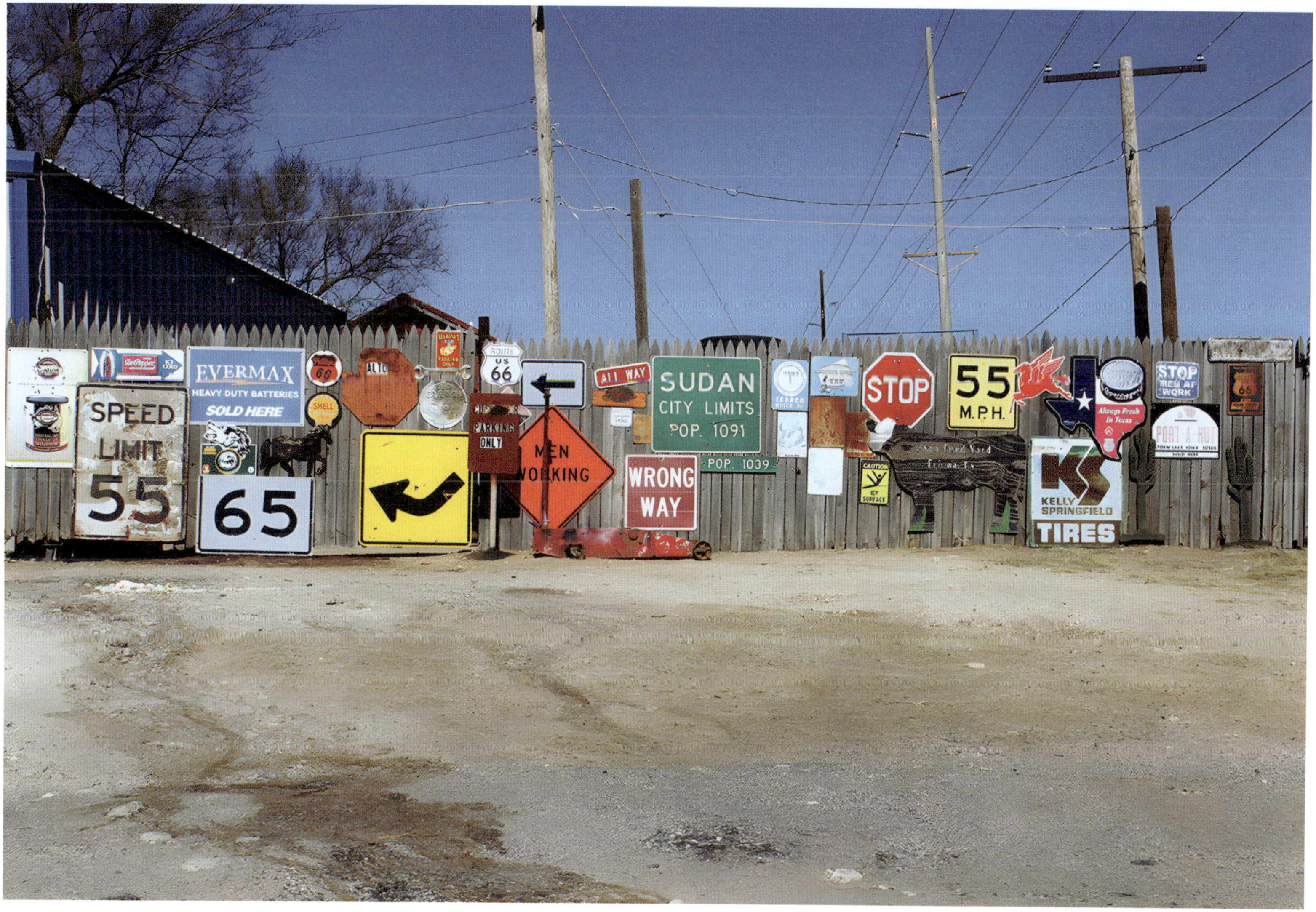

Sudan. PHOTO BY MORGAN PAGE

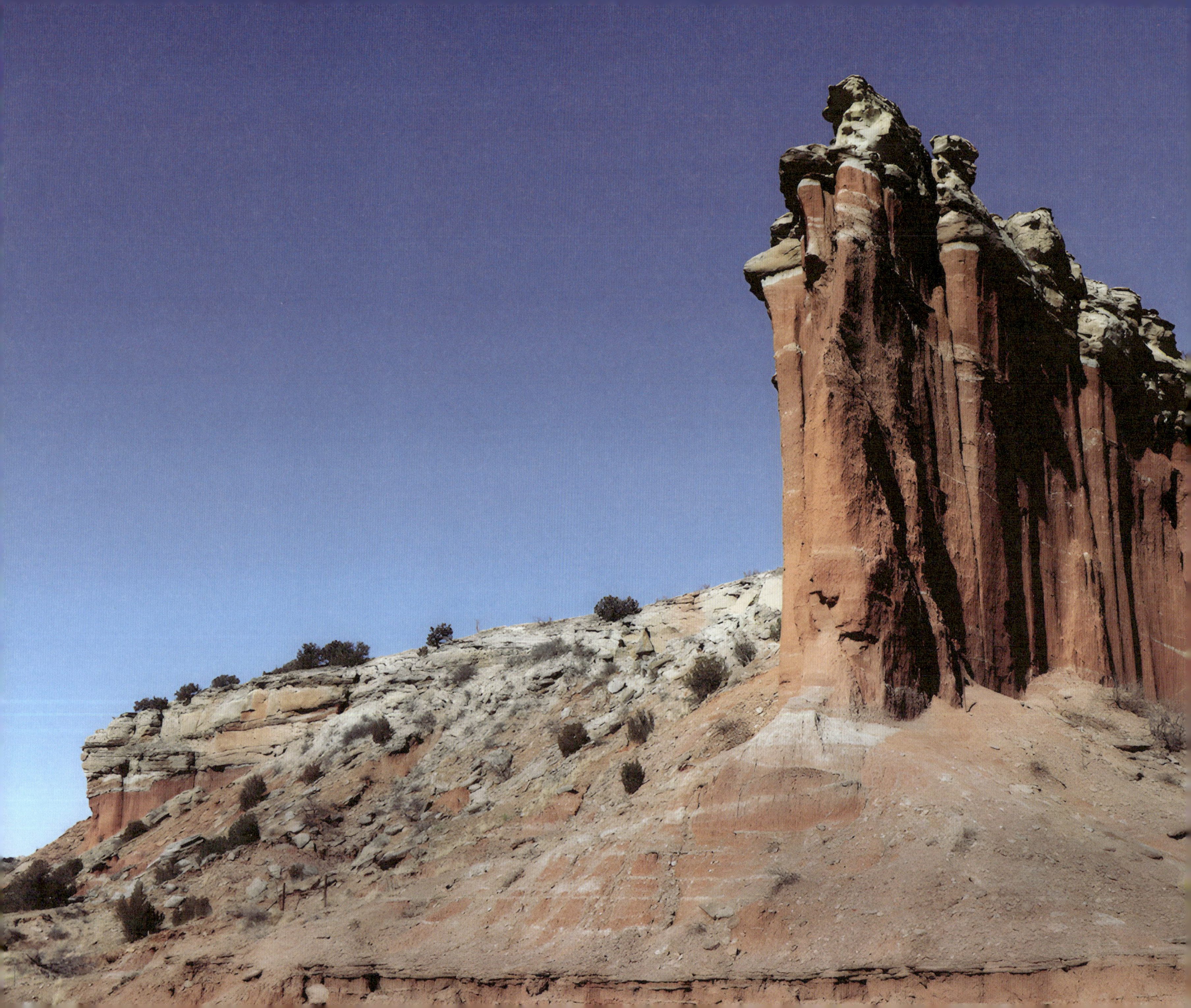

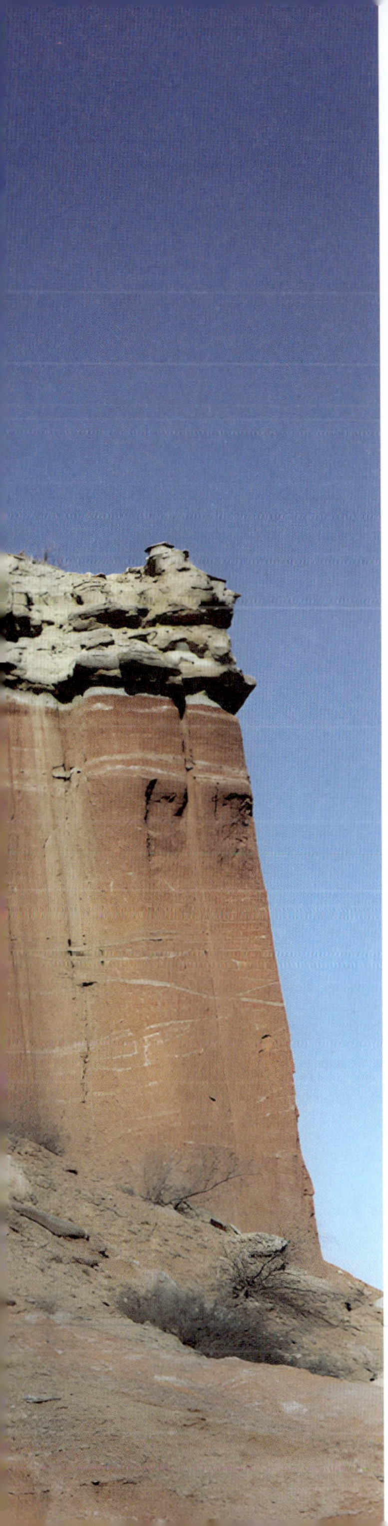

BAD HAND AT DEAD HORSE (1874)

DUSTIN RICE, WITH THE HELP OF LANCE TAHMAHKERA

When the villagers bedded down for the night on September 28, 1874, the Native tribes in Thook-Hoonko-Vee, or Deep Creek, had no idea that they had reigned for their last day as the rulers of the Southern Plains. Their camp, extending two miles along the Prairie Dog Fork of the Red River in Palo Duro Canyon, had been spotted by Tonkawa scouts. Never again would the biggest town in Texas dwell in the deep fortress. Never again would anyone seek its walls for protection. Never again would The People pass winter in freedom, by the fire, in peace.

Tule Canyon, where the killing of almost 1,500 Comanche horses took place.
PHOTO BY DUSTIN RICE

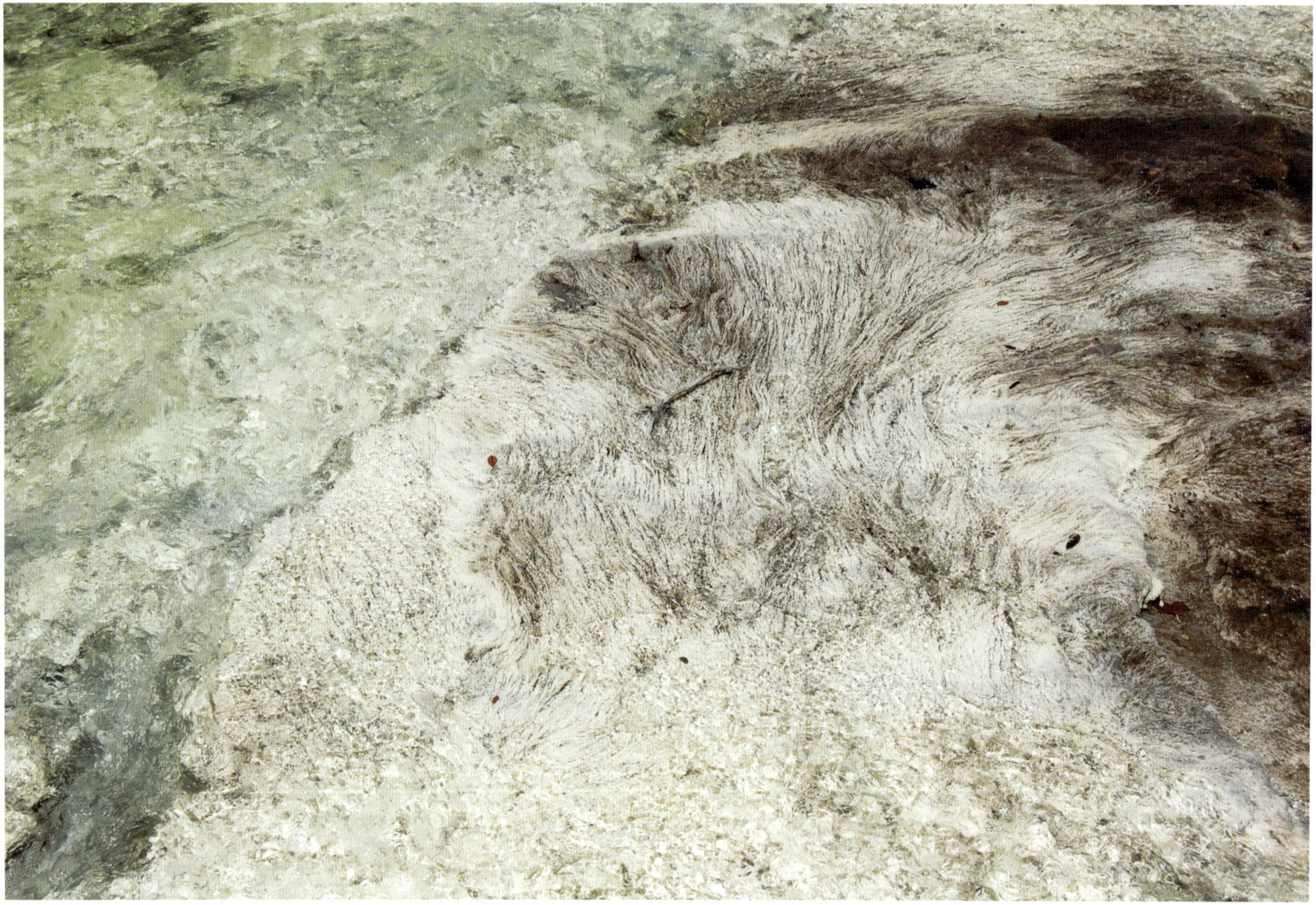
Mineral Springs in Lampasas. PHOTO BY MORGAN PAGE

Their rival was known as Bad Hand. Colonel Ranald Mackenzie lost two fingers in 1864 at Jerusalem Plank Road during the siege of Petersburg. That, along with another half-dozen wounds, kept him in constant pain, and thus in a constantly sour mood. He had a reputation for strict discipline, but he led his men from the front. He had their respect, and he had permission from Washington, DC, to use whatever tactics were necessary to get the Comanche, Kiowa, Kiowa Apache, and Cheyenne in the canyon onto agency land, into confinement on the reservation.

The plan was cold and calculated. Behind the village, slot canyons whose sheer walls dead-ended in sharp wedges served as perfect corrals for almost fifteen hundred horses. When Mackenzie's men attacked, however, there was nowhere to go and no way to get the horses out. Women and children scrambled up the cliff faces, taking only the clothes on their backs. The men followed them up, carrying only their rifles. As they reached the rim of the canyon, eight hundred to a thousand feet above, the warriors rained bullets upon the soldiers who took cover and looked to Mackenzie. "I got you in, I'll get you out!" he told his men, even as they were pinned down.

As it turned out, he didn't have to. On foot and without unified leadership, the Indigenous tribes fled into open country. The soldiers seized their entire winter food supply, source of shelter, and means of transport—and it cost the soldiers only one man. The tribes, combined, lost only three, but Mackenzie knew it was just a matter of time before they transitioned to the reservation. He had done what no one in the history of North America had yet managed to do: he had separated the Southern Plains Indian culture from the horse.

The hides and tent poles of the teepees were broken, slashed, and burned. The possessions inside were looted by the Tonkawa scouts and their wives, who had come along. Their chief, Johnson, received upward of fifty horses from the herd, and his scouts split three hundred more. The remaining horses were marched from Palo Duro Canyon to Tule Canyon, twenty miles south, where they were executed one by one with a bullet to the head.

One can only imagine the tension that filled that canyon as the long process of killing more than a thousand horses began. The relationship between a cavalry soldier and his horse was a special one. Tasking a cavalryman with killing healthy horses, be they Indian ponies or not, must have been heart-wrenching.

The thousands of pounds of rotting horse flesh in Tule Canyon turned stomachs for hundreds of miles as it carried on the wind. The sun-bleached bones were later piled up, reaching a height of over fifty feet and spreading for hundreds of yards. Eventually, they were carted off and ground into fertilizer, but the place became known as Dead Horse. The herd is said to haunt Tule Canyon to this day, stampeding at night, the thundering of their hooves like a storm without rain.

Call it karma, call it bad luck, but within a few short years, Mackenzie took a fall from a wagon, suffering a head injury in Oklahoma. He had recently been engaged to be married in Texas, but his behavior, as a result of the injury, grew erratic and hostile. His hopes for marriage were soon gone, along with his bride. He was in and out of insane asylums for at least ten years. A shadow of the proud officer he once was, he died at the age of forty-eight in New York at the home of his sister.

In the course of researching this place, I found hundreds of accounts of the heroism of the victors and how the army had cleared out the Native nuisance. I found very few accounts that reflected the Indigenous perspective. Then we had the good fortune of meeting with Lance Tahmahkera, great-great-grandson of Quanah Parker, the last Comanche war chief. He told us a story of that tragic day that was passed down to him by his grandmother. She said that McKenzie's army followed them—close enough that the Comanche could sometimes make out individuals on horseback—but the soldiers were not chasing them to engage them in a fight. They pushed them to walk as fast as they could. To wear them down. The fear the soldiers put into those that fled that day has been passed down for generations.

We made our way to Tule Canyon knowing we couldn't get to Dead Horse. It is on private land and we had no access. I don't know what we would have found if we been able to see it, but what we did find when we got to the area made our hearts sink. At the end of the canyon, across the highway from the entrance, is a reservoir built in the early 1970s, Lake McKenzie. The man who engineered the destruction of the Comanche empire has a lake named after him. The water that fills the lake runs directly past the spot where the horse kill took place. There are multiple historic monuments and markers there, and none mention the slaughter. The lake also covered and destroyed seventy-seven historically valuable archeological sites with evidence of Native culture going back more than ten thousand years.

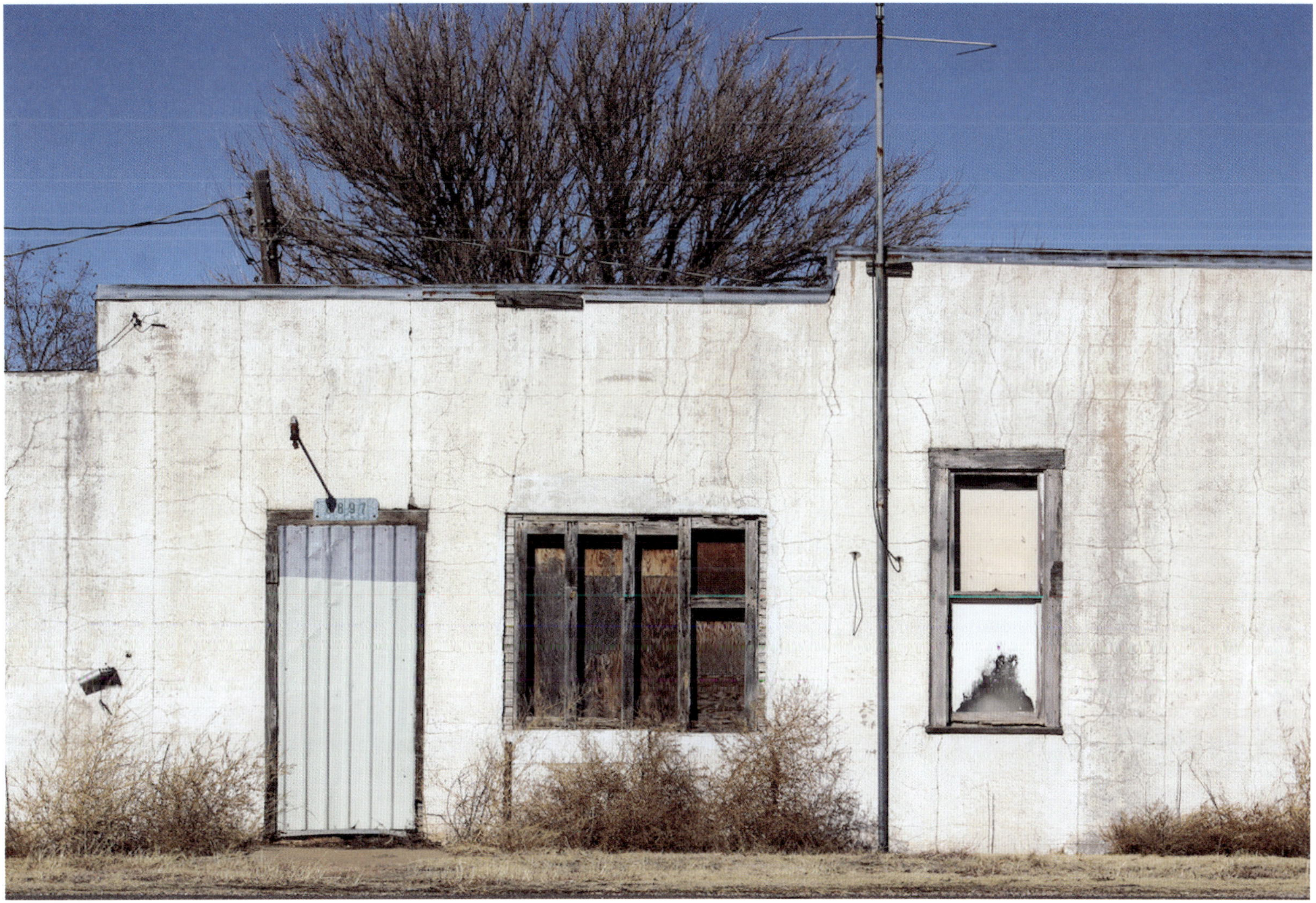

Abandoned home in Vigo Park. PHOTO BY MORGAN PAGE

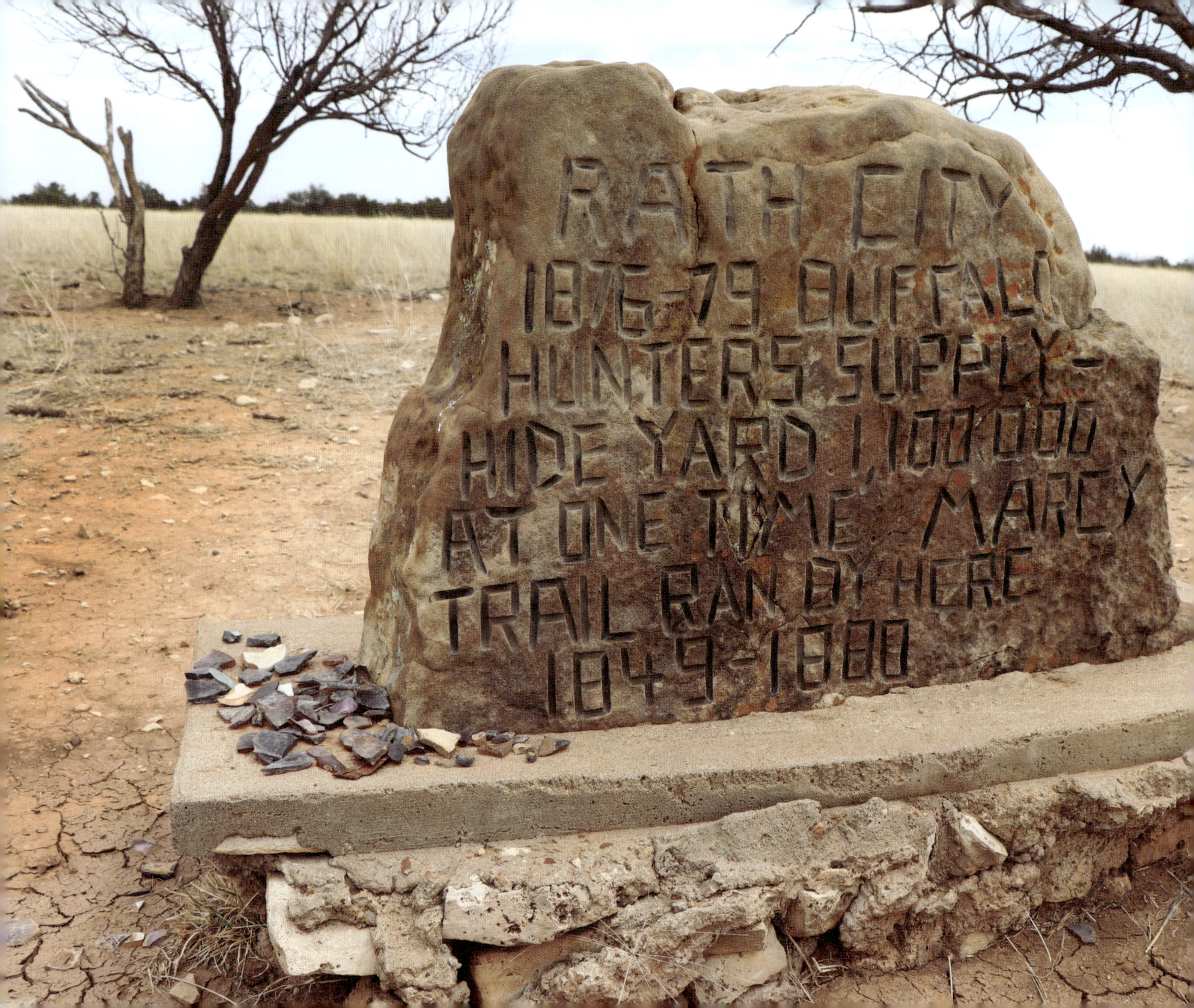
RATH CITY
1876-79 BUFFALO
HUNTERS SUPPLY-
HIDE YARD 1,100,000
AT ONE TIME. MARCY
TRAIL RAN BY HERE
1849-1880

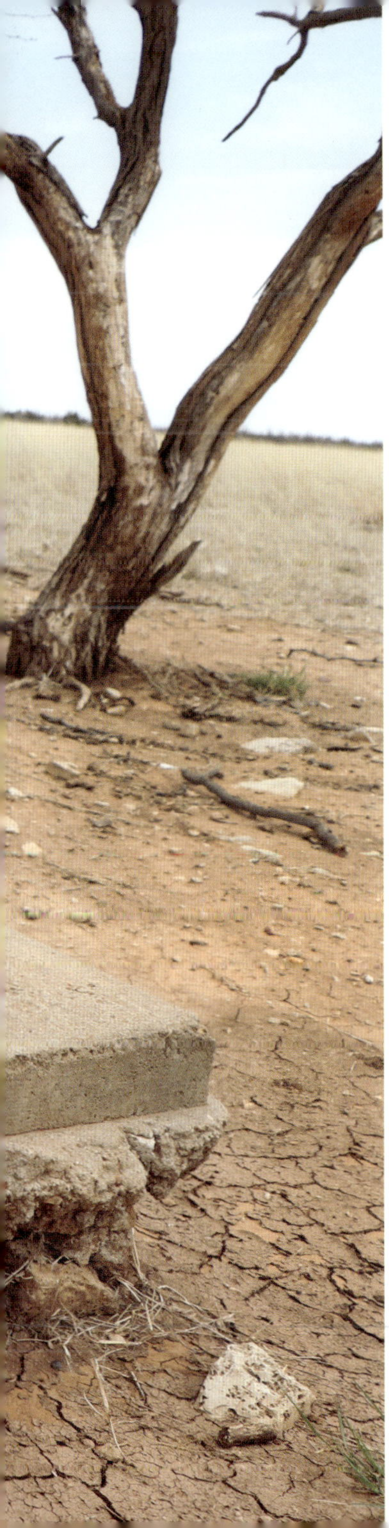

FIELD OF GLASS (1876)

DUSTIN RICE

There is a field in West Texas where, after every rain, glass grows from the ground. It glints in the grass—purple, blue, green, crystal-clear, and cloudy. Fragments of white china with blue accents, shipped from England and still sharp where they were broken, seem to push themselves out of the ground like turnips without greens. Remnants of whiskey and perfume bottles, teacups and saucers, all litter the ground in a pasture that blooms trash.

Rath City marker. PHOTO BY DUSTIN RICE

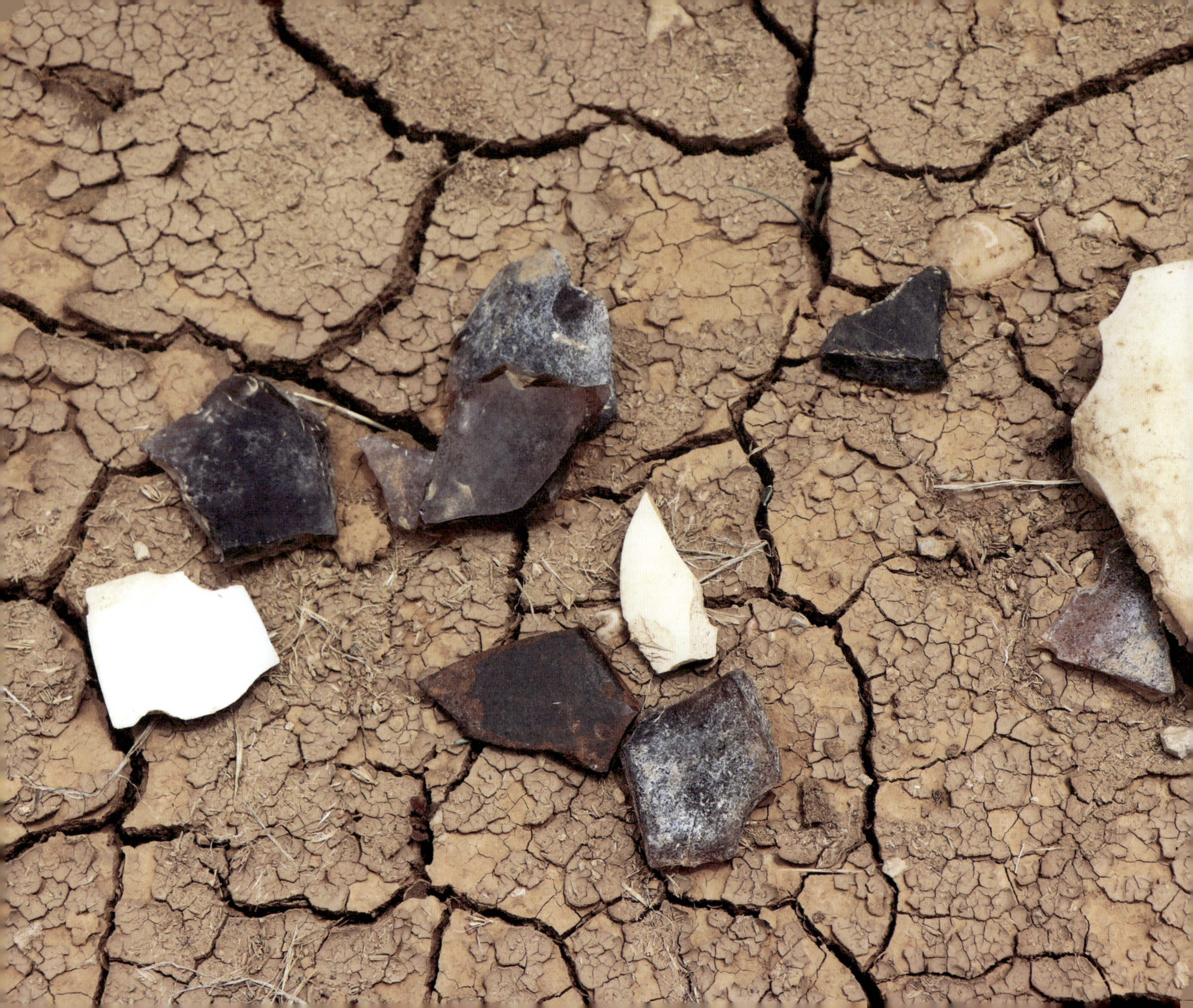

Rath City grew up overnight in 1876, as fifty wagons and three hundred frontiersmen turned this rise on the Brazos River into the last buffalo camp in Texas. It's much prettier now than it was then, when it was covered with hides drying in the trees as fat was scraped for rendering and later use in candles and lubricants. Urine (from horse, cow, bison, and human) was a key ingredient in tanning leather, so it was collected in pots. The people who did this work did not have many opportunities for bathing. They say you could smell Rath City before you saw it, depending on the direction of the wind.

If you got used to the smell (and your conscience didn't haunt you for being an accomplice to the near extinction of a species or the Indigenous people whose lives were intertwined with it), this was lucrative work. The government paid $1 per hide, as the raw material for making belts for machinery in the factories back east. As a result, the hide hunters ordered every luxury that could reach them without spoiling. Most of the items came in bottles, others in jars. The bottles and jars were almost always discarded after being emptied, and so behind every establishment there were piles of glass. For five years, they grew. One can imagine that certain businesses—saloons, brothels, laundries, general stores—would have had the tallest piles.

After the herds were gone, the town disappeared. Aside from the glass, two graves are the only evidence that thousands of people once gathered here. Eventually, the land was sold to ranchers and Rath City became a pasture. For more than a hundred years, people have gone to pick up glass and touch history. The field is private now. It's rarely visited and is left fallow to protect the history still in the ground. But if you are fortunate enough to visit, or even more fortunate to do so after a rain, then you too may see it sparkle: flashes of beauty, commemorating an ugly era.

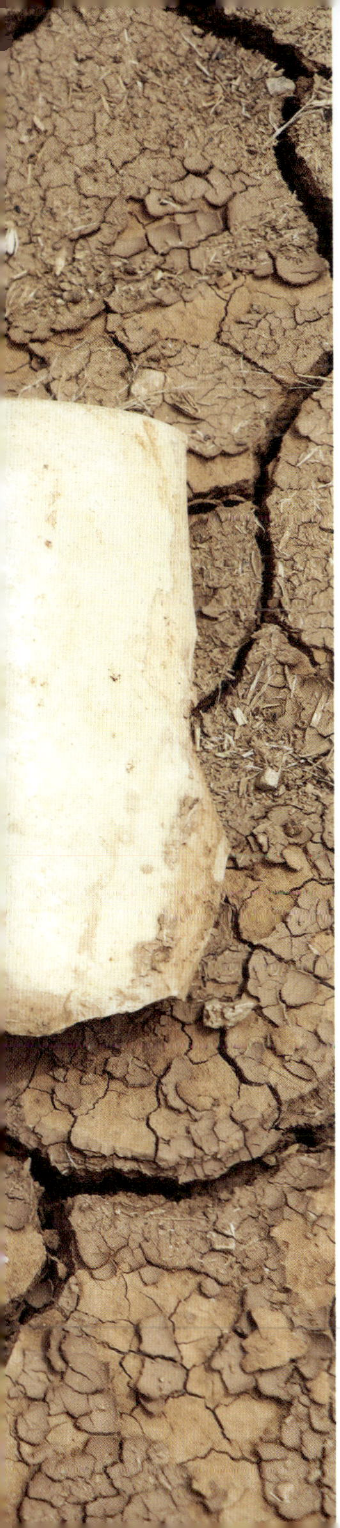

Glass found at Rath City. PHOTO BY DUSTIN RICE

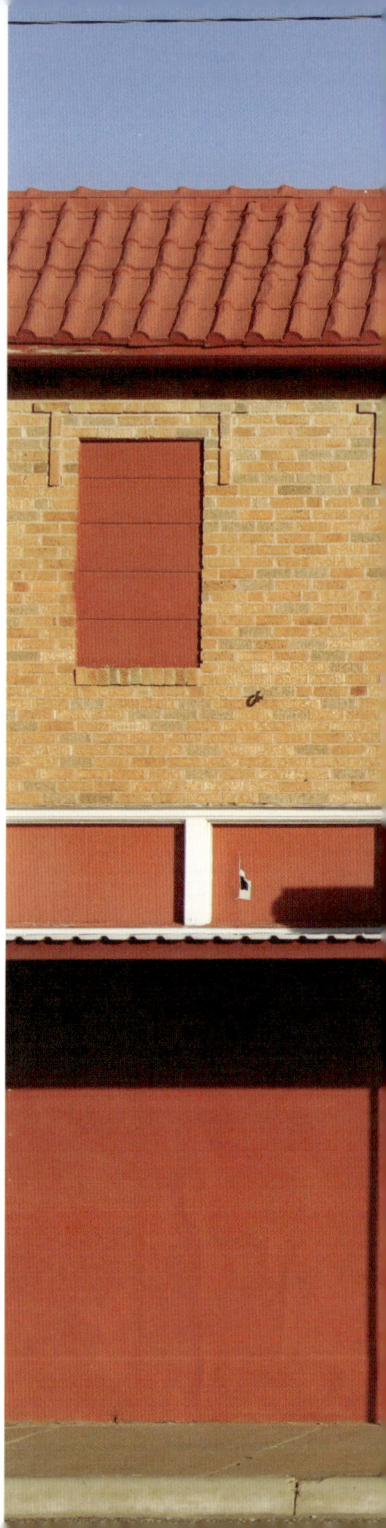

Palace Theatre in downtown Paducah, which opened November 7, 1928, with Dolores del Rio in Ramona. PHOTO BY MORGAN PAGE

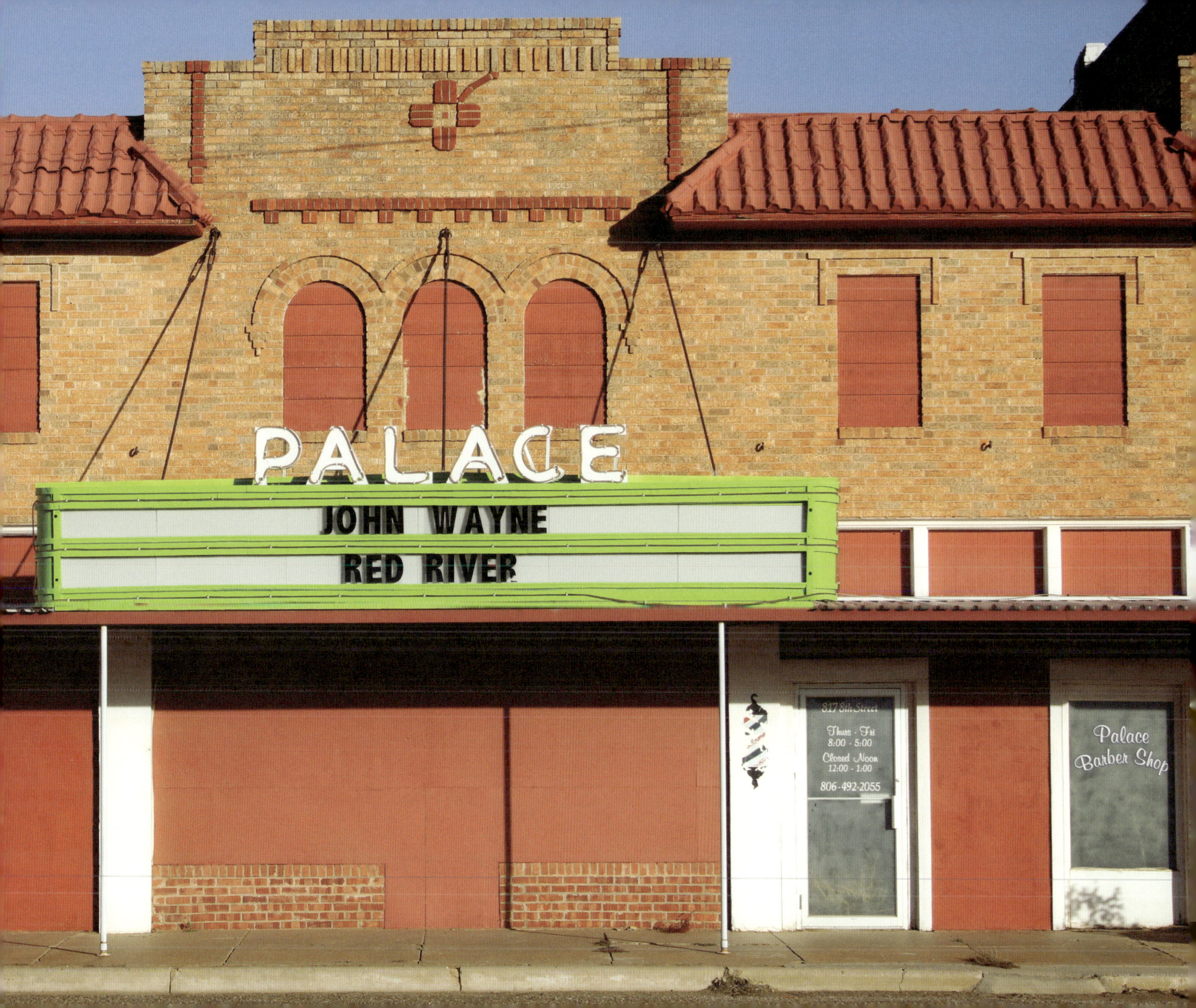

PALACE
JOHN WAYNE
RED RIVER
Thurs - Fri
8:00 - 5:00
Closed Noon
12:00 - 1:00
806-492-2055
Palace
Barber Shop

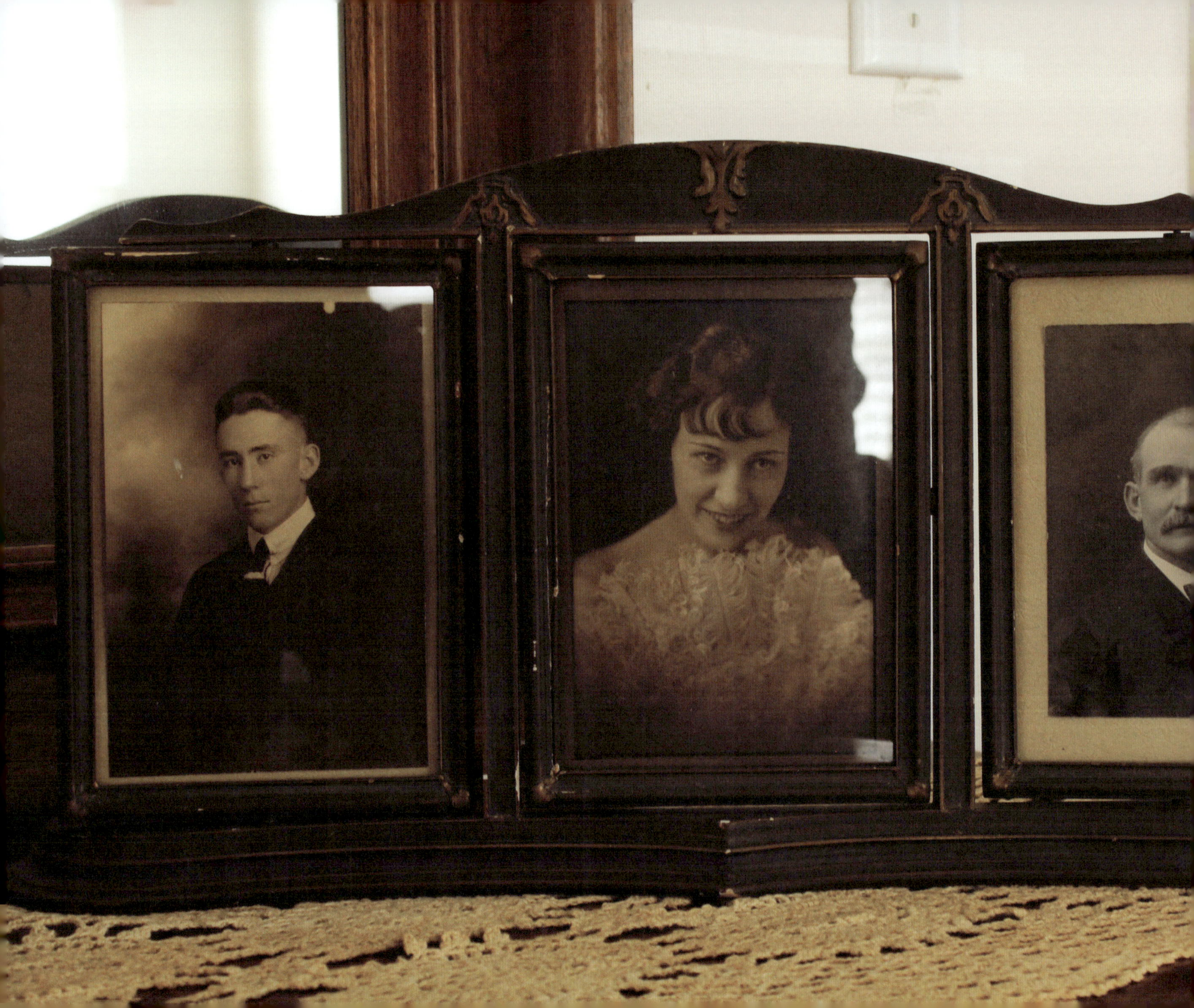

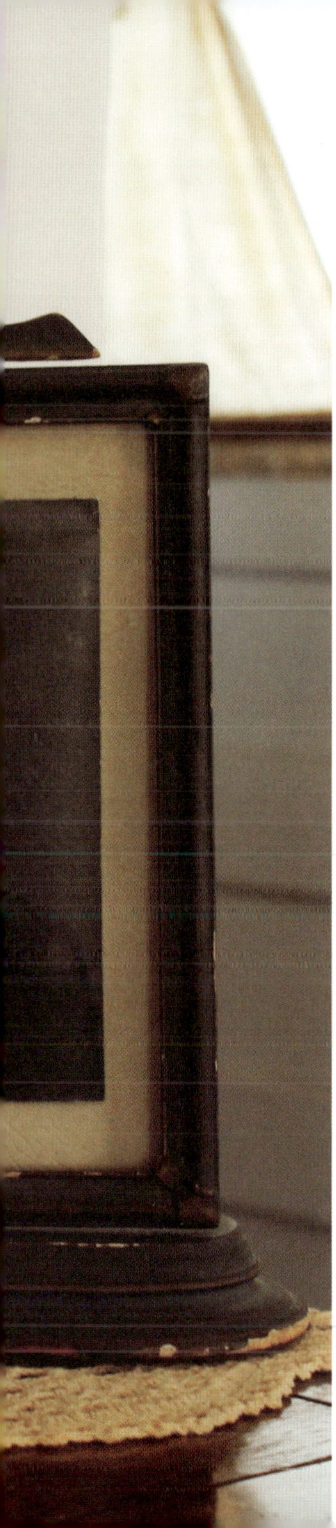

LEGENDS AND MYTHOS (1872)

DUSTIN RICE

Obbie Loving left his home in Graham, Texas, to attend college just like many other eighteen-year-olds. He was ready to make his mark on this world, ready to make a name for himself. He had spent most of his free time on the family ranch a half hour away, just outside of Jermyn. Were there parts of his life on the ranch he was going to miss? Sure. The teamwork involved in separating calves and branding them was a favorite part of his spring.

Family portraits at Loving Ranch. From left to right: Oliver Loving Jr.; Erna Loving, wife of Oliver Loving Jr.; and Oliver Loving Sr., also referred to as Oliver Loving II. PHOTO BY MORGAN PAGE

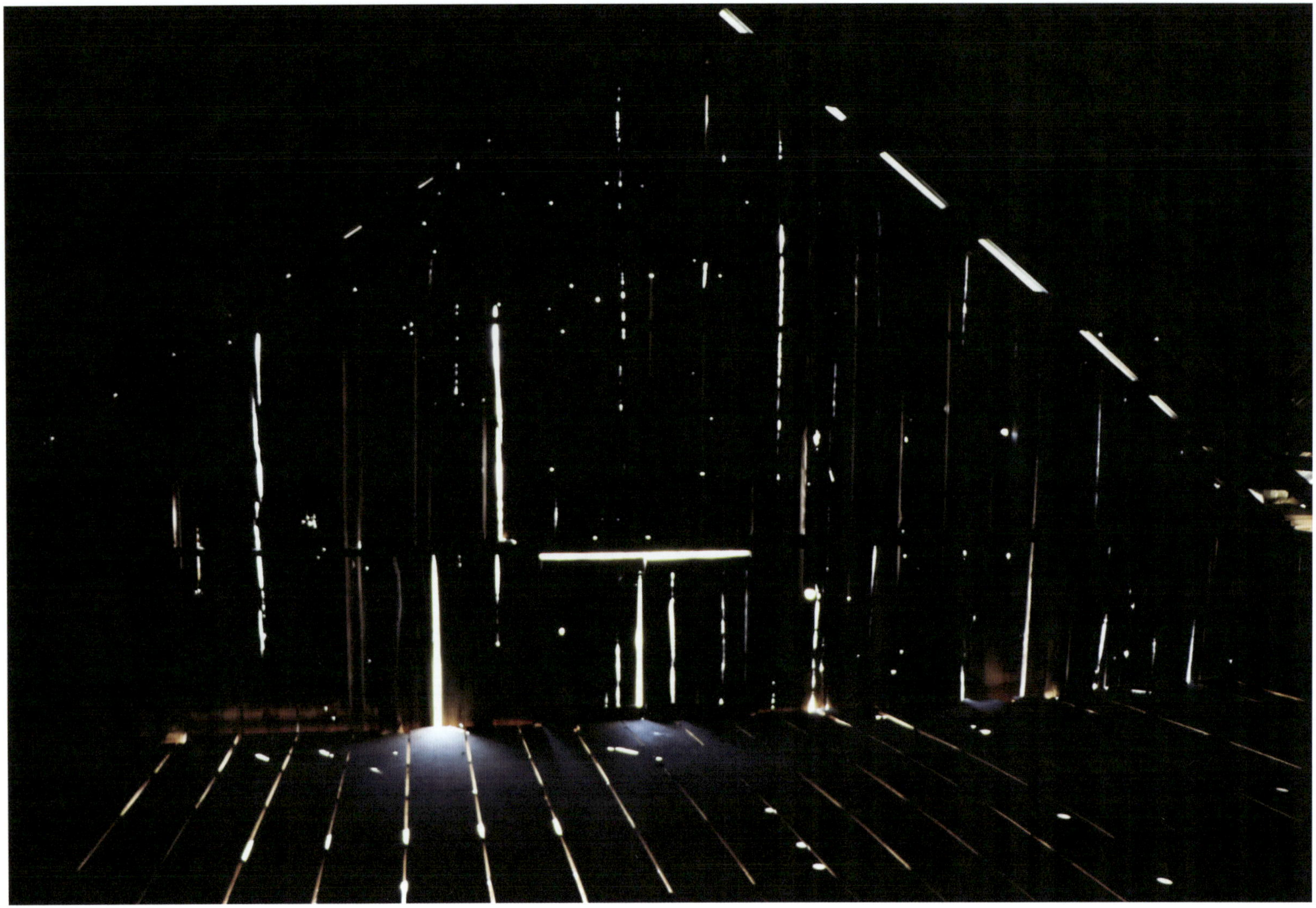

The hay loft in the barn at Loving Ranch, est. 1870. PHOTO BY DUSTIN RICE

He wondered who would be holding a hind leg in his place, rolling around in the dirt all day. But life would move on without him on the ranch; he had classes to attend. Still, when his history professor stopped in the middle of taking attendance and peered at him over his glasses, loudly asking, "Direct descendent?" he realized that maybe his name had already been made famous. His full name was Oliver Loving IV, and that name meant much more to his history professor than he knew.

In Texas, there are names that evoke memories of our history. Austin is the "Father of Texas." Crockett, Bowie, and Travis invariably elicit thoughts of the Alamo. Goodnight and Loving were the creators of the Goodnight-Loving Trail and the Texas cattle drives that followed. These names have gone beyond legend into myth. But what happens to the people who carry one of those names?

Oliver Loving and Charles Goodnight are synonymous in Texas history, but the two were very different people. Goodnight died in 1929, leaving no children; his work was in his ranching, and after his death, his work was sold and his meaningful possessions were donated to museums or willed to friends. His legacy was left in the hands of folklorists and writers like J. Frank Dobie and Larry McMurtry.

McMurtry used Goodnight and Loving as the basis for the beloved *Lonesome Dove* characters Woodrow Call and Augustus McCrae, and as a result, historical fact has been blurred with the fiction that came after. In the book, the men spend an entire career together as the representatives of justice on the frontier. The reality is that Loving was wounded on the second cattle drive the two attempted and they only worked together for a couple of years. But Goodnight really did return Loving's remains to Texas in dramatic fashion, very similar to the events in the book.

The Loving family is now eight generations removed from Oliver's passing. Their story, the one beyond the legend, is ongoing. Oliver's son James, or JC, should really be considered the person at the center of the family history, following Oliver. He started the Loving Ranch after wrapping up Oliver's continued business with Goodnight. He chose the Lost Valley in Jack County, Texas, as the location. It was the early 1870s and it was not an easy place. The family built a house and cleared the land by hand, and it's the place where they still live.

July 12, 1874, is a day that has no lasting legacy in Texas lore, but this date is significant because of what almost happened. A war party of fifty Kiowa, defeated weeks earlier at Adobe Walls, wanted revenge. Their intention was to kill and take. Had Major John B. Jones and his twenty-six Texas Rangers not been there, then many cattle, goods, and lives—as well as the lives of unborn future generations—would certainly have been taken. Instead, an engagement with Indigenous people by Texas Rangers was carried on throughout the county, ending on the front steps of the Loving Ranch. According to Thomas Horton's *History of Jack County*, two Rangers were dead and another two were wounded. This episode was the final straw for local ranchers.

JC Loving helped to found the Texas and Southwestern Cattle Raisers Association, running the organization out of his house before moving to a bigger office years later in Fort Worth. This was an effort to secure local ranches against theft, at first by Native Americans. As the Natives were moved to reservations, however, cattle still disappeared. The association's sights then turned to other ranchers, thieves, and rustlers. They kept track of brands, ensured the upkeep of records, and ultimately organized the history of Texas ranching. The association was the FBI and IRS of Texas ranching, ensuring that no rustling or brand changing went on, and it continues to this day. It was this element of Texas ranching that the Loving family would focus on for generations.

More than a century later, we found ourselves searching for

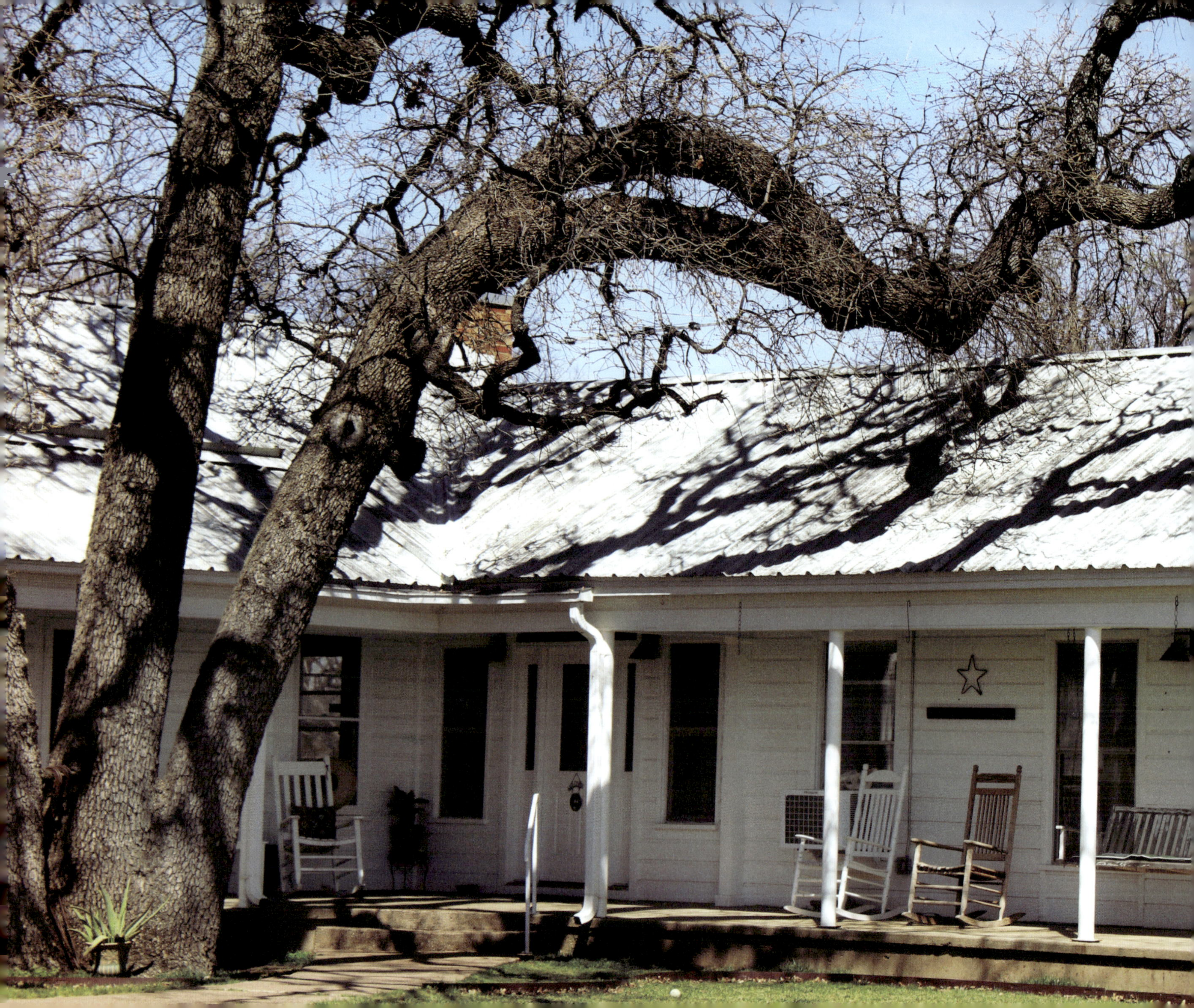

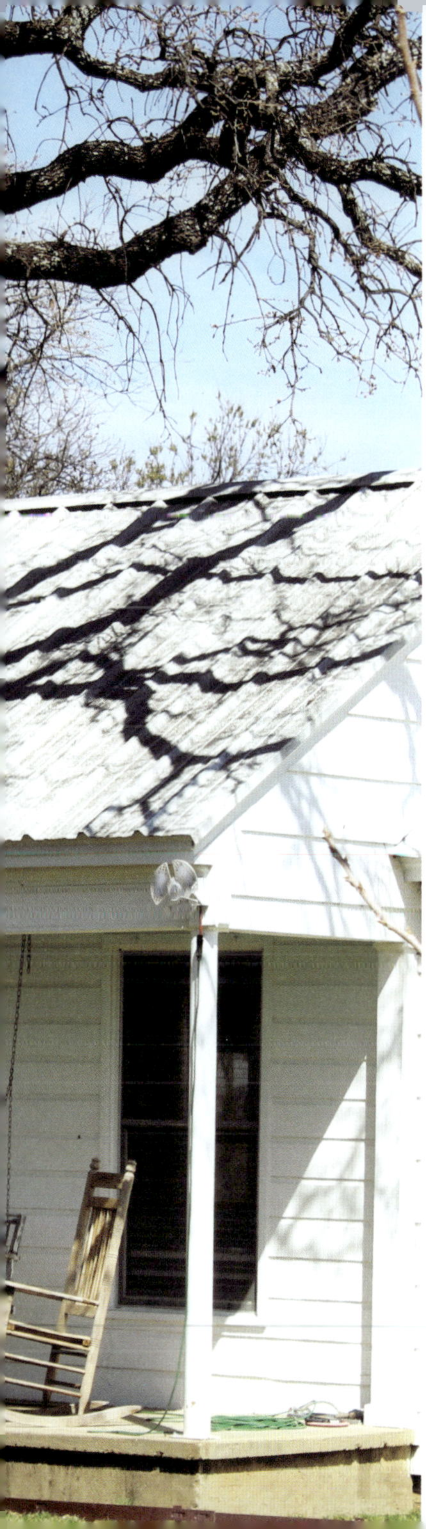

descendants of the Loving family, hoping to get information that wasn't readily available. We discovered that Oliver Loving IV was alive and well in North Texas. We reached out to one of his kin through social media, hoping for the best, and we were ecstatic to learn that she was the niece of Oliver Loving IV, or "Obbie." She said, "My uncle runs the ranch in Loving. I can put you in touch." We set up a meeting with him and he invited us to the ranch.

We arrived a little after 10 a.m., and Obbie immediately offered us a drink: "Can I get you a glass of water? A shot of tequila?" We spent a few hours getting a tour of the home and the 150-year-old barn built with square nails. We made friends with his horses and his pup, Lola, all the while being entertained and charmed by Obbie's uncanny ability to elicit laughter.

To our amazement, Obbie offered to stay in touch and help us with our project however he could. He kept his word. He lent us an important family scrapbook and a rare book about the town of Jermyn, which borders Loving. He's spoken at several of our presentations, and to this day we still text him anytime our research leads back to the Loving family. Over the years we have been overwhelmed by his generosity of knowledge, time, and spirit.

Oliver "Obbie" Loving IV was raised in small-town Texas, learning ranching as a way of life. He went on to have a career unrelated to ranching, but he has maintained the original house and kept the Loving Ranch intact and in the family. One of the many relatives of the past century and a half was the family historian, possessed of a wealth of information, and he died very young without writing or telling most of it. When that happened, most of the history of the family vanished, save for some portraits and ranching photo books. The Texas and Southwestern Cattle Raisers Association has really become the lasting family legacy. And though Obbie can't escape a history he has no real attachment to, he still puts up with people like us asking him questions about things that he often doesn't know. He just shrugs his shoulders and gives a wry smile, as if to say, "I have no idea . . ."

Loving Ranch Homestead, original construction 1880s. The home has had significant additions since then, including what is pictured here. PHOTO BY MORGAN PAGE

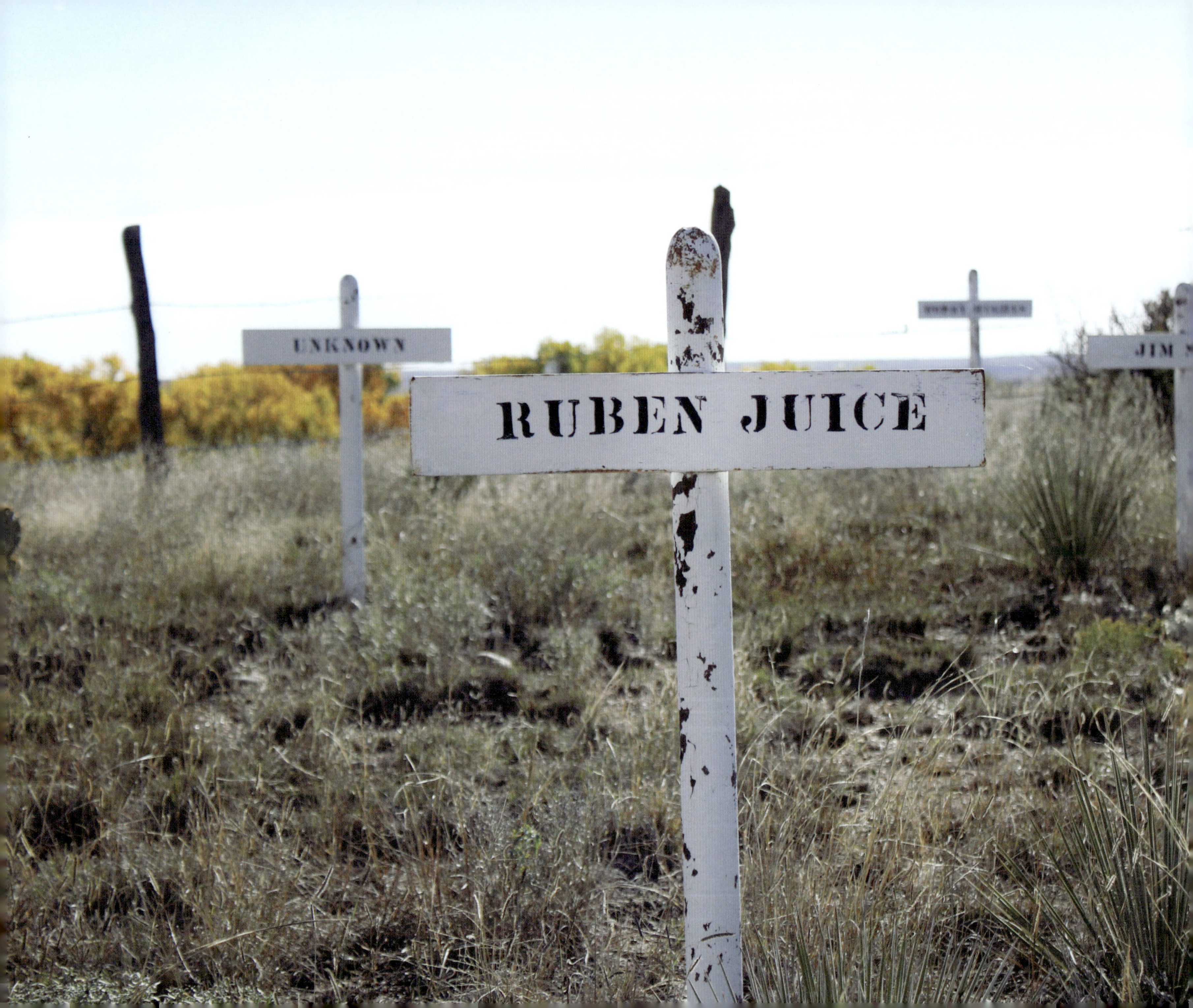
UNKNOWN
RUBEN JUICE
JIM

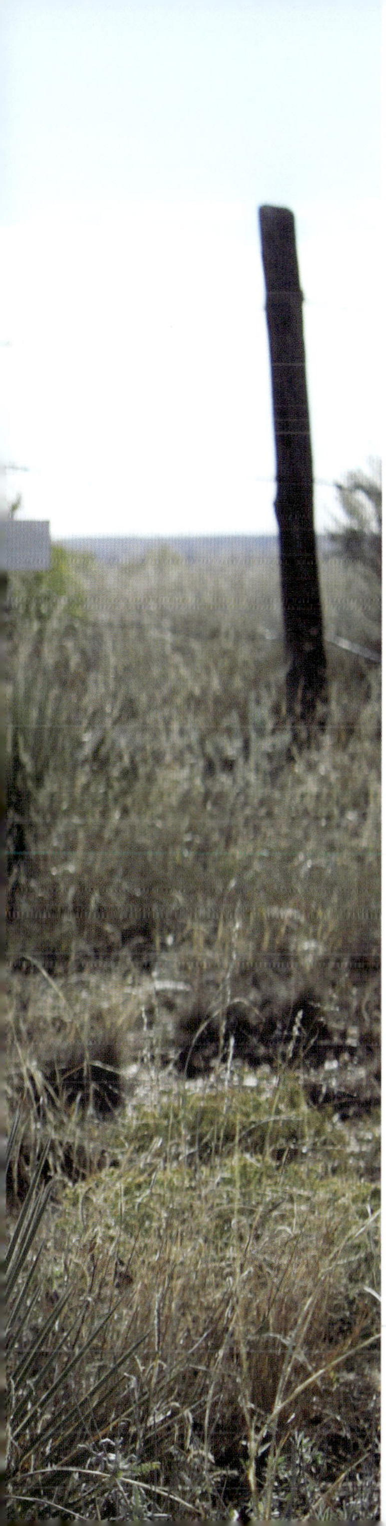

JUICE AND APPLE (1886)

DUSTIN RICE

Atop a hill in the farthest reaches of the vast plains of the Texas Panhandle lies one of the Old West's most fascinating cemeteries. It holds the bodies of the victims of one of the bloodiest and most adrenaline-filled gunfights in history—"the Big Fight"—which was better known at the time than the now-legendary shootout at the O.K. Corral.

Resting place of Ruben Juice, noted chef of Old Tascosa, at Boothill Cemetery, Boy's Ranch. PHOTO BY MORGAN PAGE

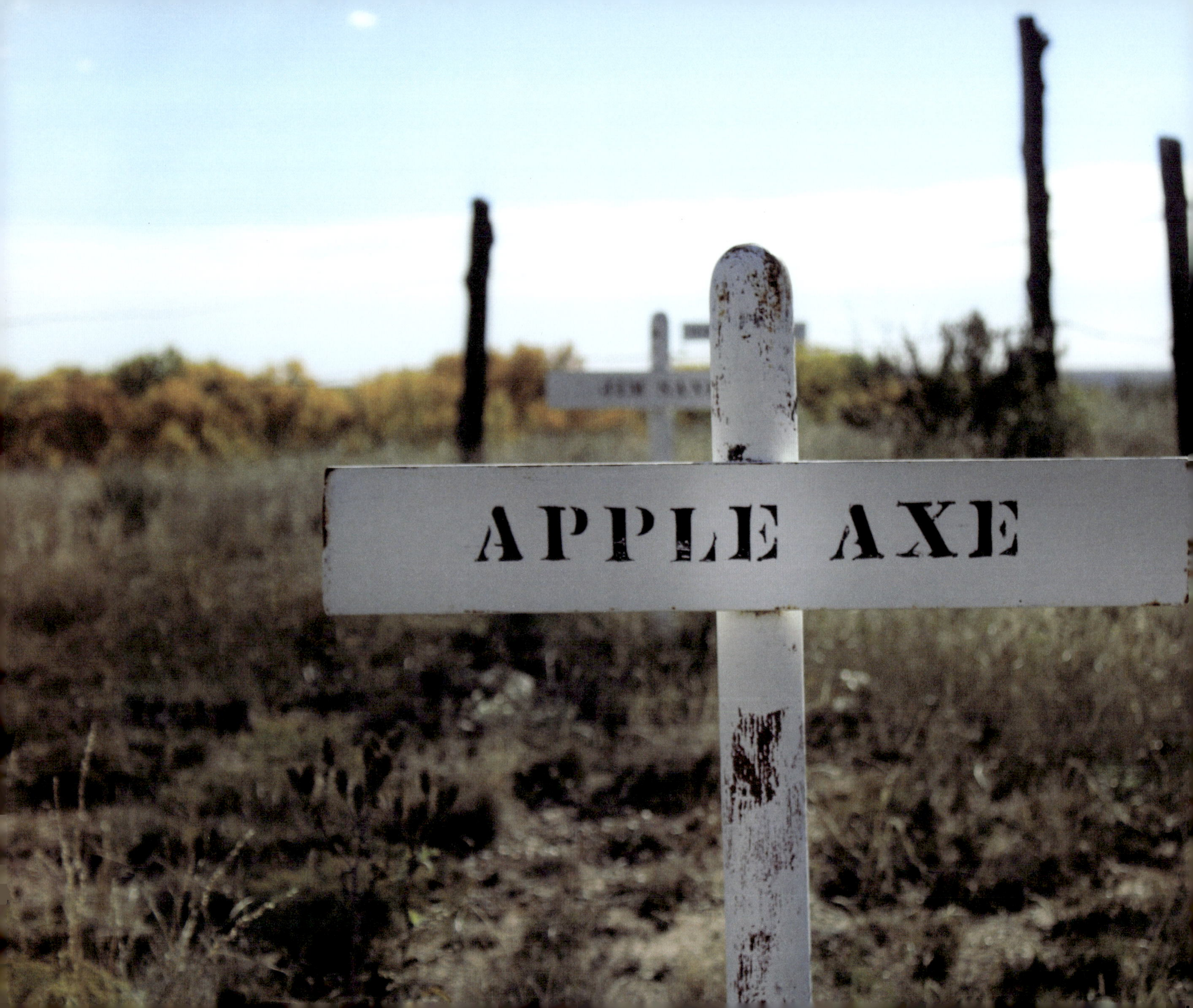
APPLE AXE

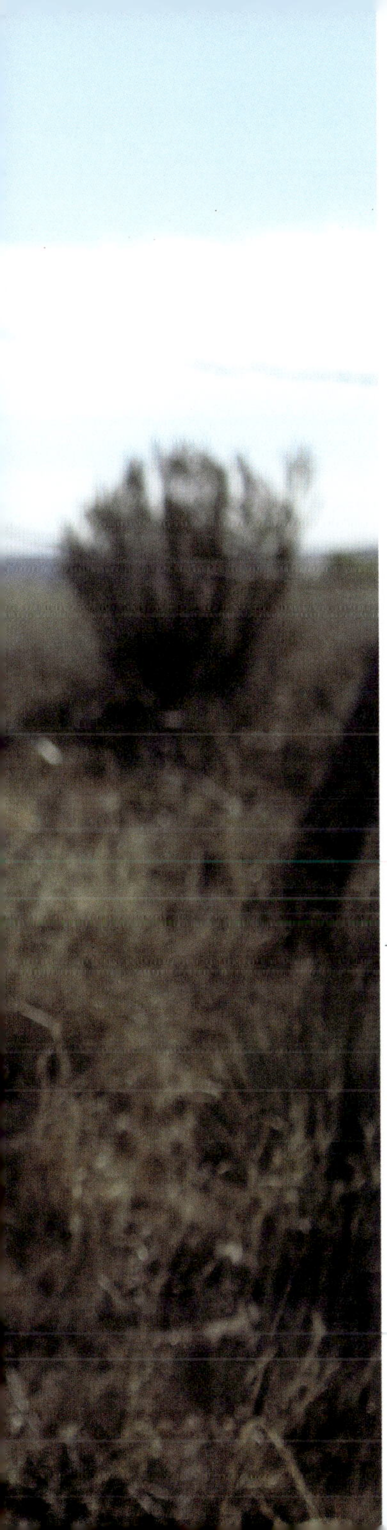

The Big Fight happened on March 21, 1886. It broke out over a woman, and the bragging of the man who won her over. It ended with four dead, two severely wounded, and just as many others lucky to get away with nothing worse than holes in their coats or hats. ("The Catfish Kid," for instance, feigned taking a gunshot, then rolled around on the ground pretending to choke until he was able to get up and run away. He is buried in the cemetery at Huntsville Prison.) The Big Fight lasted over fifteen minutes; the shootout at the O.K. Corral took only a minute, maybe two.

That is just one story buried at Boot Hill, the cemetery for the ghost town of Old Tascosa. (There are other Boot Hills across the West, all so named because the people there "died with their boots on.") Twenty-seven people are buried outside Old Tascosa and each one has a seemingly interesting story: The first interred there died over a duck. Alongside gunfighters, there is "The Dutchman," killed by The Catfish Kid. An unnamed woman and two children are stacked in a single grave due to a smallpox outbreak. There was a suicide with no record left behind but a grave, and "Big Jim" Benson was struck by lightning.

It's the ones we don't know as much about that haunt Morgan and me. We know that Ruben Juice and Apple Axe existed because of the markers on their graves and a single line that survived in Oldham County historical logs, listing their names and dates of death. The notes say that Juice "up and died," and Apple "went with him." Theirs is a story I wish I could write, but can only imagine.

Tascosa was a town that lit up like a match. It burned bright for a few years in the 1880s and was mostly gone by the turn of the twentieth century. Billy the Kid passed through before he claimed to have killed twenty-one men (actually more likely four to eight) in Lincoln County, New Mexico. Juice might have served him dinner every night he was there, considering there were only one or two places to eat, and Apple probably "went with him . . ."

Resting place of Apple Axe, Boothill Cemetery, Boy's Ranch in Old Tascosa. PHOTO BY MORGAN PAGE

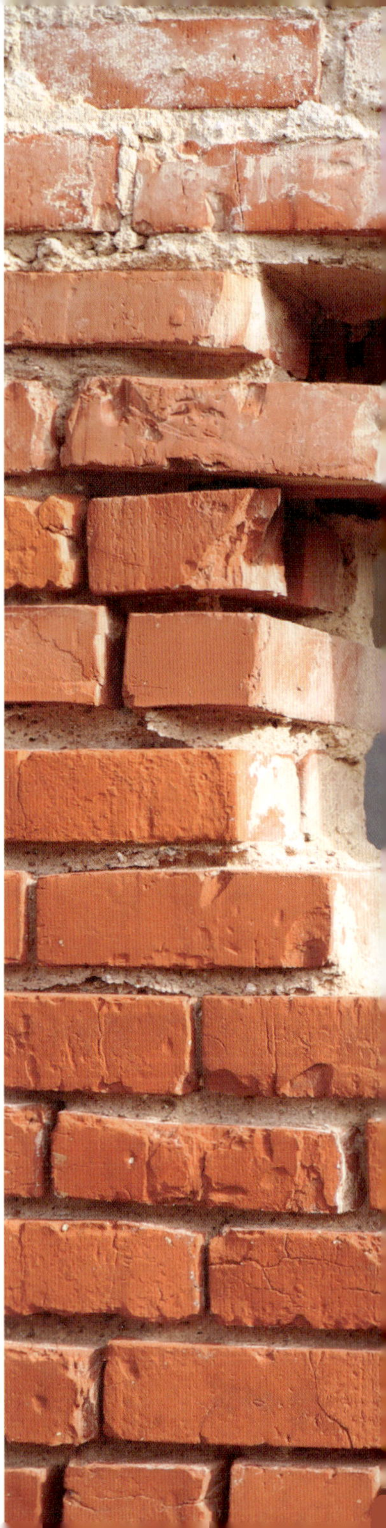

Abandoned building holding old ice machines and appliances, Stamford.
PHOTO BY DUSTIN RICE

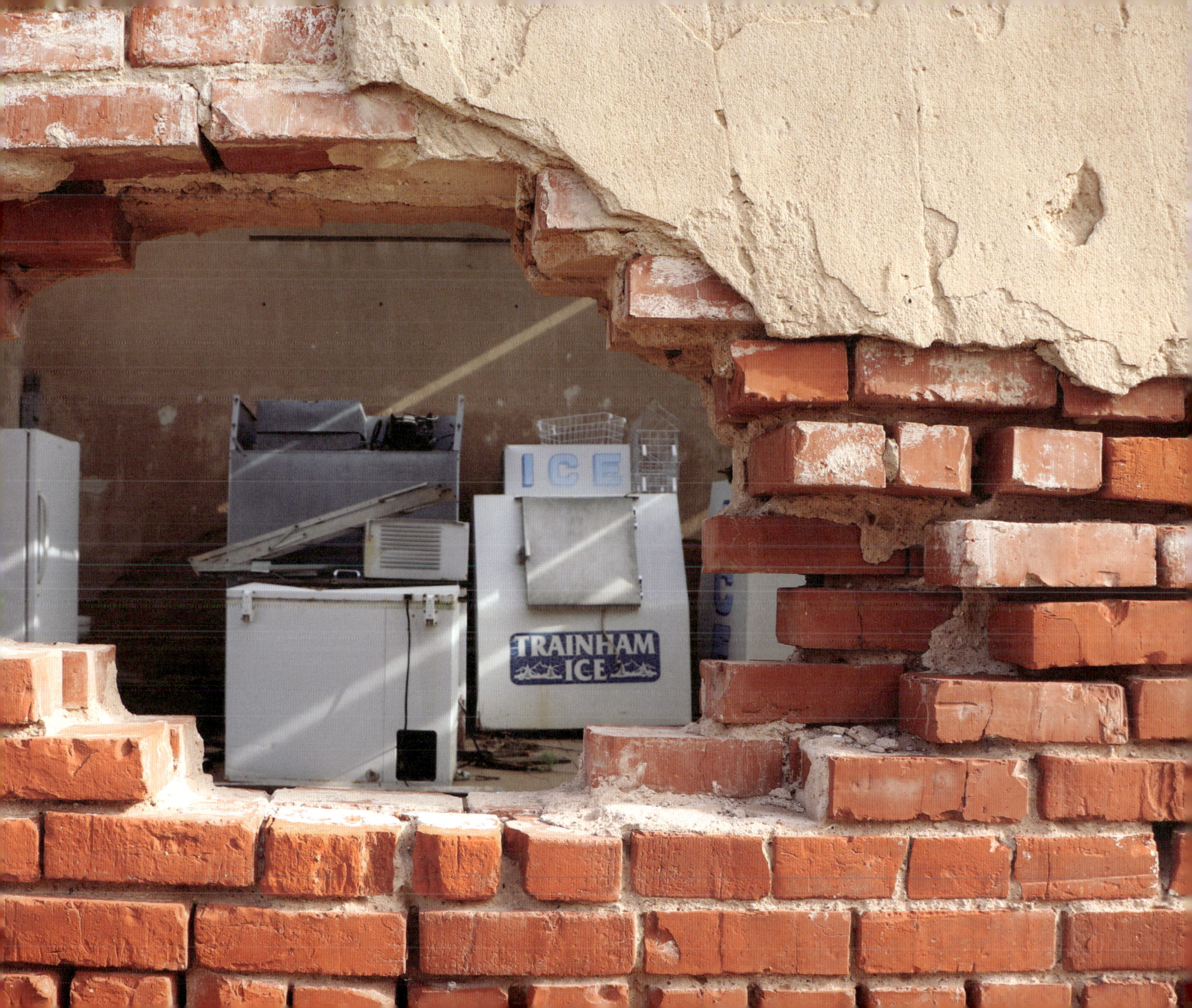
ICE
TRAINHAM
ICE

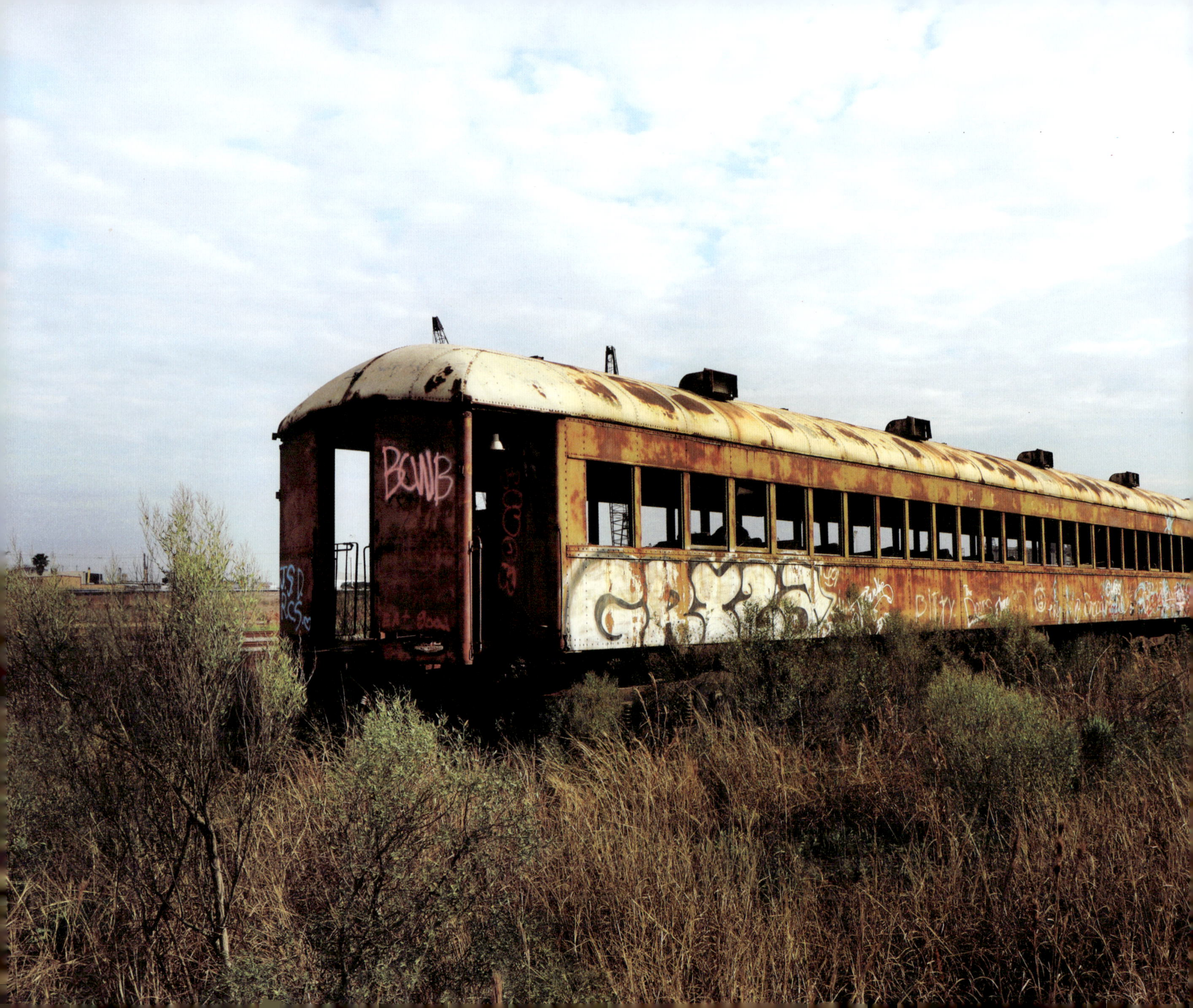

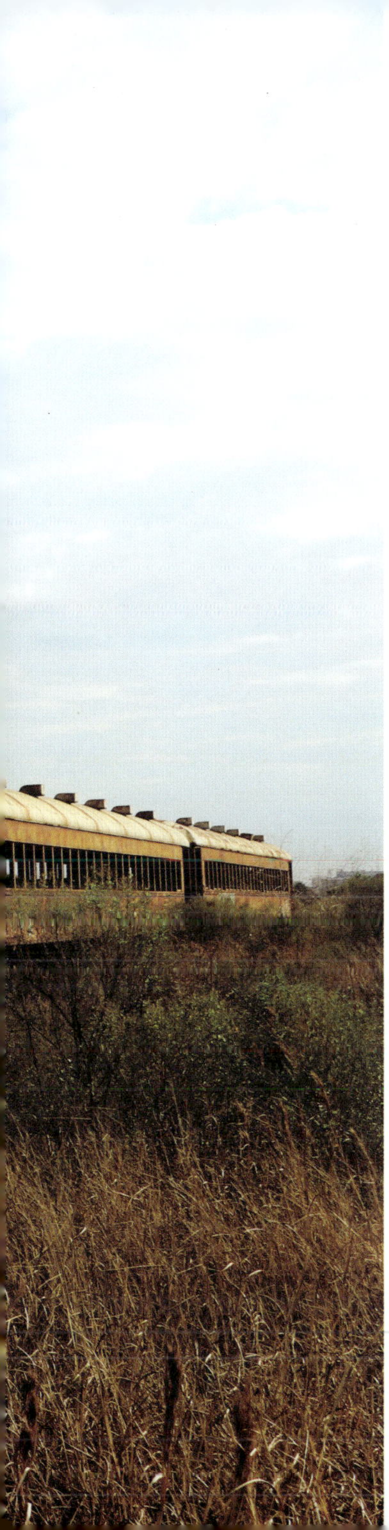

GOOD INTENTIONS (1899)

DUSTIN RICE

For three-quarters of a century, there existed a network that exploited the innocent, uprooted and displaced the naïve and unwitting, and ripped apart already tattered and frayed families—all in the name of charity. It was called the Orphan Train. It was all but unknown across the United States that Texas had become an open market for children.

Old passenger cars on abandoned tracks by the channel, Galveston. PHOTO BY DUSTIN RICE

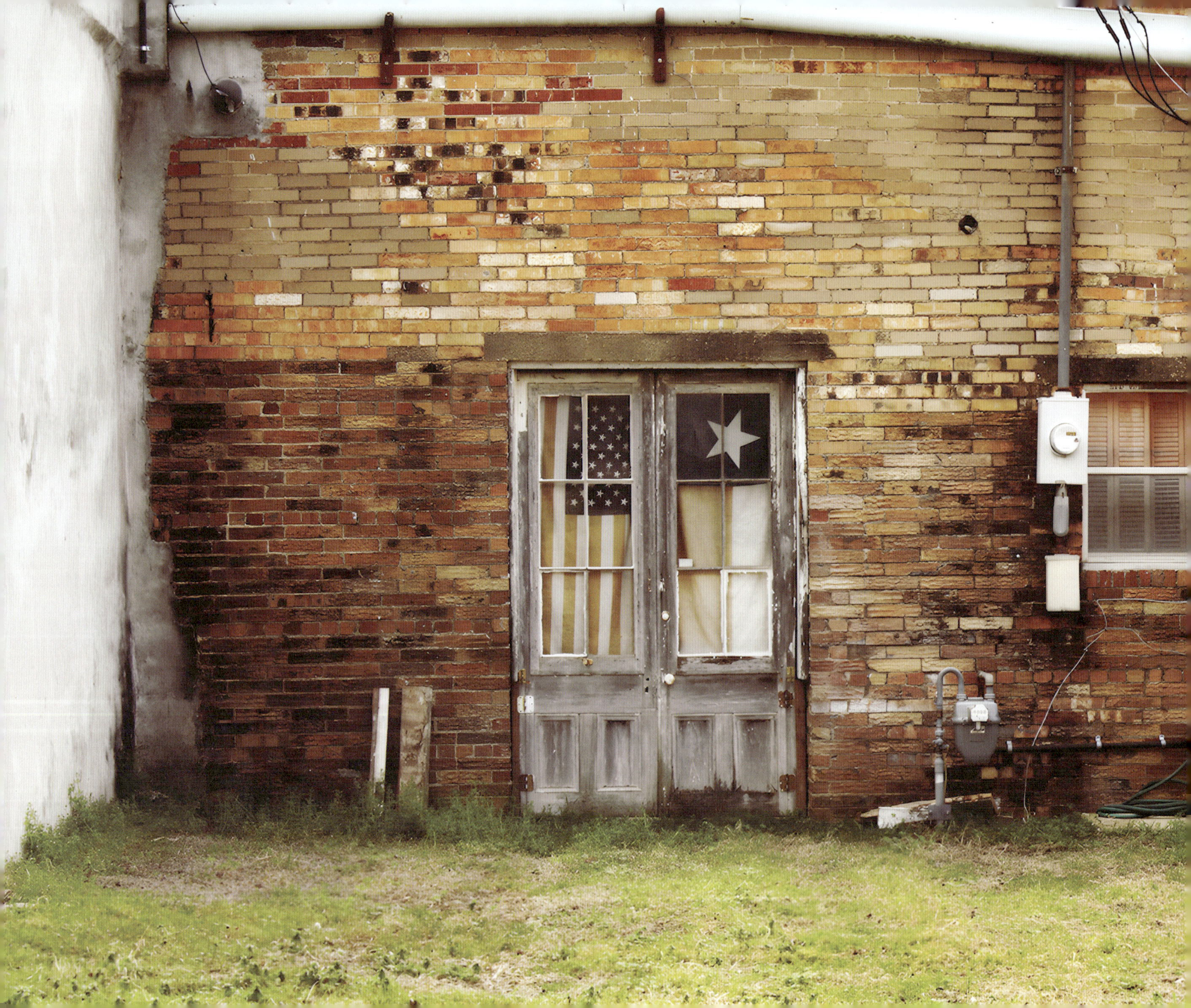

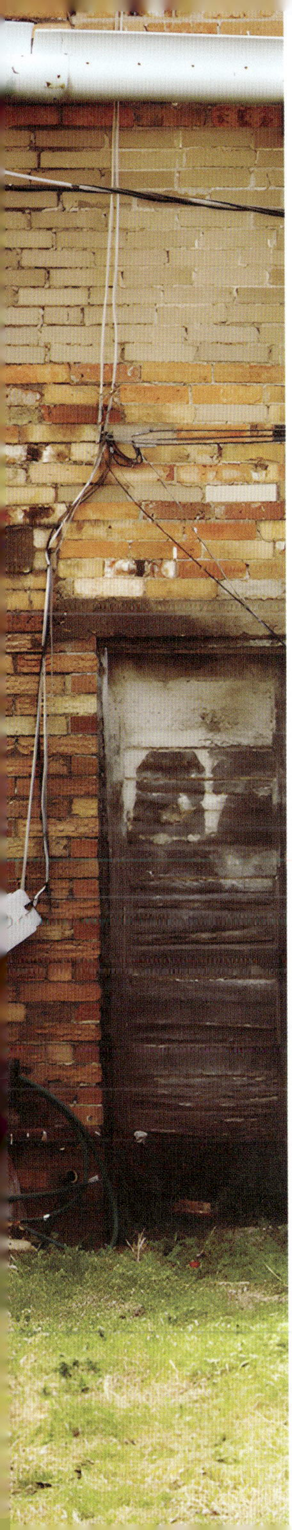

A backyard in Calvert. PHOTO BY MORGAN PAGE

By the mid-nineteenth century, the streets of East Coast cities were crowded and filthy, hardly the place for kids. If they were running the streets, it was assumed that their parents were either dead, drunk, or broke, or they just didn't care. The solution arose from the myth of the West. The homesteads out west on the fertile plains could become the home for these miscreant waifs. So the children were shipped west by train, with Texas receiving more than most states.

As railways expanded, so too did the network of cities and towns that could accept children. As the program grew, there were inquiries about requesting specific hair and eye colors. Town halls became auction sites, though no money was exchanged. A new vocabulary emerged, with children being "placed out" on a "trial," and potentially "re-placed" if things didn't work out for the foster family. Though agreements concerning good treatment were signed, these parents were often doing little more than hiring farmhands. The children were inspected for their ability to work. It was cheap labor for the families if they could afford the food and had the room.

The unlucky ones bounced from home to home through one town, then were on to the next, and so on until they found a more permanent place. The really unlucky ones were hostages to forced labor, living in horrible conditions—or worse, abused in other ways. This was sadly not uncommon. Others made it to the end of the line.

At places where the railroad ended, places like Galveston, the options were limited. When children reached Galveston, they were greeted by women dressed in black and white, the nuns at the Catholic orphanage. If they weren't from a religious family, this would probably have been very confusing. The nuns were introduced as Sister Mary this and Sister Mary that and then the kids were ushered to their bunks at the St. Mary's Orphan Asylum, located near the beach. One particularly sad group came in mid-1900. They would be the last orphans received by the asylum.

On September 8, 1900, a tremendous hurricane hit Galveston. As the first floor of the orphanage flooded, ninety orphans and ten nuns moved to the second floor and waited while repeatedly singing the hymn "Queen of the Waves." The nuns tied clothesline from their waists to the wrists of the children. Some were recovered this way after the building collapsed and was washed away in the night. Though no one knows exactly how many lives were claimed, estimates reach as high as twelve thousand, though most reports settle around eight thousand. The victims were buried not far from where the orphanage once stood. The exact location of the graveyard is not agreed upon, but it is said to be near the seawall that protects the city today, as well as near a grand hotel, the Hotel Galvez.

The children who were lost that day are said to run the halls of the hotel. Unable to rest, they keep guests up at night. They pinch and prod, scatter clothes, and bounce balls. Laughter can be heard in the hallways, spots of cold felt in the rooms, and guests report feeling immense sadness at the thought of children.

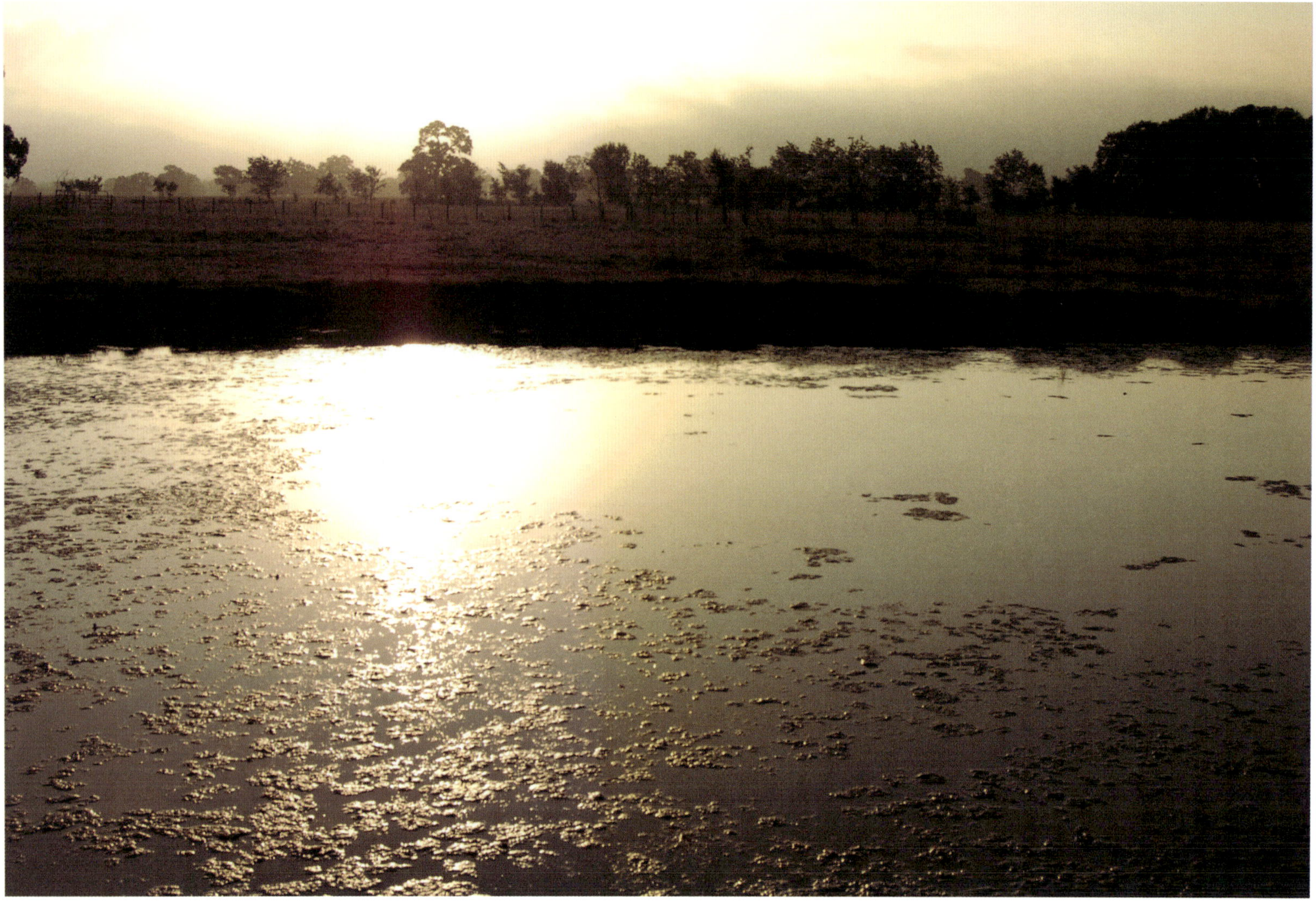

Pond at daybreak, Normangee. PHOTO BY MORGAN PAGE

One day, not seeking the macabre, Morgan and I were on a family vacation and happened upon the Hotel Galvez. It was barely even a conversation when we agreed to go in: it was research for the book. The lobby was being remodeled, bustling with workers and full of activity. We took our time, eating brunch in a restaurant there. If anything supernatural happened we didn't notice, despite sitting in the exact spot where ball bouncing and laughter are said to occur.

Afterward, we made our way to the railyard that sits on the north side of the island, right by the docks that the cruise ships launch from. Galveston isn't a town we would normally have included in our research or our project, but exceptions are made in some cases. I had seen images online and on social media of some abandoned passenger railcars in Galveston and I had to see them for myself. After some research, I found them (Google Maps is an amazing resource). They are right off 37th Street; a dirt road leads to within fifty feet of them. They probably date from the first half of the twentieth century, and are marked with C. T. & C. R. Y. on the side. That's for the Chicago Transfer and Clearing Railway Yard. The cars had to make their way over eleven hundred miles, only to die a slow death at the mercy of the salty air.

Though they are not of the same era as the Orphan Train, I see them as a fitting representation of the story. They carried people around the greater Chicago area, then were discarded, as there were too many of them. They were passed around until they made their way to the end of the line and weren't even seen as fit to scrap.

I walked in and around the cars, getting a feel for what they once were. The seats are tattered and springs are exposed. The windows were long ago busted out, and the glass-strewn floors buckle and warp as you step on the worn-out carpets.

As I walked, I noticed something odd. Toward the end of the second car there were sheets up on both sides of the car to act as a windbreak. Where the seats had been ripped out, the cleared space held a king-size mattress, complete with box springs, gleaming white in its surroundings. I had stumbled upon someone's bedroom. There was no one around, but that probably wasn't going to last. I backed out and climbed down from the car, glad it was at least of use to someone.

It had been a gloomy day up to that point, but as I made my way back the sky seemed to open with sunlight and I captured the shot you see at the beginning of this essay. It was about three minutes after I left the anonymous bedroom on the train. As we left we saw a man carrying a couple of plastic bags and headed in the direction of the cars. I'm willing to bet it was his bedroom

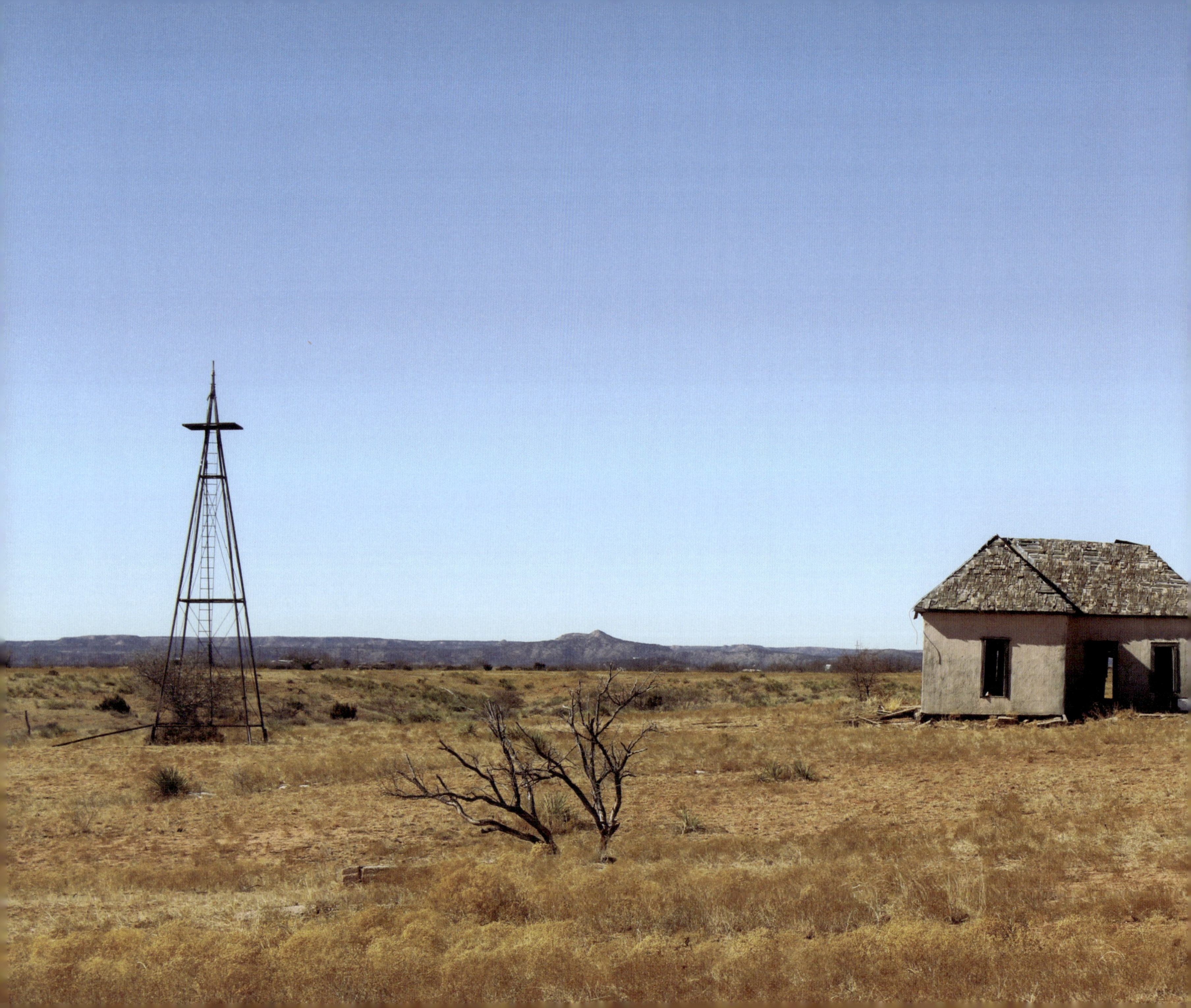

GRACE FROM AMARILLO (1907)

DUSTIN RICE

Though the house we were shooting was just outside of Quitaque, a short drive down the craggy caprock from the sprawling expanse that is the Panhandle prairie, I was struck by the pure sparseness of the life that must have been lived there. I was suddenly flooded with bits and pieces of stories I had heard growing up: details from stories of life on the vast plains about an hour and a half north of the house we saw in front of us. It reminded me of one person specifically, Callie Grace.

Callie Grace's mother, Blanche, died a matter of weeks after she was born, as a result of complications from the birth. Her father, Odie, dropped his three children off in the doorway of his mother's house, one not unlike the house in Quitaque. They had been a loving family for roughly six years,

Abandoned sharecropper home in Quitaque. PHOTO BY MORGAN PAGE

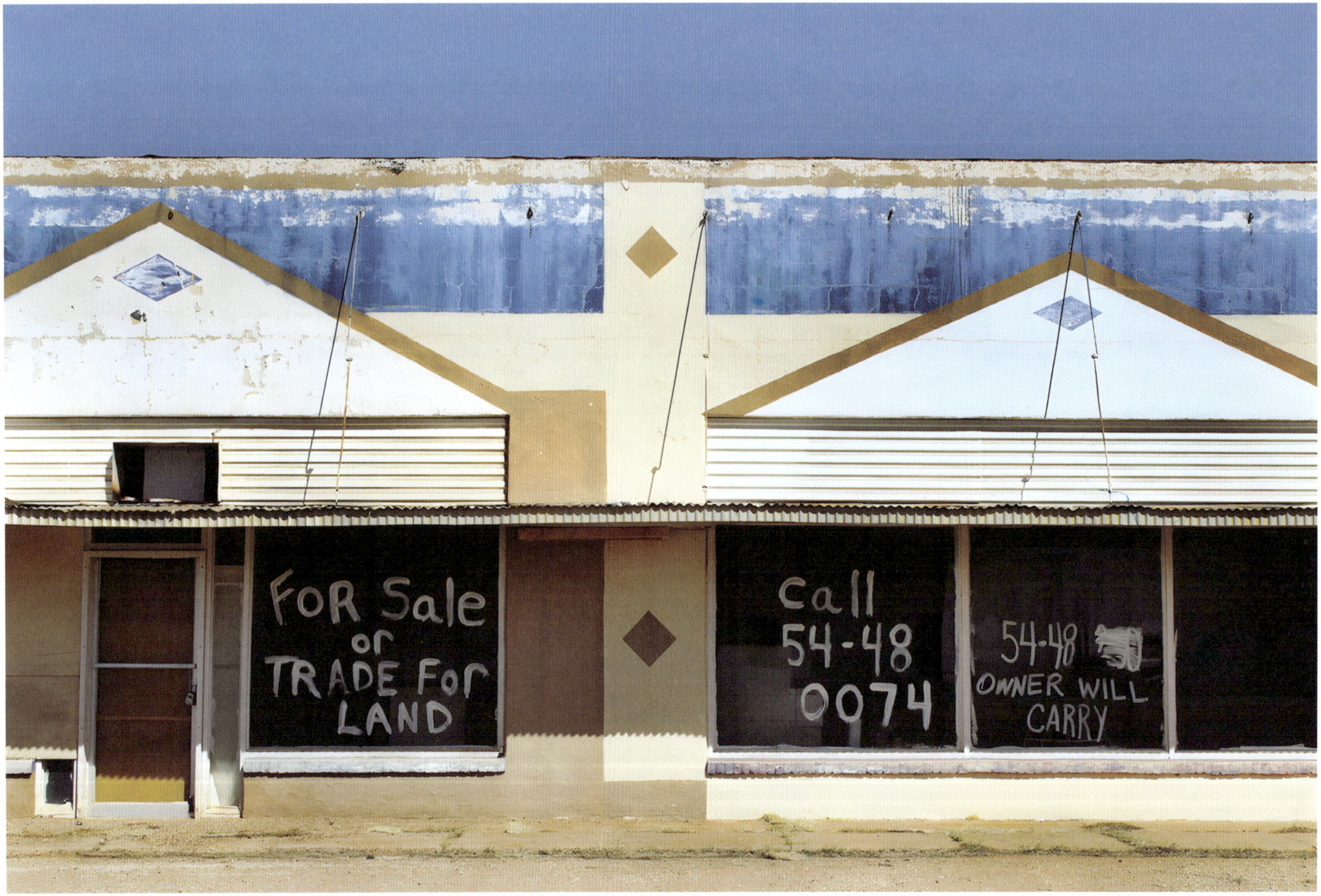

For sale or trade for land, Needmore. PHOTO BY MORGAN PAGE but Odie told his mother, Sallie, that he couldn't bear the loss of his dear Blanche, and so he left. (No one really knows where Odie went until his passing, but on June 10, 1908, he was gone. The family has always maintained that his death was from a broken heart.)

In the early 1900s, Amarillo was just a Panhandle town with denizens as rough as the winters. Horseback and buggy were still the most common forms of transportation and guns were kept on hips. Sallie had managed to raise two grown men, Mose and Odie, and send them out into the world, and what she got back was some joy, but mostly heartbreak.

At this point Grace's grandmother had already had a life of heartache. Her husband had left with her sister, but they left a little boy behind. She was raising him when she was also left with Odie's three children (two boys, plus Grace). The pair would return only to take the boy she had raised. It was a purely evil thing for them to do and she never quite recovered.

Her other son, Mose, was the successful proprietor of the Cozy Corner Bar in Dalhart, Texas, until he was murdered by a drunk in late 1909. The murderer was released on a $2,500 bond and was never seen again. That meant that Grace had lost her mother, father, and uncle all in a year, and Sallie had lost both of her sons.

Amidst all this, Grace was loved. As she and her brothers grew up in Amarillo, Amarillo grew up around them. By the mid-1920s, Grace had become a flapper, rebelling somewhat against the ranching lifestyle that characterized the town. She smoked, she went out, she danced. She fell in love with a young man named Horace. They married and had children. They made it through the Depression by having jobs that were essential. She worked for the Bell Telephone Company, directing phone calls on the switchboard. He worked for Santa Fe Railroad as a dispatcher and Morse code messenger. They wrote each other letters when he was away, and she kept those for the rest of her life.

With all the chaos and heartache that surrounded her early life, it would have been easy for Grace's heart to harden, but she chose otherwise. She was a doting mother to her three children, two girls and a boy. Grace loved all of God's creatures. She would pick up crickets off the floor in the grocery store and set them free outside. She rescued a turtle from the side of the road that had been hit by a car. She cleaned him up as best she could and glued him back together. Because of a broken leg, Sam the turtle lived in a box under Grace's bed for the rest of her life. He was bathed twice a week and loved bananas. He outlived her by a decade.

I didn't meet Grace until 1982, when she was in her mid-seventies. Grace was my great-grandmother. She loved to visit with family, but struggled to hear the conversations, as a result of decades spent wearing loud headphones at the switchboard. (Her daughter later became an audiologist.) But even with her poor hearing, Grace loved to tell stories. If you could get a question across, and it sparked something in her, she'd prattle on and on.

I knew very little of her story when I stopped that day in the caprocks and imagined what it must have been like to be born on this prairie. I had not heard about the traumatic childhood that my great-grandmother endured. I only knew the angelic, four-and-a-half-foot sparkplug who drove a Mustang II poorly because she could barely see over the steering wheel. Later I was determined to find out more, so I talked to my Aunt Ramona, her daughter, and asked my dad some questions, too. He mentioned a scrapbook that my Nanny, Grace's other daughter, had made a decade or two earlier. The handwritten stories, names, and dates that she spent hours putting in the scrapbook offered a wealth of family information. I never would have pieced Grace's story together without Nanny's help. Although Grace passed in 2004 at ninety-six years old, I feel like I am still getting to know her.

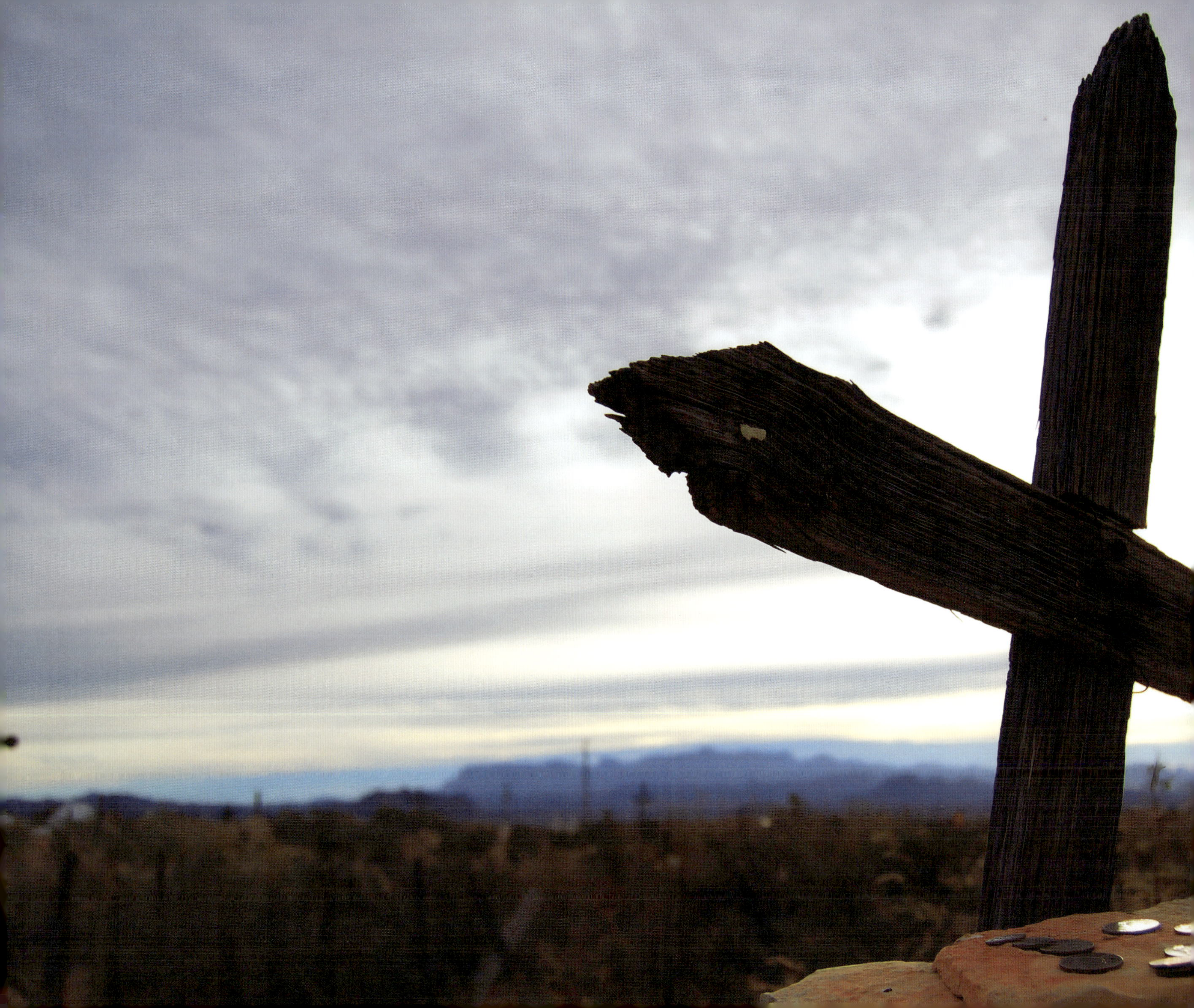

DEVIL IN THE MINE (EARLY TWENTIETH CENTURY)

DUSTIN RICE

Native Americans extracted cinnabar from the Terlingua area for thousands of years. They used it to make vermilion, a color they painted on cave walls by spraying it from their mouths. Over time, this was very toxic and likely shortened the lives of many Indigenous people. They had no way of knowing they were handling a poisonous mineral; they probably just liked that it looked beautiful and lasted for generations. The Chisos Mining Company, however, knew exactly how toxic that material was. They refined the cinnabar and ultimately used Terlingua's resources to exploit a people, a region, and in effect the entire economy of early twentieth-century Big Bend.

Chisos sunrise in Terlingua. PHOTO BY DUSTIN RICE

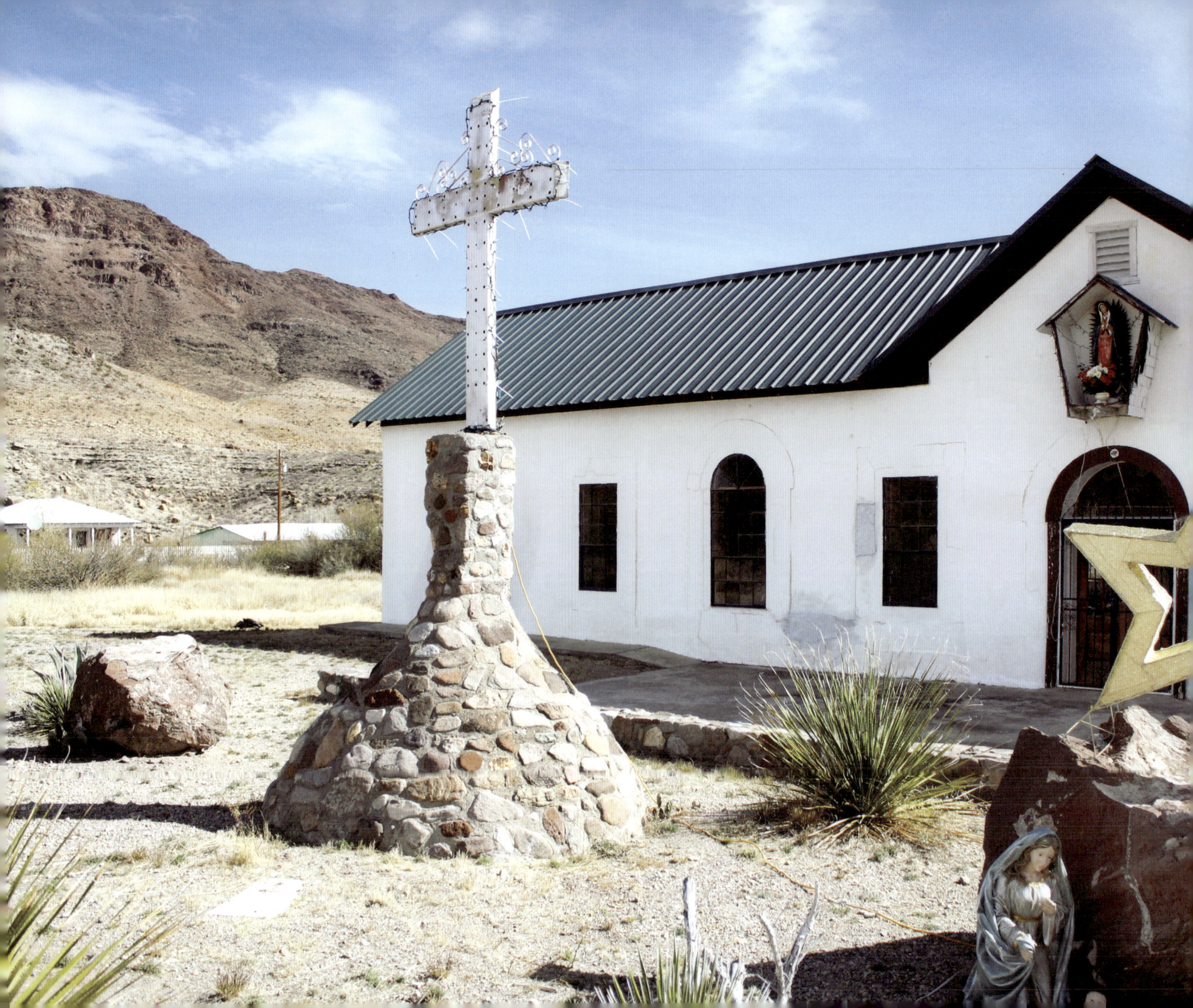

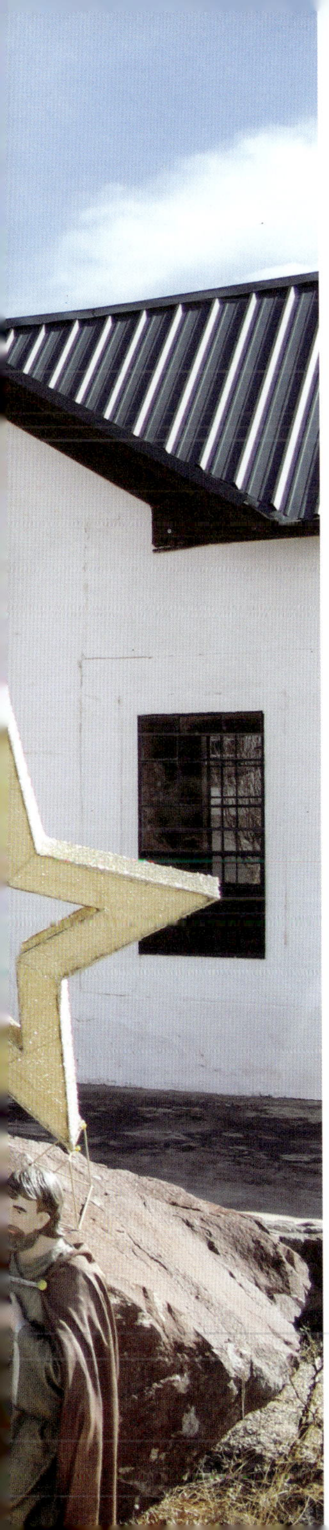

Howard E. Perry knew extravagance. Even while living in the desert, he maintained his membership in the New York Yacht Club. This extravagance came at the expense of the Mexican miners, who died of mercury poisoning while pulling ore from the ground. A sickening disparity emerged between the man in the mansion on the hill and the men who worked for him. Workers toiled for pennies a day, unaware of the horrific nature of their impending deaths: most developed mercury poisoning within five years of working in the mines.

Mercury poisoning is a nightmarish fate. What begins with uneasiness and a decline in general health eventually spirals into madness. Famously, the term "mad as a hatter" came from haberdashers' use of mercury in hat-making and their subsequent tendency to end up in an asylum. Plenty of those buried in the west side of Terlingua Cemetery suffered the same fate: the men there died young, mostly in their thirties and forties, victims of the Chisos Mine. Perry died in Boston, aged eighty-six.

One can imagine that the dangers of life in the mine, including illnesses and collapses, as well as the inherent dangers of living in one of the last wild west towns—drunkenness, gun violence, and diseases of all kinds—combined to make Terlingua one of the country's most uniquely appalling places in the early twentieth century. It's ironic that the Chisos Mining Company chose that name, presumably just taking the name of the mountains without giving it a second thought. "Chisos" translates as "ghosts" in Spanish. Who knows how many ghosts the Chisos Mine ultimately made? For starters, you can visit several hundred graves in the Terlingua Ghost Town Cemetery, where the men who lost their lives to the mine are buried.

Sacred Heart Catholic Mission Church in Shafter, est. 1890.
PHOTO BY MORGAN PAGE

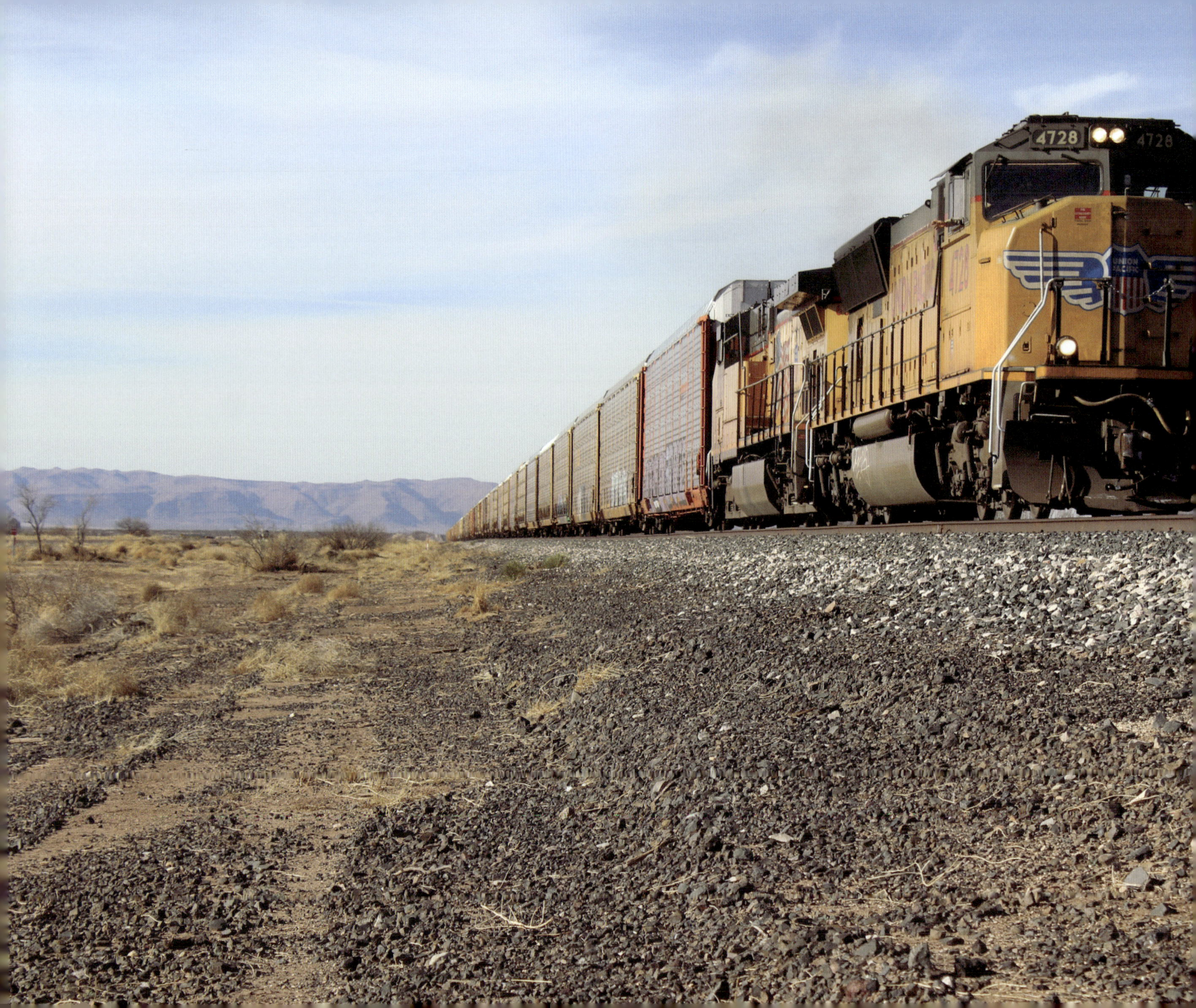
4728

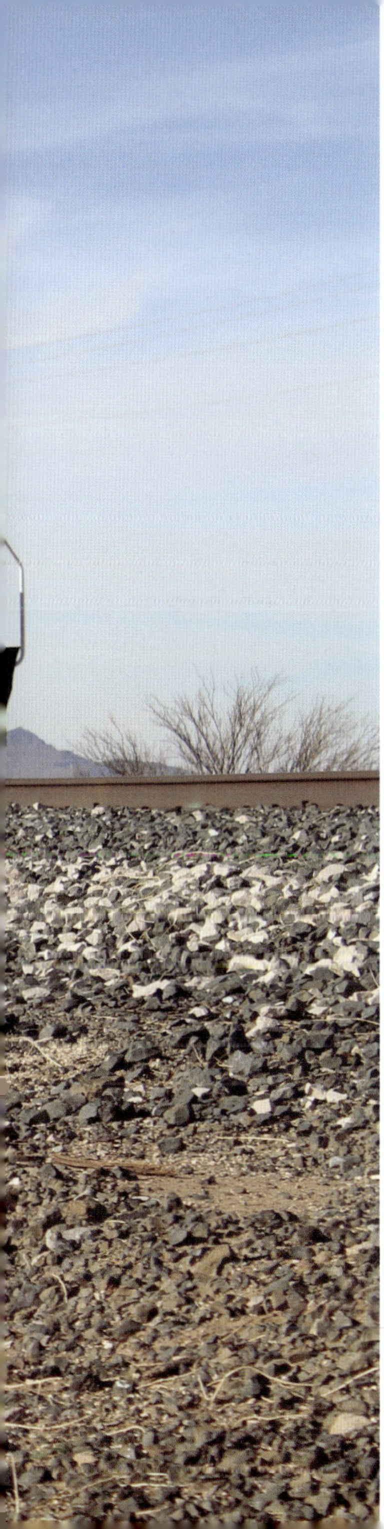

THE EXPRESS MANAGER (1912)

DUSTIN RICE

We were on a weeklong expedition in West Texas, and Big Bend was now in the rearview mirror. Though we had left home with a list of towns forming a scavenger hunt of histori cal people and places, we had learned that some of our greatest finds would be unplanned. Whenever something mysterious or captivating caught our eye, we would jump out of the car and get to work photographing and taking notes. So when I spotted a historical marker on a deserted highway just past Sanderson, we stopped.

Not the same type of locomotive or car, but a train on the same track as that described in "The Express Manager," Hwy 90. PHOTO BY DUSTIN RICE

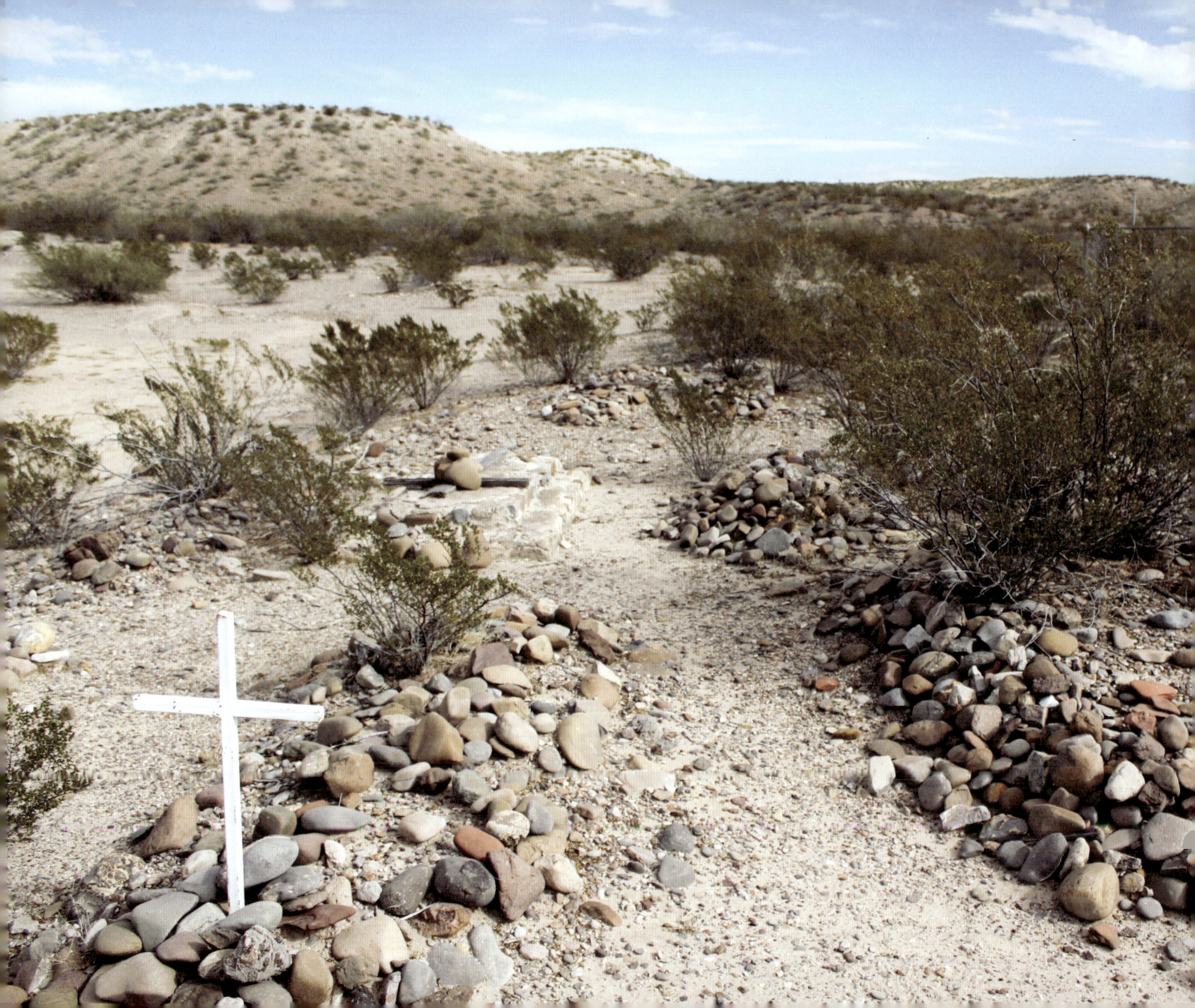

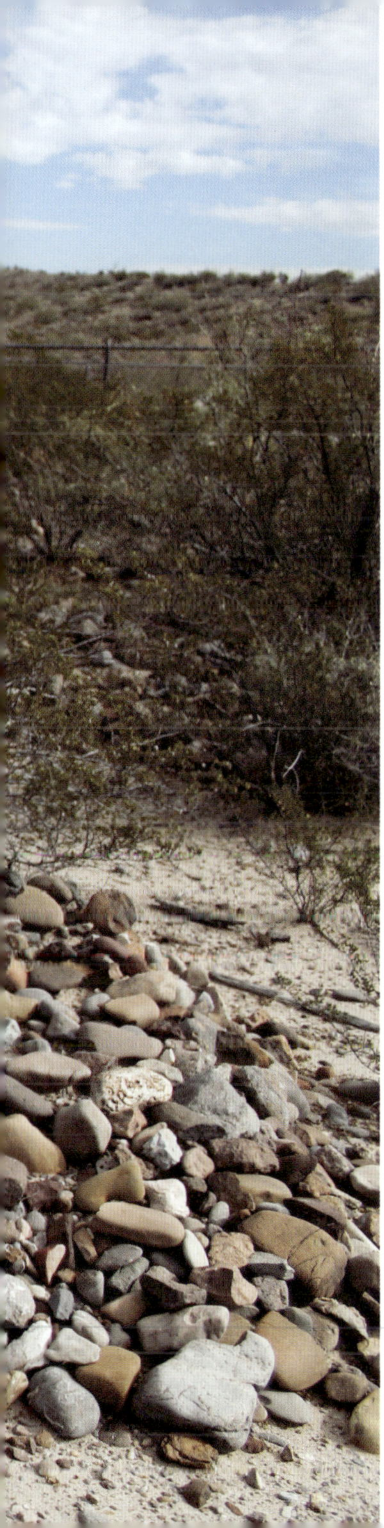

The surroundings were so empty and desolate that I wondered what noteworthy event could possibly have happened out there. The violence of the marker instantly brought to mind a quote:

> It is better to be the hammer than the anvil.
> EMILY DICKINSON

Despite being an avid reader of Texas history, I had never come across this quintessentially Texas story involving an unlikely hero pitted against masked robbers in the Wild West. When the #9 Galveston, Harrisburg, & San Antonio locomotive left Dryden shortly after midnight on March 13, 1912, the night seemed just like any other to the express car manager for the Wells Fargo Company. To keep busy on the mundane overnight route, David Trousdale decided to organize packages for the next few stops. The train had gone only a few miles when it slowed. Trousdale knew something was amiss, but he didn't go near the door. He heard approaching footsteps, and a familiar voice from an engineer or porter called out to him. Trousdale finally looked out to find a man standing there, rifle in hand, bandana as a disguise. The train was being robbed.

Trousdale had no way of knowing that the man behind the mask was something of a celebrity. Ben Kilpatrick was a member of the Wild Bunch, along with Butch Cassidy and the Sundance Kid. "The Tall Texan" had just gotten out of prison after serving ten years of a fifteen-year sentence for a previous train robbery, and his partner, Ole Hobek, had served time with him in Atlanta. Ole, by all accounts, wasn't very smart.

Unarmed and facing an unknown number of perpetrators, Trousdale was led to the front, where he found Ole with the engineer. The robbers ordered that the passenger cars be disconnected, and they pulled away together in the locomotive and the remaining cars. All the robbers wanted were the Wells Fargo packages on Trousdale's car. As the express manager, Trousdale was responsible for at least trying to defend Wells Fargo's property.

The robbers stopped the train after a mile or so, at Baxter's Curve. This section of track was perfect for a train robbery: isolated and empty, it made for an easy getaway through the hills on horseback. They'd left an eleven-year-old boy, the self-proclaimed "Cimarron Kid," to tend the horses, which they had shod backward to confuse anyone tracking them.

Kilpatrick prodded Trousdale back to the express car with his rifle, cursing him the whole way. Trousdale put Kilpatrick at ease by declaring he didn't get paid enough to fight, and he

Cemetery in Balmorhea, a sea of unmarked graves. PHOTO BY MORGAN PAGE

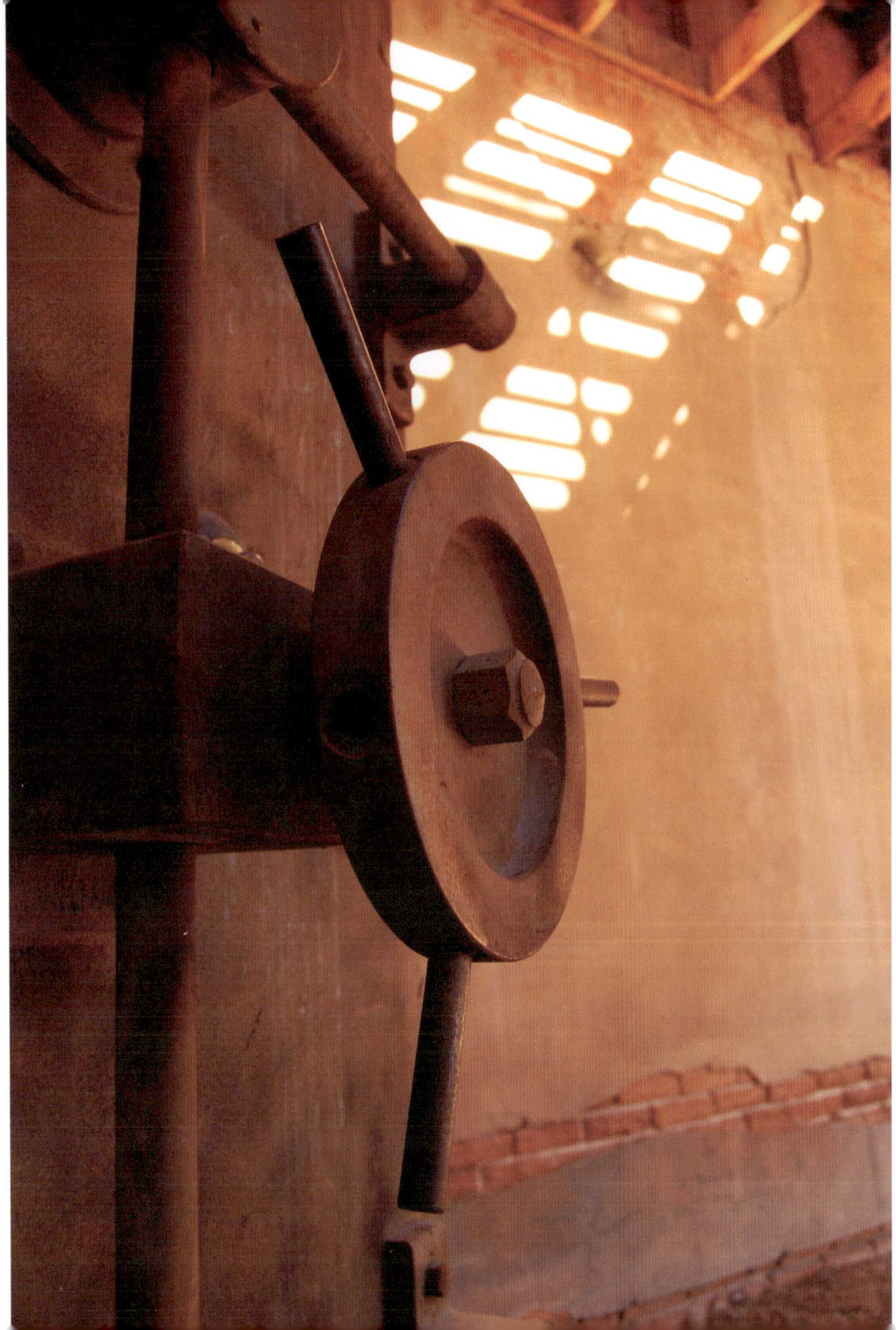

Bank vault in Barstow. PHOTO BY DUSTIN RICE

stood aside as the robber rummaged through the cargo, looking for items of value. Sensing an opportunity, Trousdale pointed Kilpatrick in the wrong direction, leading him away from any valuables and wasting his time.

While Kilpatrick's back was turned, Trousdale had a lucky find. He came across an ice maul, a mallet used to break up ice in crates of oysters. He quietly tucked it inside his coat. Trousdale then called out to Kilpatrick, directing him to a package on the floor and stating that it held more value than any other package there.

Kilpatrick leaned his rifle against the wall. As the robber bent down to go through the parcel, Trousdale withdrew his hidden hammer and swung with all his might. The blow landed at the base of Kilpatrick's skull and "unjoined his head from his neck," as Trousdale later said. Trousdale struck him a few more times for good measure, and "knocked his brains out." Taking quick inventory of the weapons at hand, Trousdale gave them to his mail clerk and helper. And then, they waited. And waited.

After two hours, Trousdale fired a single shot through the roof, finally eliciting a response from the slower of the two would-be robbers. Unsure of what to do, Ole called out Kilpatrick's alias for the evening: "Frank?!" When he didn't hear his own alias, "Pardner," in return, he poked his head around the corner. Trousdale zeroed in on him and shot Ole above his left eye as he peered in. Ole died where he stood.

The train pulled into Sanderson at about five that morning, long overdue. Confused townspeople helped unload the bodies as the sheriff questioned the crew. Pictures from an impromptu photo session with the corpses made their way into papers across the nation, and grateful passengers heaped praise on Trousdale.

They weren't the only grateful parties: Trousdale eventually received over $2,500 from the federal government, Southern Pacific Railroad, and Wells Fargo. In addition, Mr. Wells and Mr. Fargo personally presented him with a gold watch, and the train's passengers bought him a watch fob with a diamond in a Texas star. As for Ben and Ole, they had been unceremoniously thrown into a hole.

We headed east from the marker; the rest of the story had ended behind us, in Sanderson. To think I would never have thought to dig further if it weren't for a random marker on an empty highway. The marker I read that day packed an entire night's events into a few lines: it had the terms "train robbery," "bludgeoned . . . with an ice mallet," and "killed the other with the first robber's rifle." It proves that even in the most desolate places in Texas you can find history waiting to be uncovered.

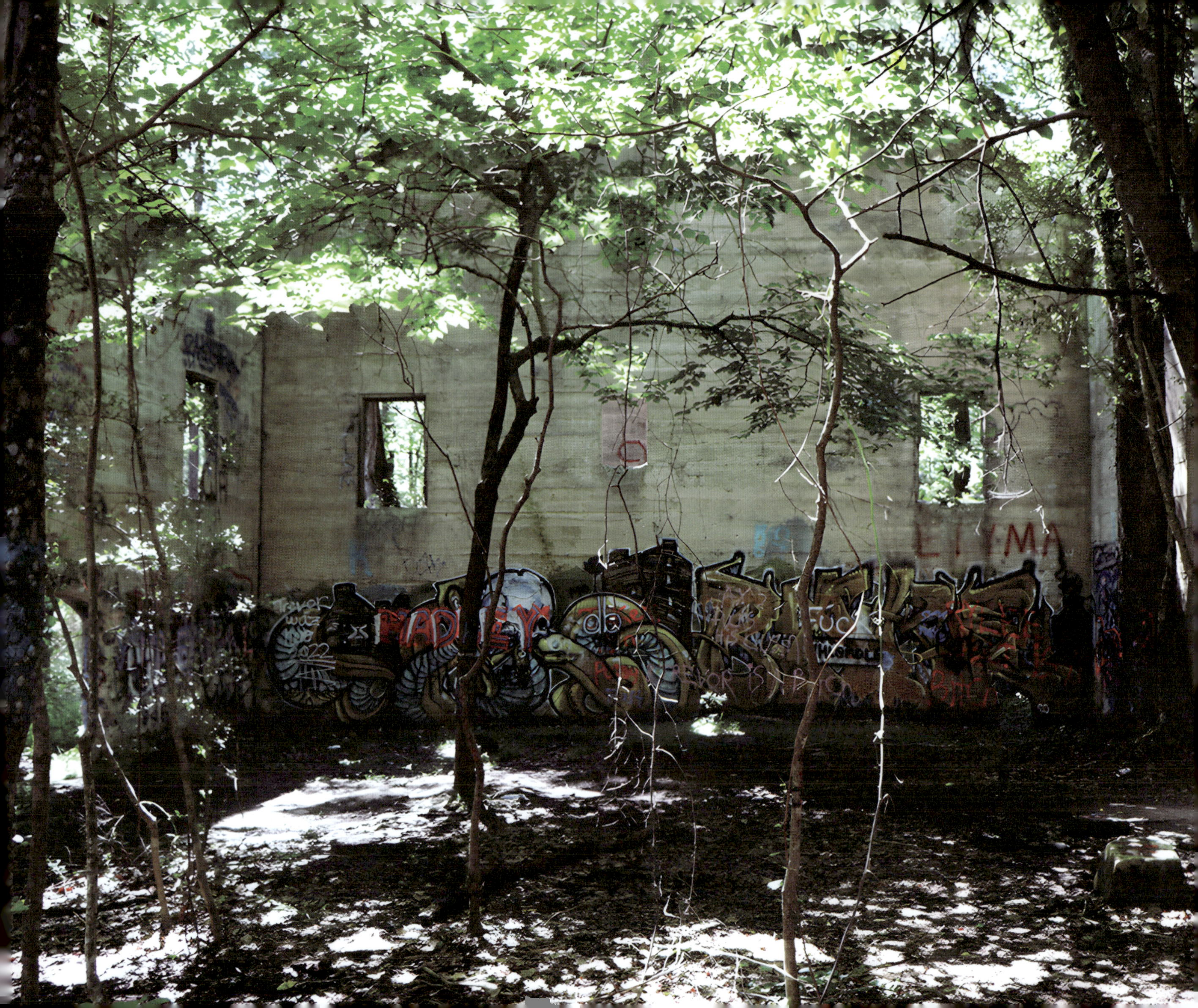

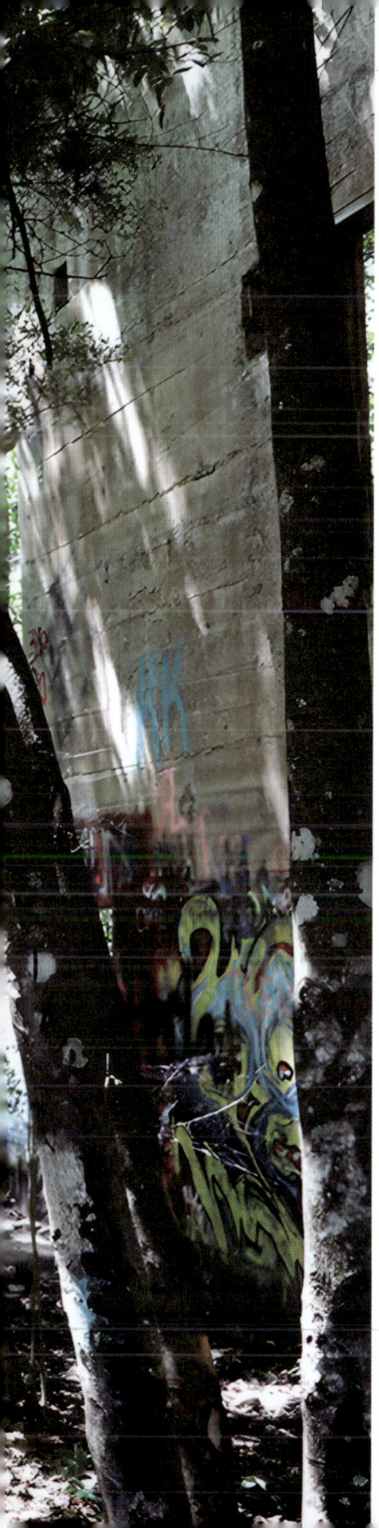

ANGELINA'S LESSONS (EARLY TWENTIETH CENTURY)

DUSTIN RICE

Morgan and I visited hundreds of towns and thousands of structures for this project. Almost all of the places we visited have one thing in common—they are on or near a road. But one was different. Angelina National Forest, deep in the East Texas Piney Woods, includes the former town of Aldridge, the remains of which have sat beside the Neches River for almost 120 years. The former sawmill community is only accessible on foot, and after researching it for months, it had become my white whale.

Aldridge Sawmill. PHOTO BY DUSTIN RICE

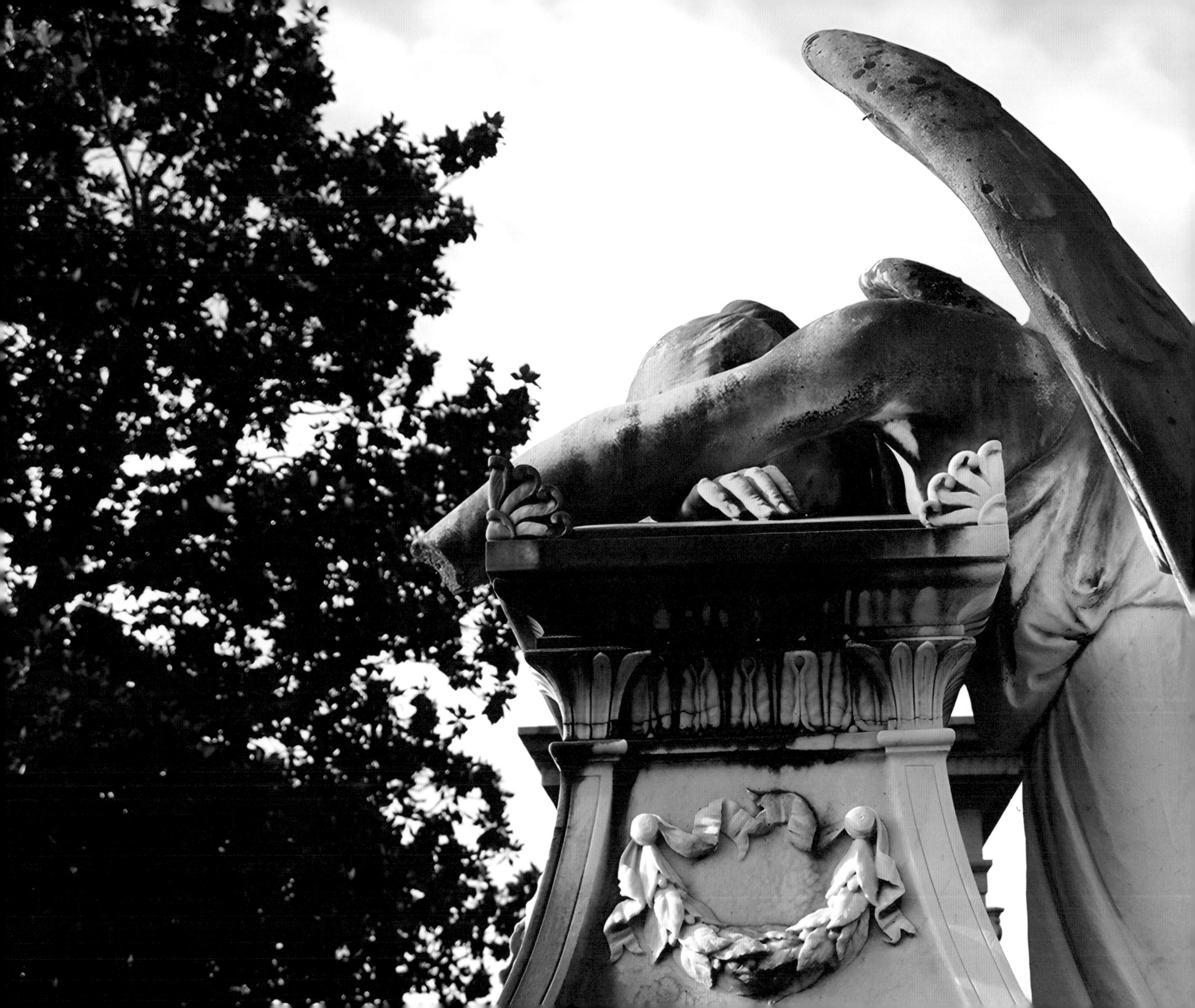

To start, I had seen that we would need to go to Boykin Springs Recreational Area, between Zavalla and Jasper. The road was under construction. From the highway, we could see that the recreation area was shut down, locked behind a barricade. We were six and a half hours from home. I was not letting one barricade stop us. We gathered what we needed and began our hike. Turns out it was a thirty-minute hike to the start of that trail to Aldridge. At this point, Morgan—four months pregnant—said she wasn't going the rest of the way. Fair enough, and with her blessing I told her I would be back in a couple of hours and not to worry; it wasn't that far.

I knew I had messed up right from the start. The sign for the mill said two and a half miles at the start, double what I had just told my pregnant wife. Rather than backtrack, I decided I would just go faster. I ran where I could, jogging most of the way out to the mill. The trees were marked with yellow tags that had arrows. I was paralleling and crossing back and forth over a creek, and I looked at which way the creek was flowing to keep my direction. The trail was fairly easy. About two-thirds of the way out, I saw a sign for the mill. I was making great time. I remember the hair on my arms standing on end because I was so excited to see this place. I felt like a kid; this was going to be a highlight of our project.

The Weeping Angel on the grave of William Scott Youree, Scottsville, one of five famous angels in Texas by Frank Teiche.
PHOTO BY DUSTIN RICE

As I rounded a corner and came through some overgrowth, I saw colors that shouldn't be out in the green of a national forest: pink and blue graffiti, presumably left by previous visitors (or more likely bored teenagers), let me know that I was in Aldridge.

Three concrete structures, cavernous and completely out of place, make up what's left of the Aldridge sawmill. The mill was active from the early 1900s until 1927, consuming great swaths of old-growth pine trees until they had cleared the lumber completely and transport to the mill became unprofitable. At its peak, the mill produced 125,000 board feet a day. The noise—boilers and saws, trucks and trains—must have been deafening. I bet if it were still going, Morgan would have heard it from where she was waiting in the car. The mill employed over five hundred men who brought families, making up a town of perhaps fifteen hundred people deep in the forest.

It was a walk through history as I was shooting, my mind spinning as I walked from one behemoth to another. I could see the boiler belching steam and the saw chugging back and forth, though they had been still for a century. I could hear operators yelling over the noise of it all, children playing in the distance. It's not often in life that you get to be utterly alone in a place and it speaks to your soul. I have visited ruins

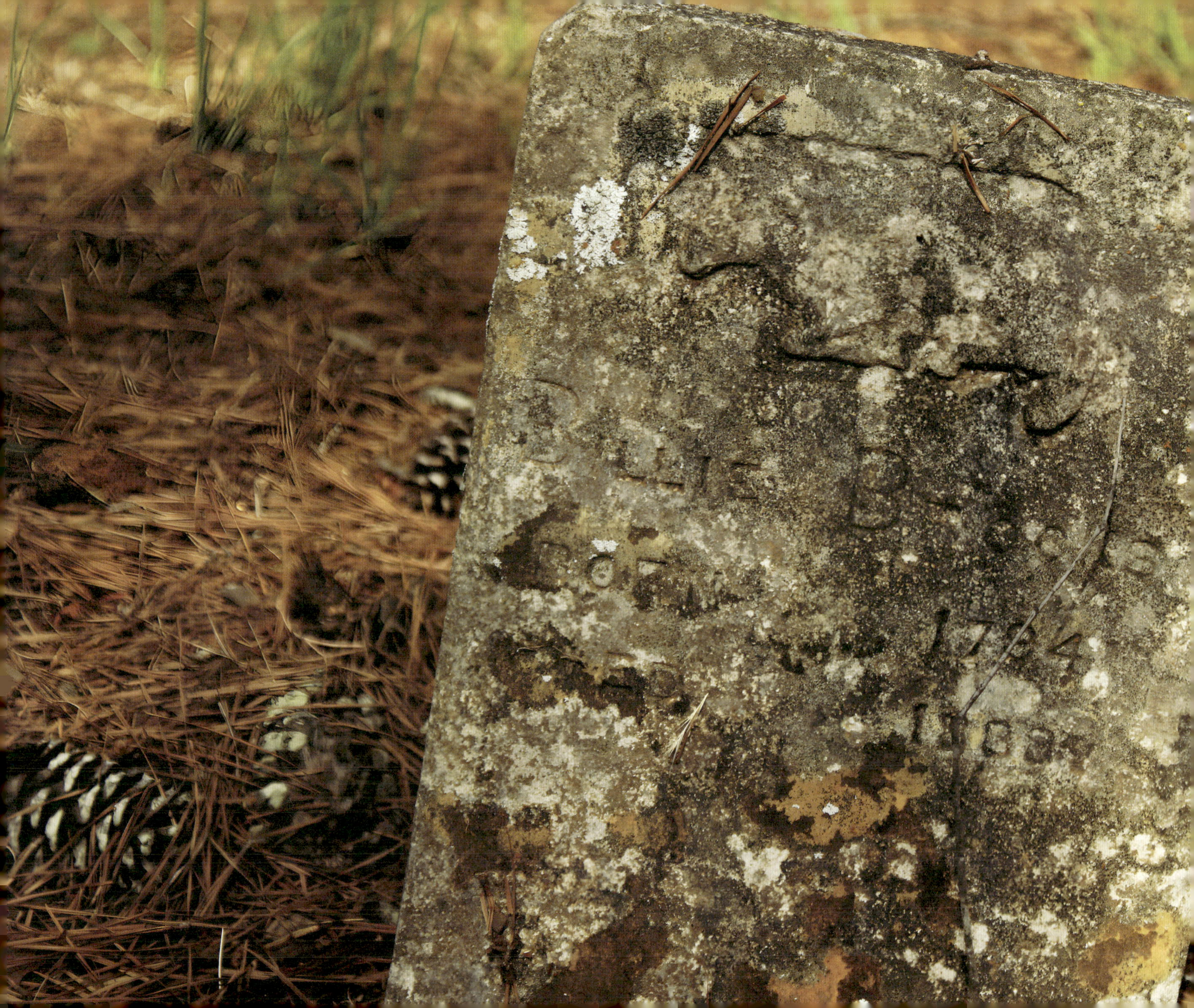

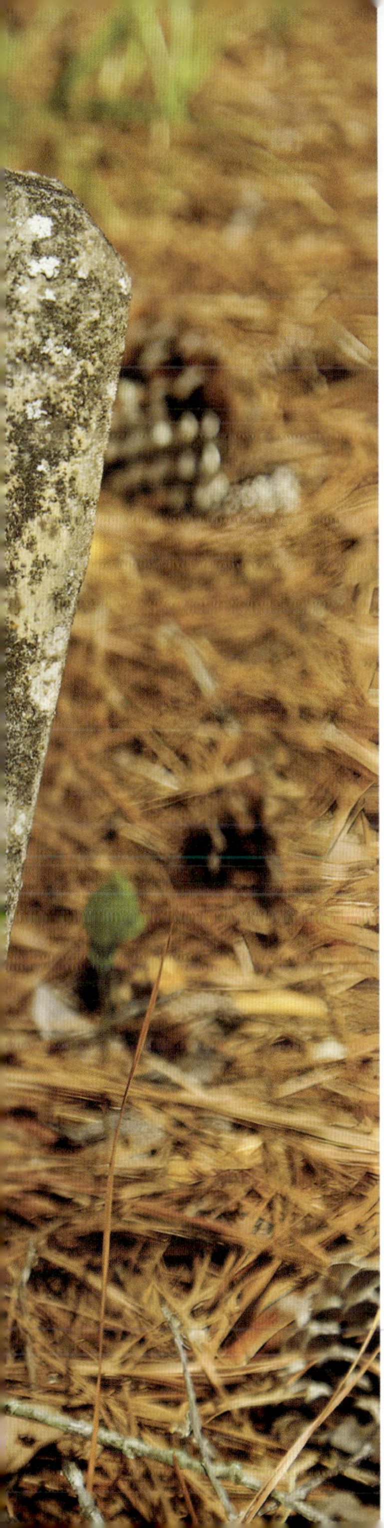

on tours and seen ancient sites with guides, but this was different. This place was mine alone. I found it, I researched it, and here I was by myself. It was like playtime as a kid. But when the fun was over and I was ready to leave, I had a lot of time to make up. I lit out, jogging and then running where I could.

As I was drinking the last of my water, I saw a yellow tag in front of me. That was strange. It was taking way too long to get back, and I had started to think something was wrong. I don't get turned around easily, but maybe I had gotten on a wrong trail. The water in the creek was even running the wrong way. But it was when I got to the sign, the one that said the mill was ahead, the one I was so excited to see before, the one that was two-thirds of the way out to the mill, that I knew I had really messed up. I had gone about two miles in the wrong direction, running and jogging most of the distance of about seven miles; I was out of water, and now I had to turn around. So I turned back, seeing some things for the fourth time, totally defeated.

I knew Morgan was probably having a panic attack by now. Phone service in the forest was nonexistent, and I had left long-range walkie-talkies sitting on the table in my garage. I was on the verge of panic myself. I went through a list of all the ways I had messed up, but I still couldn't figure out how I had gotten to where I was. There's one way in and one way out. Then I saw it, even saw my own footprints. At the end of the trail, about a quarter mile from the trail-head, is an open area I should have recognized. You can cross the creek to the left and finish, or you can be a moron and meander in a circle and head right back out where you just came from, like I did.

By this time, I was cramping and sore, though somewhat relieved. I knew Morgan was none of these. The walk back to the car from the recreational area was one of the longest walks of my life. It was uphill under a hot sun, and only partially paved. I saw Morgan get out of the car as I came into sight. I was limping and cramping but overjoyed to see her. She informed me that she had talked to the forest rangers and they told her to give me another hour, and that time was just about up. The Forest Service was about to come looking for me.

The whole ordeal had taken about four hours but felt like an entire lifetime, a roller-coaster from excitement and elation to disheartened panic. Was it worth it? The reader can decide that for themselves. I just know that I won't soon forget that it pays to bring as much water as you can hold and pay attention to signs.

Next to the Scottsville Cemetery, separated by a fence, is another cemetery thought to be where slaves were buried. These gravesites are much less decorative, and some are altogether unmarked. Billie Brooks, 1794 to 1888. PHOTO BY MORGAN PAGE

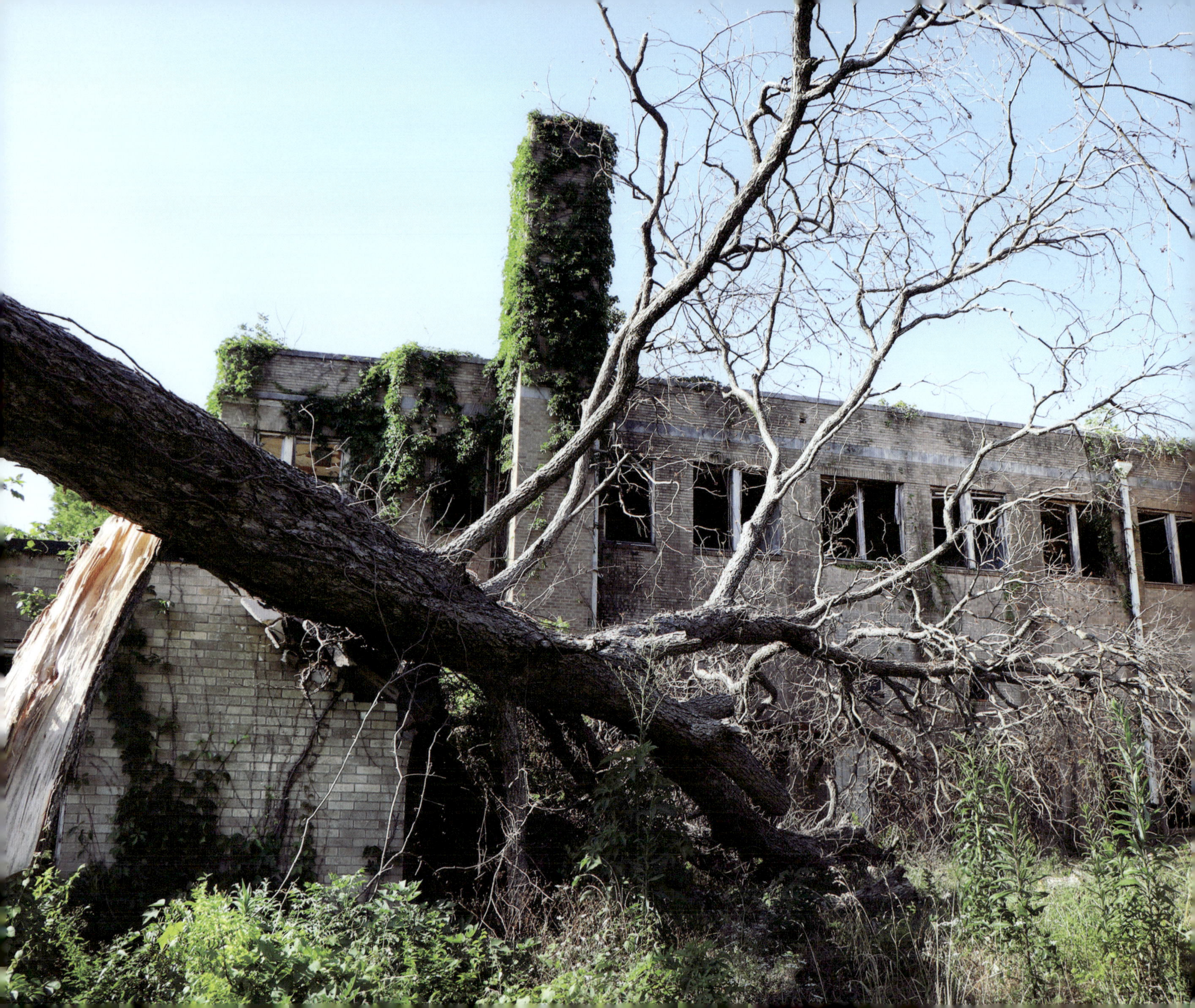

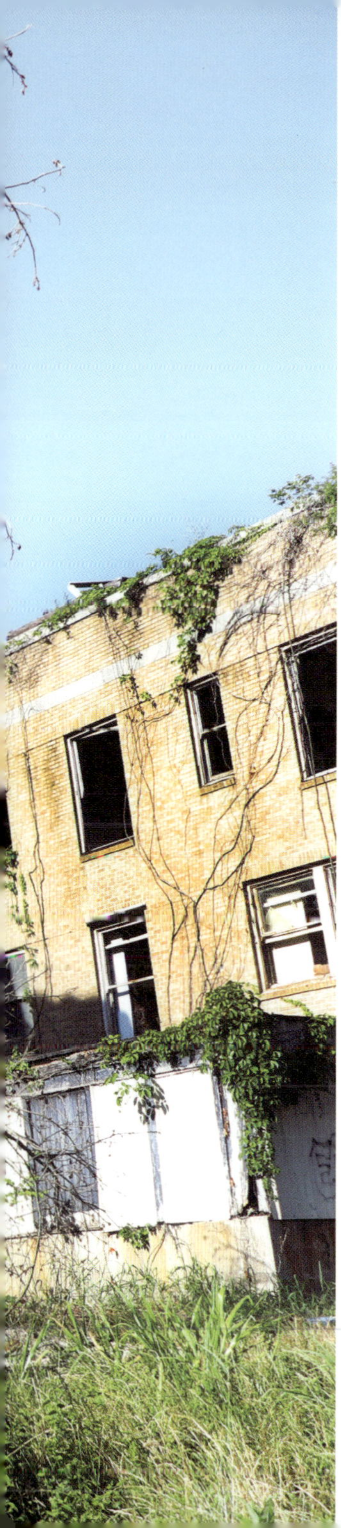

THE DARK HALLS OF THE T&P (1920s)

DUSTIN RICE

Each time we enter a left-behind place, it elicits a response from us. A vibe, an aura, whatever you might call it: there is an automatic reaction when we visit a site that was once inhabited, but is no longer. There can be an uplifting feeling, particularly in schools, like an optimism that remained behind. Sometimes I've felt joy for no particular reason, a giddiness that I couldn't explain. Other places have a weight, a palpable heaviness. Some of these visits have been downright unpleasant. Sometimes there's a feeling, as if from a very deep and primordial place, that says, "Get out. Get out immediately." This was the feeling I got upon visiting the former hospital of the Texas & Pacific Railroad in Marshall, Texas.

Exterior of the Texas and Pacific (T&P) Hospital, Marshall. PHOTO BY DUSTIN RICE

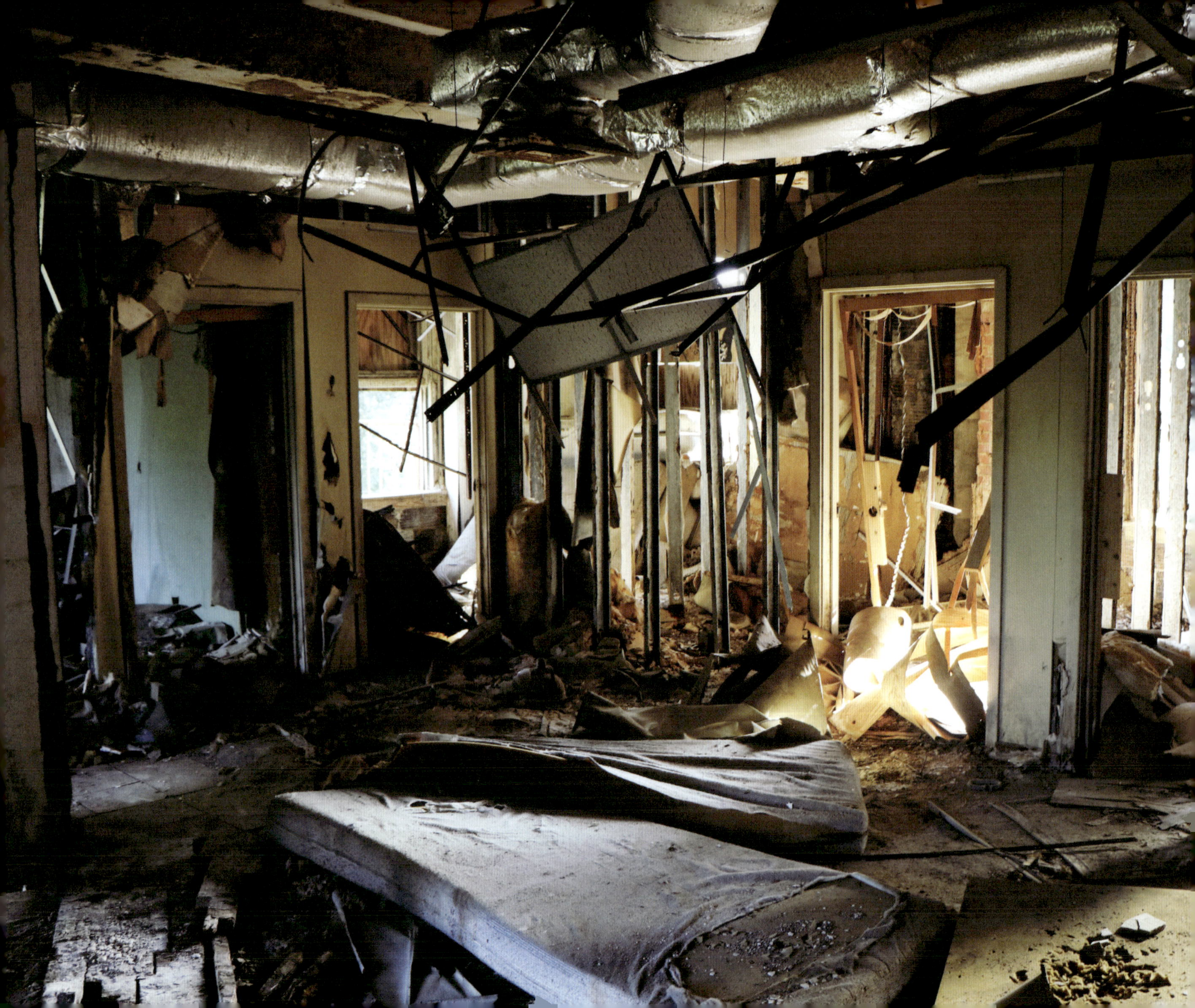

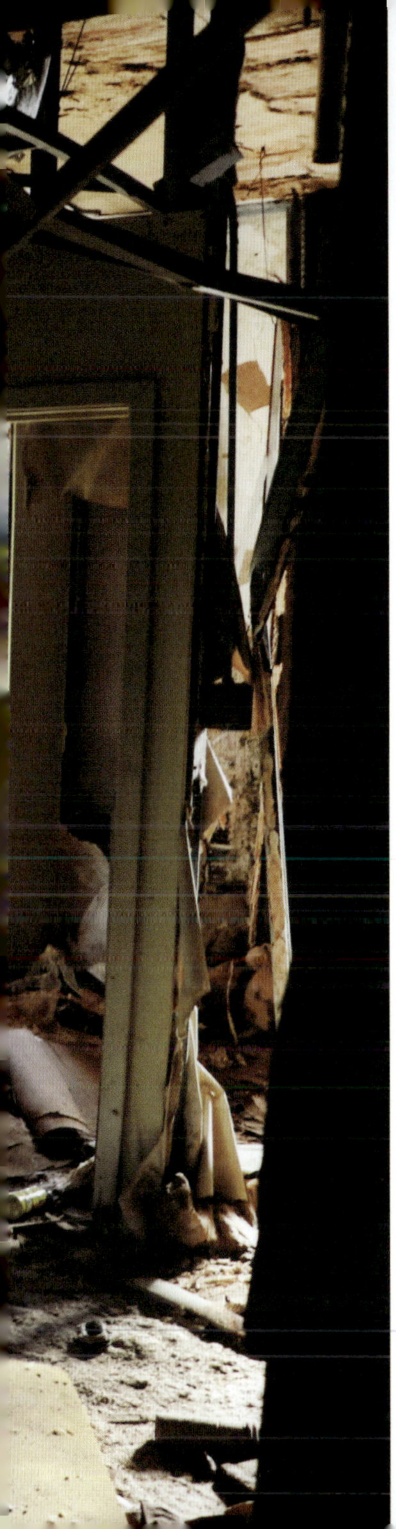

It was easy to drive past the drab building on Grand Avenue in the heart of Marshall. We missed it and had to turn around before we were sure we had found it. Covered in vines and with boarded-up windows, it sat right in the middle of a modest neighborhood. Abandoned for well over forty years, it checked every box for me as a place I wanted to document for our project.

I couldn't wait to go in as we pulled up. Morgan and I have differing mindsets when it comes to visiting these places. Most of the time she is content to take exterior shots. She will enter if she can, but tall grass or even the slightest chance of a run-in with wildlife will generally limit her interior shooting. For this one, it was going to be just me going in. We talked it over: we would each go off for an hour or so and check in with each other later, which is how we often do it. Off I went.

The history of the place intrigued me. In the 1920s it was one of the most state-of-the-art medical facilities of its time, operating for over fifty years as a railroad hospital, almost unique at the time. The T&P, one of the oldest and longest railroad systems in Texas, was forward-thinking. The company assembled railway surgeons, some of the most specialized healthcare workers of the time, and made the hospital into one of the best trauma centers of its day. The building was constructed in the Modern Style: characterized by long, clean lines, made up of concrete, glass, and metal, and devoid of ornamentation. It had over a hundred rooms, a capacity that was absolutely vast for the time. The worst injuries from throughout the T&P network were sent there. New techniques were developed to prolong the lives of the injured, preventing many fatalities. As an unanticipated consequence, the hospital housed a large number of trauma victims who endured untold amounts of pain in long-term care. The sounds in the halls must have been nightmarish.

I went in, and the excitement to shoot that I had felt dissipated. I immediately felt I was being judged. I felt like a ghoul. Or, more accurately, it seemed as if someone, or something, was telling me I was a ghoul for being there. They weren't wrong, and I felt immoral for having wanted to be there, but I was already there . . . so I pushed on.

I had entered from the back and started searching the bottom floor. There was pain in those walls. There was agony in the mortar between the bricks. I sped up, something I never do. I usually find myself going at a snail's pace to soak in what I'm shooting, but this time I hurried myself along, not wanting any of this soaking in. I felt like I was being chased from empty space to empty space. The mattresses drew my attention: I knew to my core that every person who had lain on one of them had not wanted to be there. No one ever spent a comfortable night there.

Interior of the Texas and Pacific (T&P) Hospital, Marshall.
PHOTO BY DUSTIN RICE

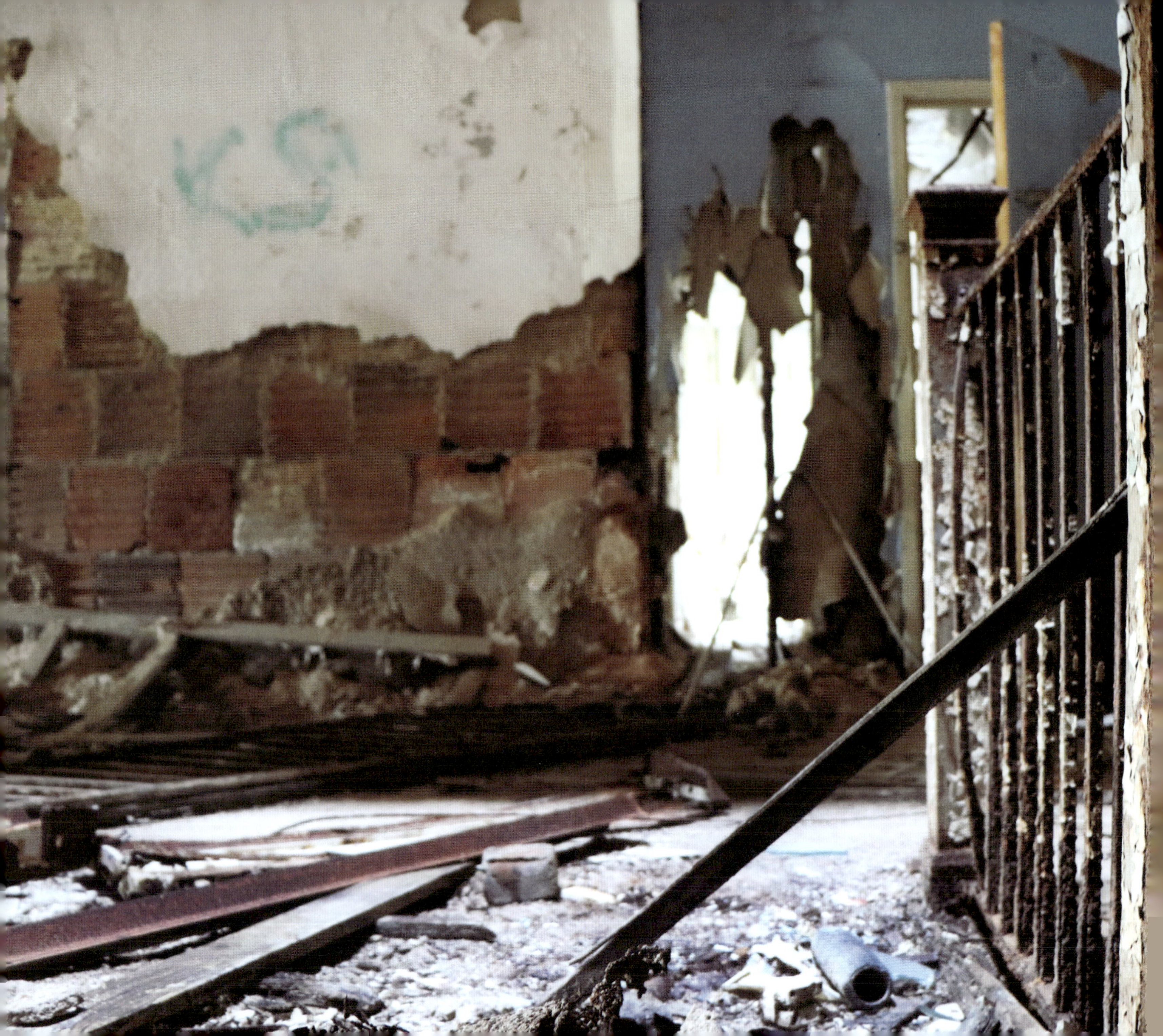

Over fifty-plus years as the flagship medical center for one of the largest railroads in the country, the facility housed an unknown number of patients. Suffering from everything from broken bones to crush wounds, paralysis to sepsis, some of them slowly died there, and others painfully endured. Those who survived and were able to leave must have been traumatized anew by coming back for follow-ups or the fitting of prostheses, or to participate in research benefitting the care of others. The hospital's experimental techniques saved lives, but this progress came at the expense of submitting some of its earliest patients to what must have seemed like torture.

I struggled to find my way through the building's maze of hallways. Time seemed to slow as I mounted the stairs to the upper floors. The faster I tried to go, the more lost I felt. Floor by floor, I made my way up, finally getting to the top. I smelled chemicals when I arrived there, a scent that definitely should not have been there: my mind went to chloroform for surgeries and bleach for the bloody floors. Either way, it seemed like my signal to go. My visit was over, and whatever I had hoped to see or find was not there. What *was* there was something else, something tangibly bad.

After I left, I did more research on the hospital. I found out that for a brief time in the 1980s, it was used as a juvenile detention center. I felt the terror those youths must have felt. Dread. Impending doom. When I had been there less than an hour I was almost clawing to get out; it would have been a waking nightmare to be forced to live there. There's nothing a child could do that would warrant trapping them in a place like that.

Walking out of that building was like shedding a skin, or like leaving the lair of a great creature who had held me in its grip. I still don't know what I had thought I would find when I mapped out our visit, but what I got was definitely something else, something unexpected, unwanted. There was something there in the halls of the T&P Hospital. And it was dark.

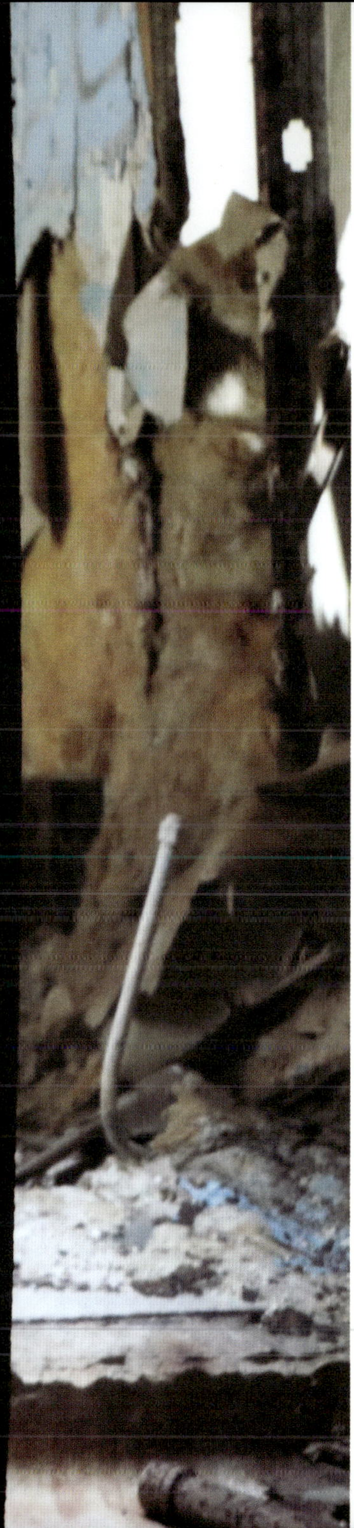

Basement level of the Texas and Pacific (T&P) Hospital, Marshall. PHOTO BY DUSTIN RICE

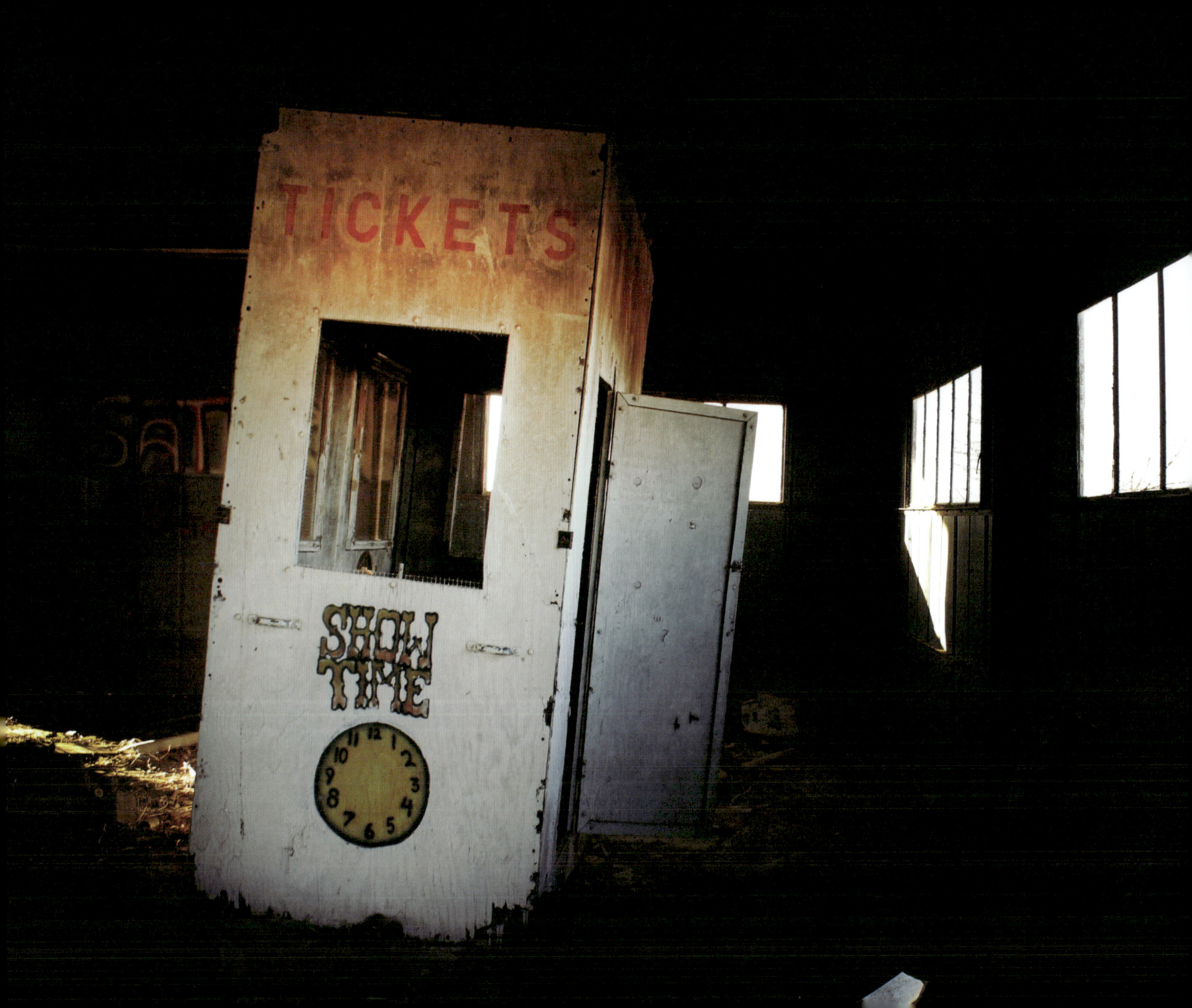
TICKETS
SHOW TIME

THE ROAD BETWEEN MANKINS AND DUNDEE (1925)

DUSTIN RICE

Imagine, if you will, the year is 1925, and you're driving down Highway 82, then called Seymour Road. You have driven this road before, so you know there's absolutely nothing to see on the seven-mile stretch between Mankins and Dundee. You're minding your own business when suddenly you see ahead of you, coming in your direction, a convertible car with a monkey on a leash, jumping up and down in the passenger seat as it approaches. You slow down, and even stranger sights meet your eyes . . .

Original ticket booth from the D. S. Dudley Show, found in a garage on the same lot as Cheyenne Dudley's home, Mankins. PHOTO BY MORGAN PAGE

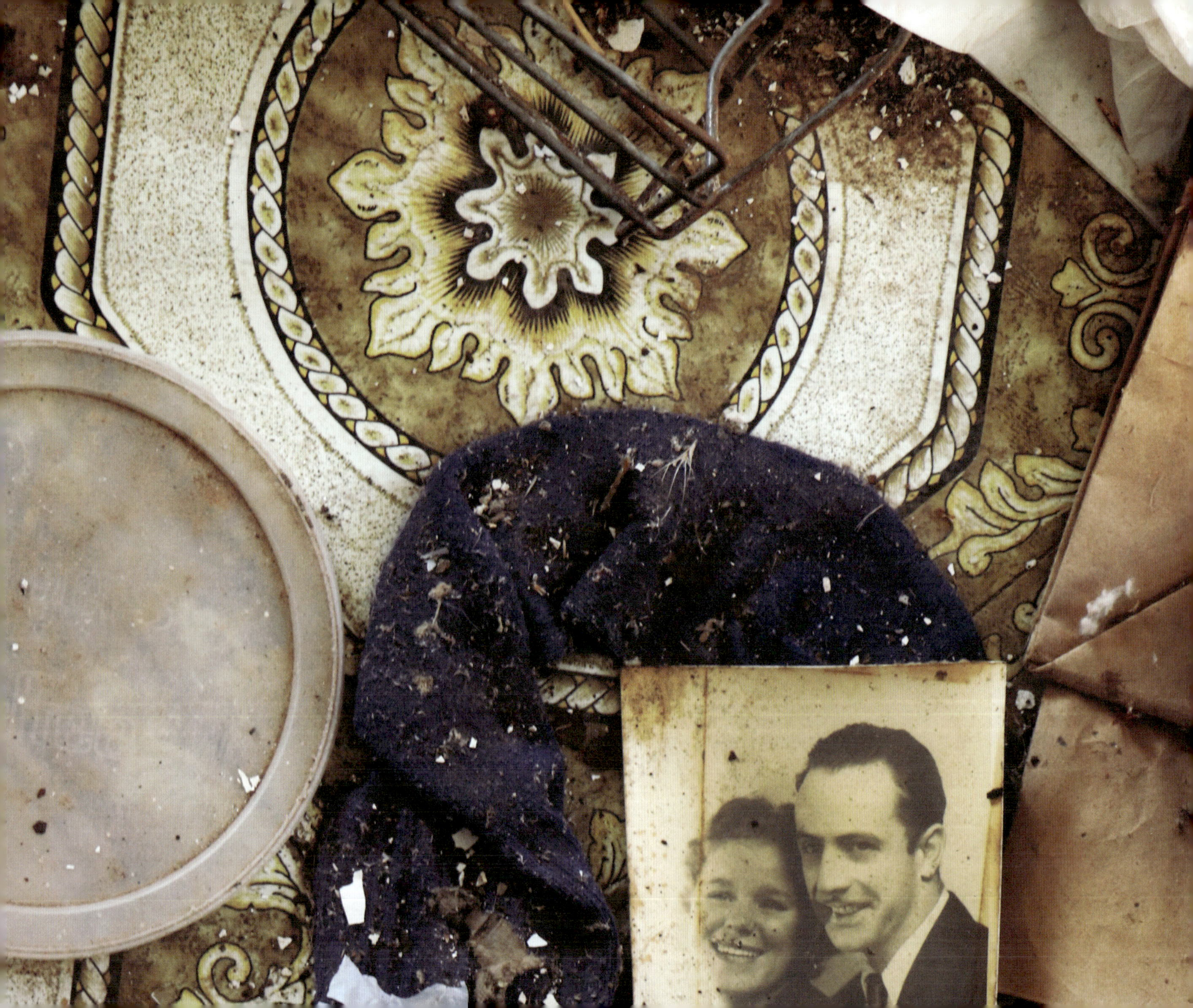

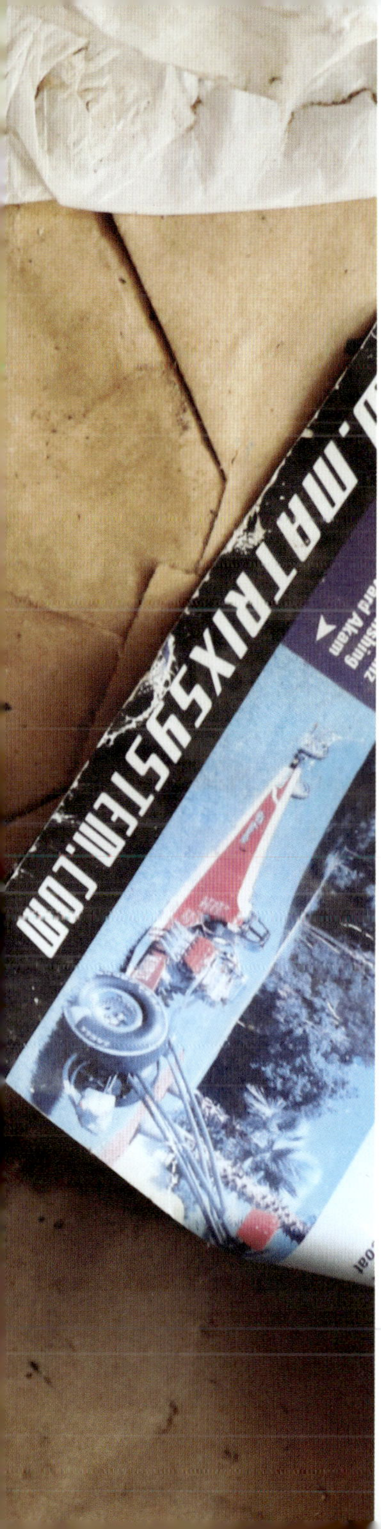

In the years between World War I and the early 1970s, Mankins was the offseason home of a traveling circus called the DS Dudley Show. For eight months of the year, the town was nearly empty as the 250 performers and their families packed up and hit the road. The other four months, however, the performers patrolled this stretch of highway. According to local legend, the elephants would walk with trainers wherever the trainer felt like going: exercise is exercise. Lion tamers would walk cubs on leashes, and strongmen would see someone changing a tire and lift the car for a laugh. A carny once went shopping at the Dundee Store with an eight-foot boa constrictor around her neck—at a time when no one had ever seen such a big snake except in pictures.

The DS Dudley Show was owned by Dick "Cheyenne" Dudley. Dudley bought the circus, and, following his service in World War I, took the show on the road. It was styled after Buffalo Bill Cody's Wild West show, which was popular around the turn of the twentieth century. Dudley's circus soon evolved, incorporating carnival rides, exotic animals, and sideshow attractions. An elephant, zebras, lions, and tigers lived behind Dudley's house. Bearded ladies, contortionists, trick ropers, and Native American role players toured with the group and all were welcome to stay in Mankins during the offseason. Dudley himself spent the offseason placing ads in newspapers where the circus would visit the next year, filling open positions, and auditioning new acts. He had no time for roadside shenanigans.

Cheyenne Dudley's circus made this unremarkable stretch of highway one of the most eye-popping roads in Texas and probably caused a few fender benders among unsuspecting travelers. The DS Dudley Show endured and entertained through good times and hard, touring through the Depression, World War II, and even after Dudley's passing. His children took over for some time, but eventually roadside circuses and sideshows fell out of favor. Around the same time that summer blockbusters took over movie theaters, the DS Dudley Show performed for the last time. The gas shortage of the 1970s combined with a lack of societal nostalgia paused the tour, and it just never started again.

Two of the first places Morgan and I ventured to after undertaking our project were Dundee and its neighbor, Mankins. They were just a few miles down the road from us then, and we loved the idea that a circus once spent its offseason in the area. We passed Mankins by as a place to shoot the first time we were there because everything was overgrown, but we did notice all the old carnival rides out back and always thought we would return and shoot them, given how close they were. As time passed and our project grew, we went further and further away and just

Photograph found on the floor of Cheyenne Dudley's home, Mankins. PHOTO BY DUSTIN RICE

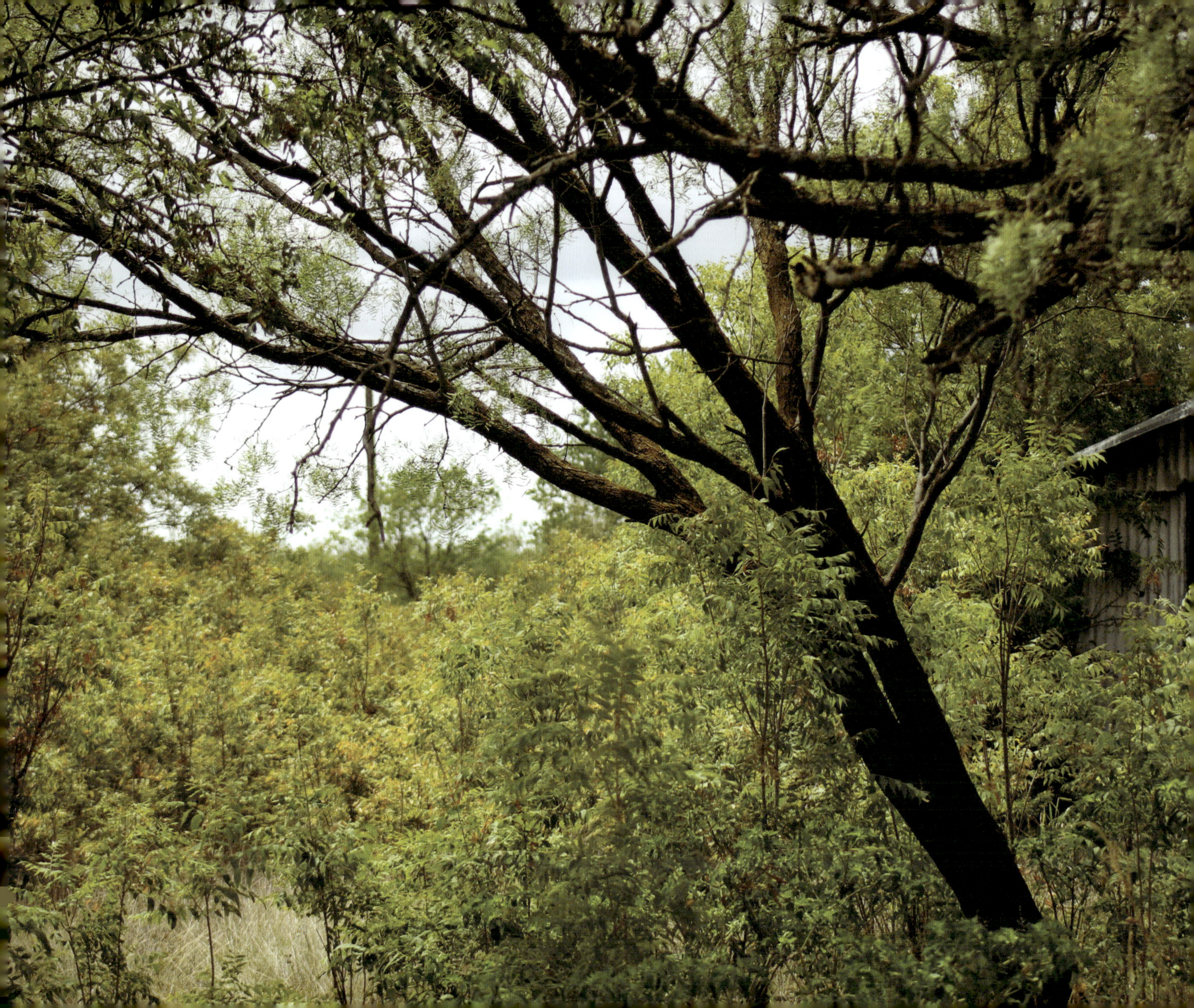

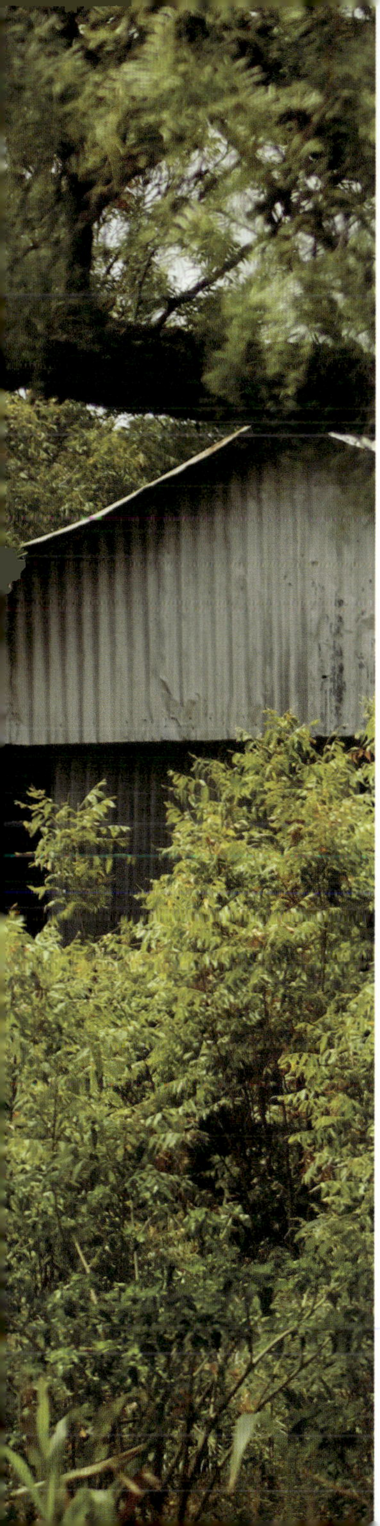

never really circled back. Then about two years on, we did drive through, and the entire highway had been moved. It now went right through the back yard of the old Dudley property and right over where the old rides were. We never came back and now it was gone. Who knows what was there that we could have documented? We did go back to see the house and storage building that are still standing, but this remains one of the great what-ifs of our travels.

We learned a hard lesson about taking advantage of the opportunities that are presented to us. We are now keenly aware of how fleeting the subjects we are covering can be. We have seen several times that, when we revisit places, almost inevitably something we have shot is gone. Whether rotted, blown down, moved, replaced, or covered by a highway, such things are not always viewed with reverence by others. Time is always marching on, right over the things we love. So now we stop when we see something, even if it's right down the road, because we don't know if it will be there the next time we drive by.

Buried in Dundee. PHOTO BY MORGAN PAGE

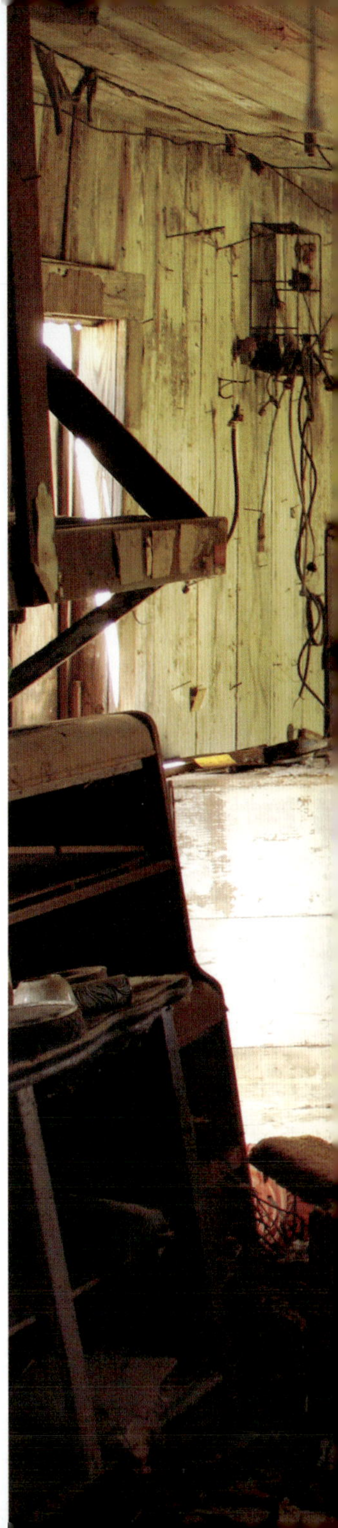

Abandoned store in Dundee. PHOTO BY MORGAN PAGE

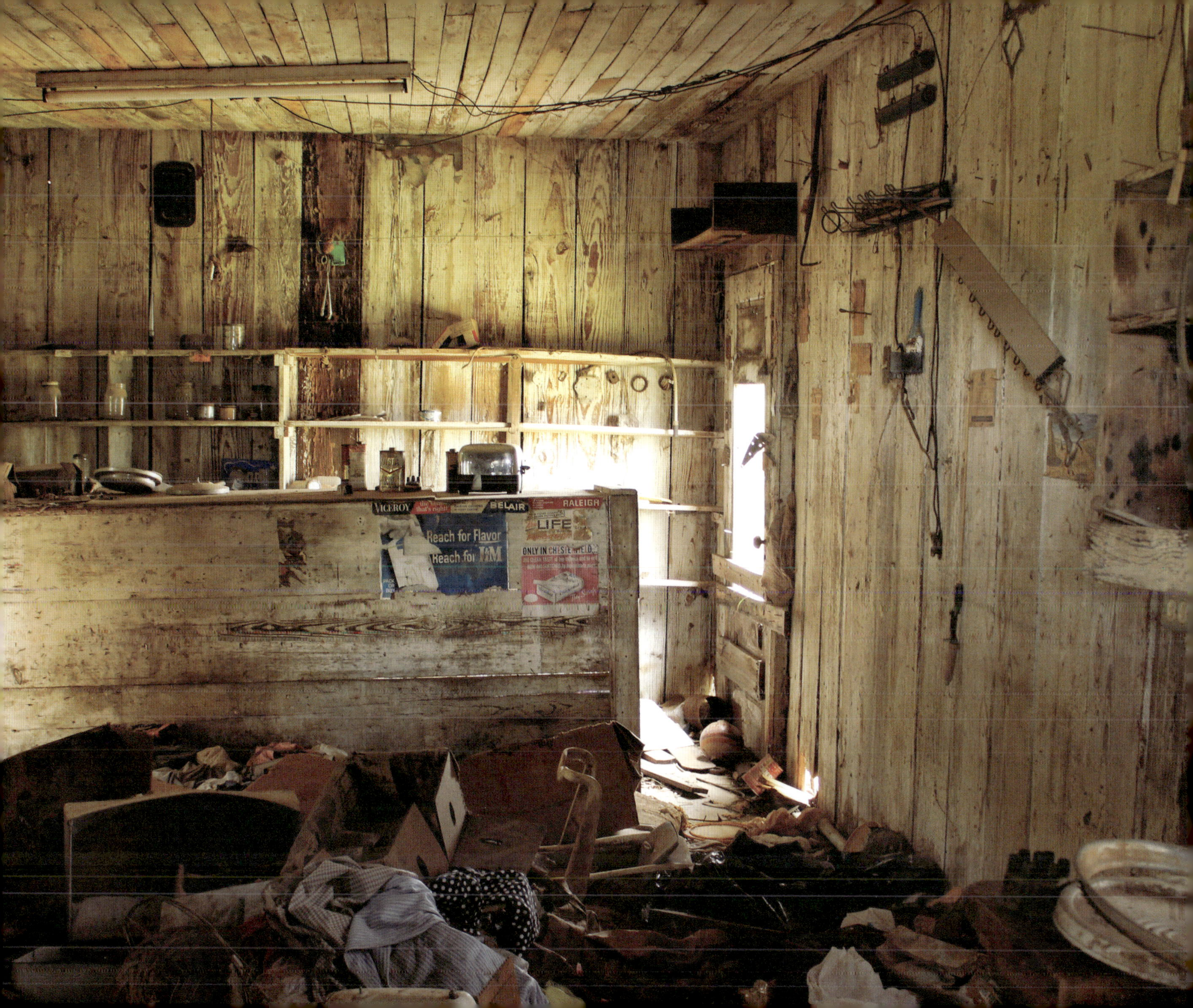
VICEROY
that's right
BELAIR
RALEIGH
LIFE
Reach for Flavor
Reach for L&M
ONLY IN CHESTERFIELD

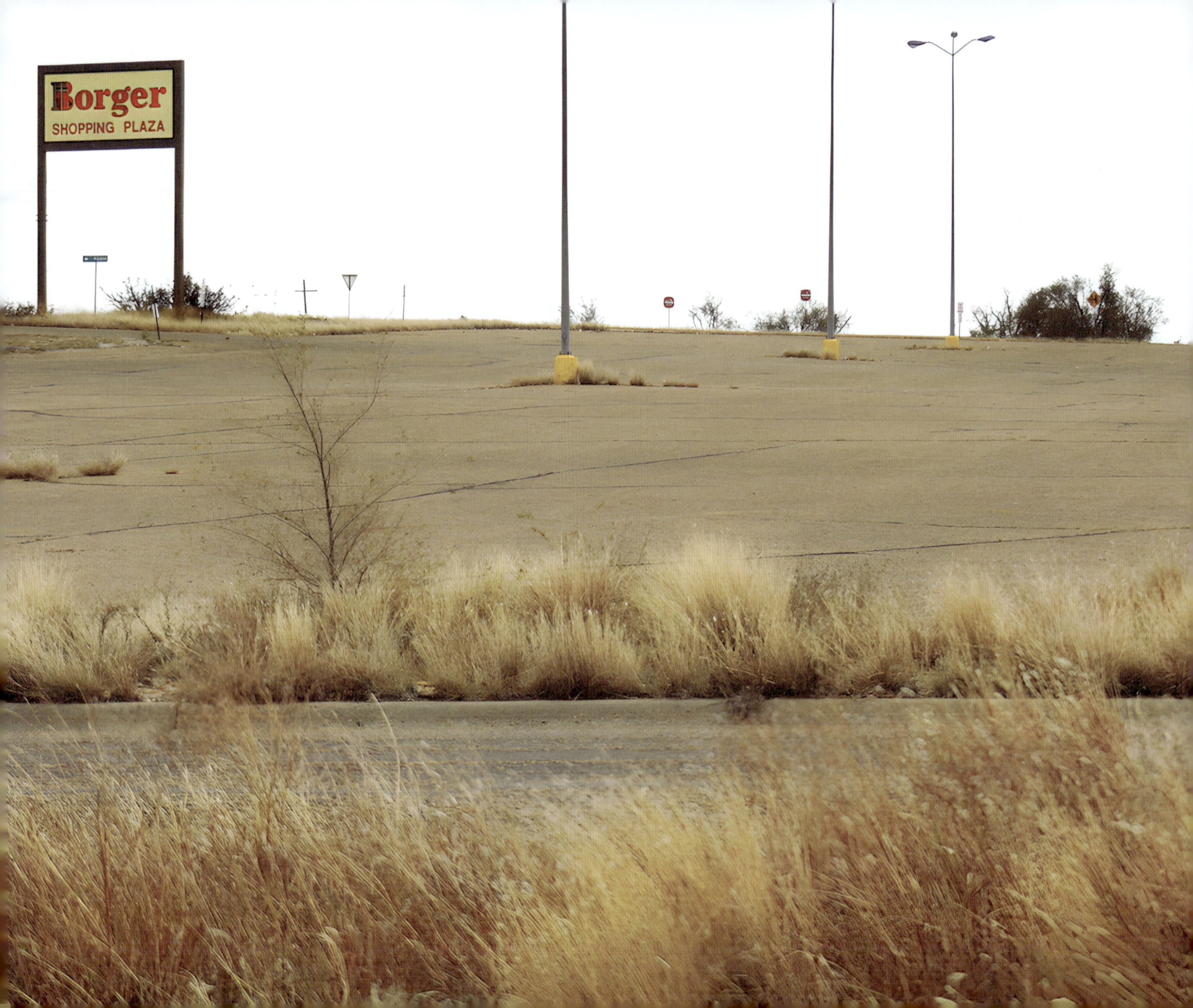
Borger
SHOPPING PLAZA

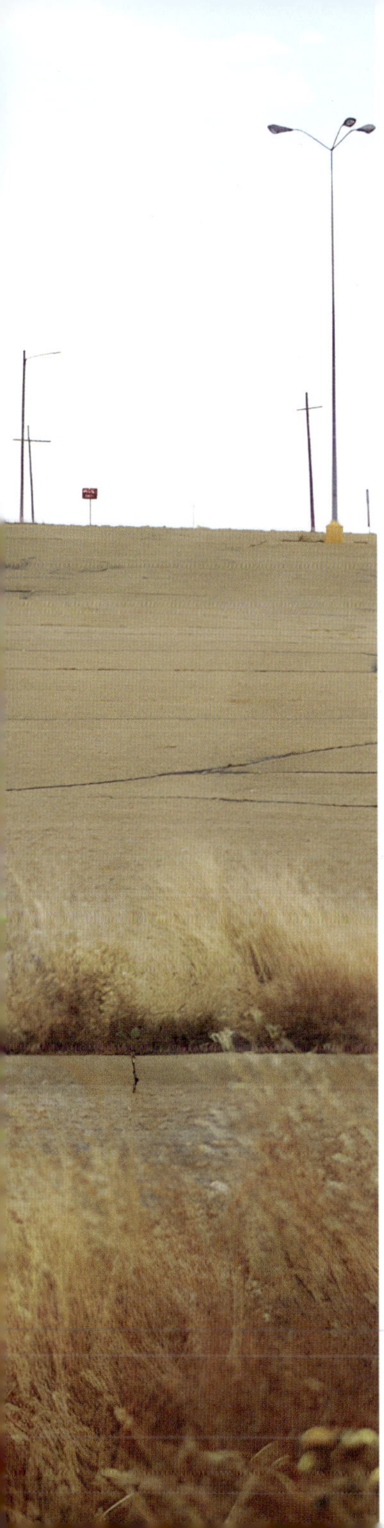

BOOGER TOWN (1926)

DUSTIN RICE

Asa "Ace" Borger left Oklahoma on horseback in January 1926. He had done some land deals on his way west from Missouri, and a businessman named "Slick" had shown him that, under the right circumstances, with the right timing, one man can make a town just spring up out of nowhere. That was what Ace planned to do, and his time had come. Word was just getting out that oil had been struck in the Texas Panhandle. It would be the beginning of the end of his life.

View from abandoned Kmart parking lot in Borger. PHOTO BY MORGAN PAGE

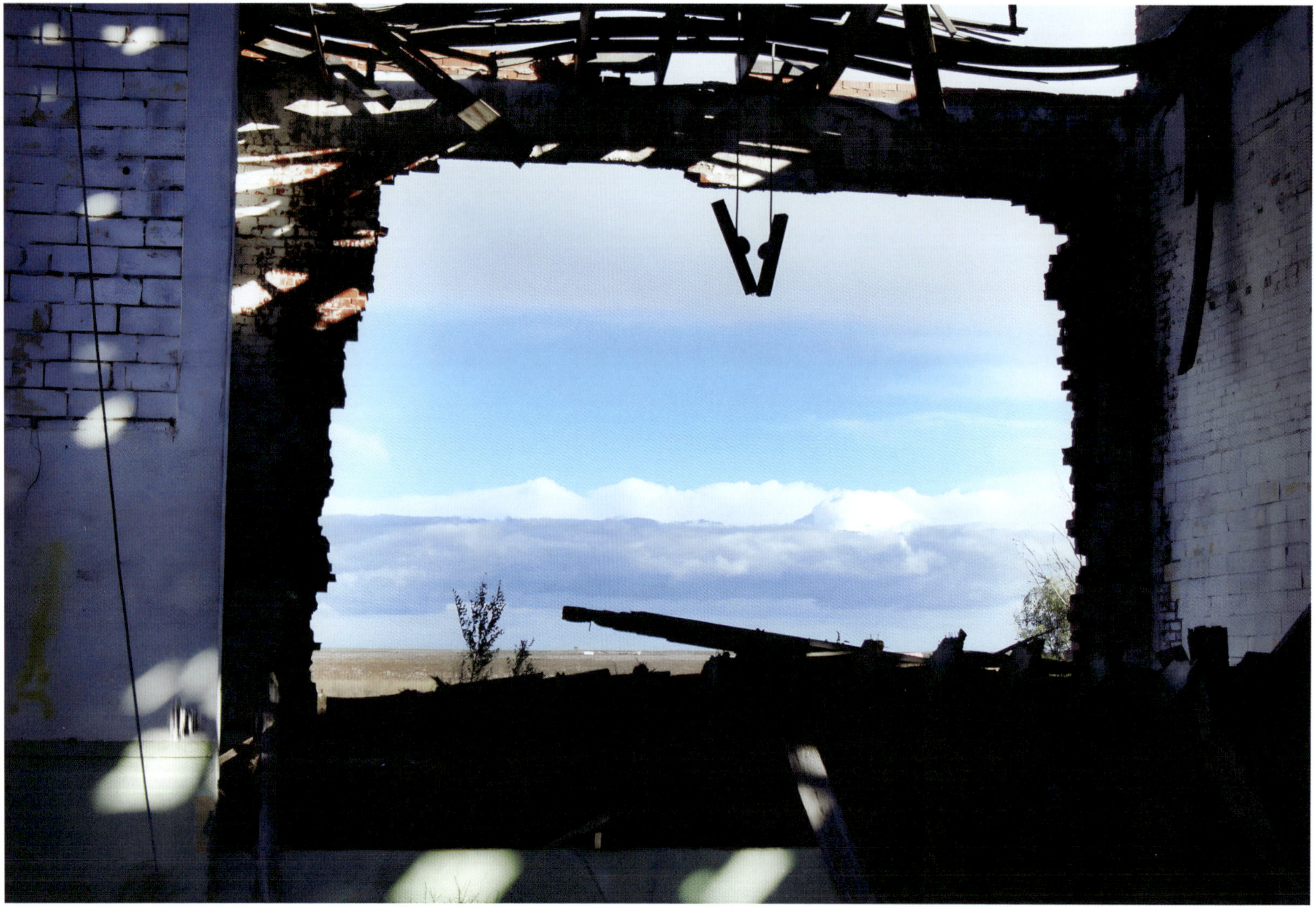

Perico. PHOTO BY DUSTIN RICE

When Ace rode up to the oil rig one bone-cold morning, he had a question for the boss: Whose land were they on? The boss pointed him toward the ranch house, and after a short meeting he became the proud new owner of 240 of the ugliest acres in the Panhandle. He had paid $12,000. The land was rugged, rolling, and dry—frozen in the winter and hell on earth in the summer. But Ace did not care about the conditions aboveground, for he knew what was under the land.

Once Ace filed the necessary paperwork, the town of Borger was born. He plotted the lots and streets and sent money to advertise news of "BLACK GOLD FOUND!" in the Amarillo papers and beyond. The first day of lot sales topped $100,000, and in six months Ace cleared $1,000,000 in land sales.

It didn't take long for the criminal element to come to town. Ace invited his cronies to set up and incorporated the leaders into a sham city government that only existed to organize the crime. "Two-Gun" Dick Herwig, the new town sheriff, was also the town's "protection" for prostitution—in short, the town pimp. Flying in the face of prohibition, "Shine" Popejoy, so-called King of the Texas Bootleggers, licensed illegal liquor to every bar and flophouse in town, monopolizing the trade and setting high prices across the board. The bogus government became known as the "line," and this organization covered up murders, peddled drugs, and promoted prostitution and liquor. They even harassed citizens for cash on the street by fining them for made-up infractions on the spot, demanding so-called line contributions.

Booger Town, as Borger was known in those days, burned white hot and eventually caught the attention of law enforcement down in Austin; in 1927, a double murder and its subsequent cover-up caused the Texas Rangers to be called in. Legendary Ranger Frank Hamer called it the worst crime ring he had seen in Texas. While some arrests were made and offers to leave town accepted, things quickly returned to the way they were, if not worse, as soon as the Rangers left.

Eventually an honest district attorney came along and legitimately prosecuted crimes in Borger for the first time ever. He was honest and unflappable and incapable of being bribed, so naturally he was murdered as he got out of his car one night late in 1929. The murderer was never caught, but the story gained so much attention that the Rangers were immediately called back in and martial law was declared, based on their reports and arrests. The crime ring was finally ended. Saloons were locked up, stills demolished, and arrests made with no option for lawbreakers to head out of town. The deputies and sheriffs were disarmed, the town's leadership was disbanded, and the Texas Rangers and state troopers took over. Legitimate elections were held, and the reorganization of the town was underway. Despite being the man who set up the whole scheme, Asa Borger was never prosecuted for any crimes.

Ace met his end on the steps of the post office in 1934. He had neglected to bail county treasurer Arthur Huey out of jail. Huey had been arrested for embezzlement and Ace had a hand in the scheme; Huey took Borger's failure to post bail as an insult. He emptied his .45 into Borger, then grabbed Borger's own .44 and shot him with that as well, all in broad daylight. Huey somehow got away with claiming self-defense; some say the jurors thought Borger had it coming to him.

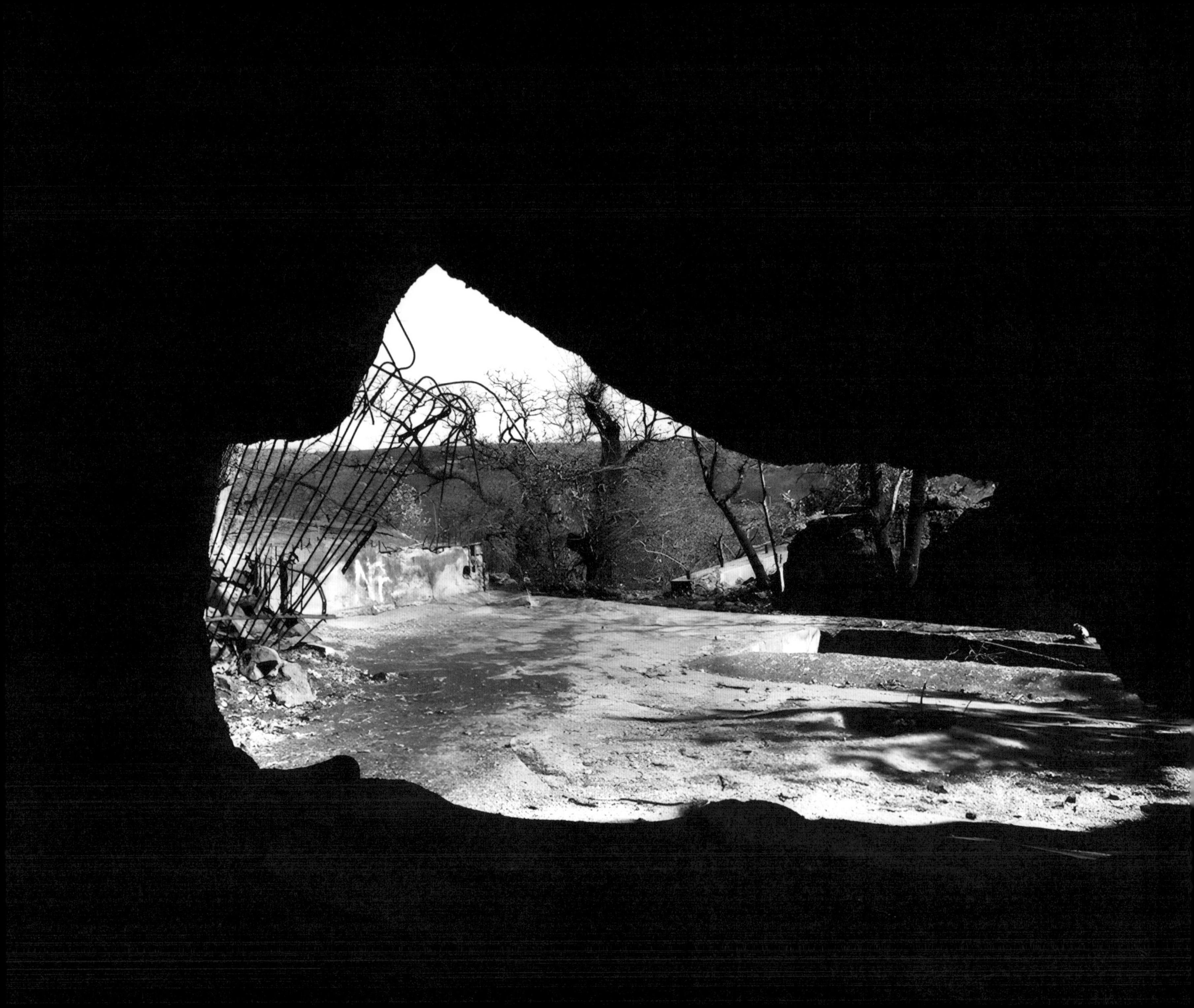

THE LITTLE ZOO UP THE HILL (1927)

DUSTIN RICE

After hearing rumors of an abandoned zoo only a couple hours from home, Morgan and I knew we had to make it a part of our project. It was in Cisco, a town I had driven past at least fifty times on I-20, the road between Dallas and Abilene, though I had never stopped.

It had taken just under a year for the zoo's concrete to be poured and its wrought iron to be erected. The back side of the town's brand-new dam, built in 1923, was the chosen location. The zoo would be right next to another new entertainment venue, the world's largest concrete pool. Built by a local construction crew and manned by local unemployed laborers, Cisco's latest attractions became a weekend travel destination in the late 1920s for people from hundreds of miles around.

View from the bear cave at the abandoned zoo in Cisco. PHOTO BY DUSTIN RICE

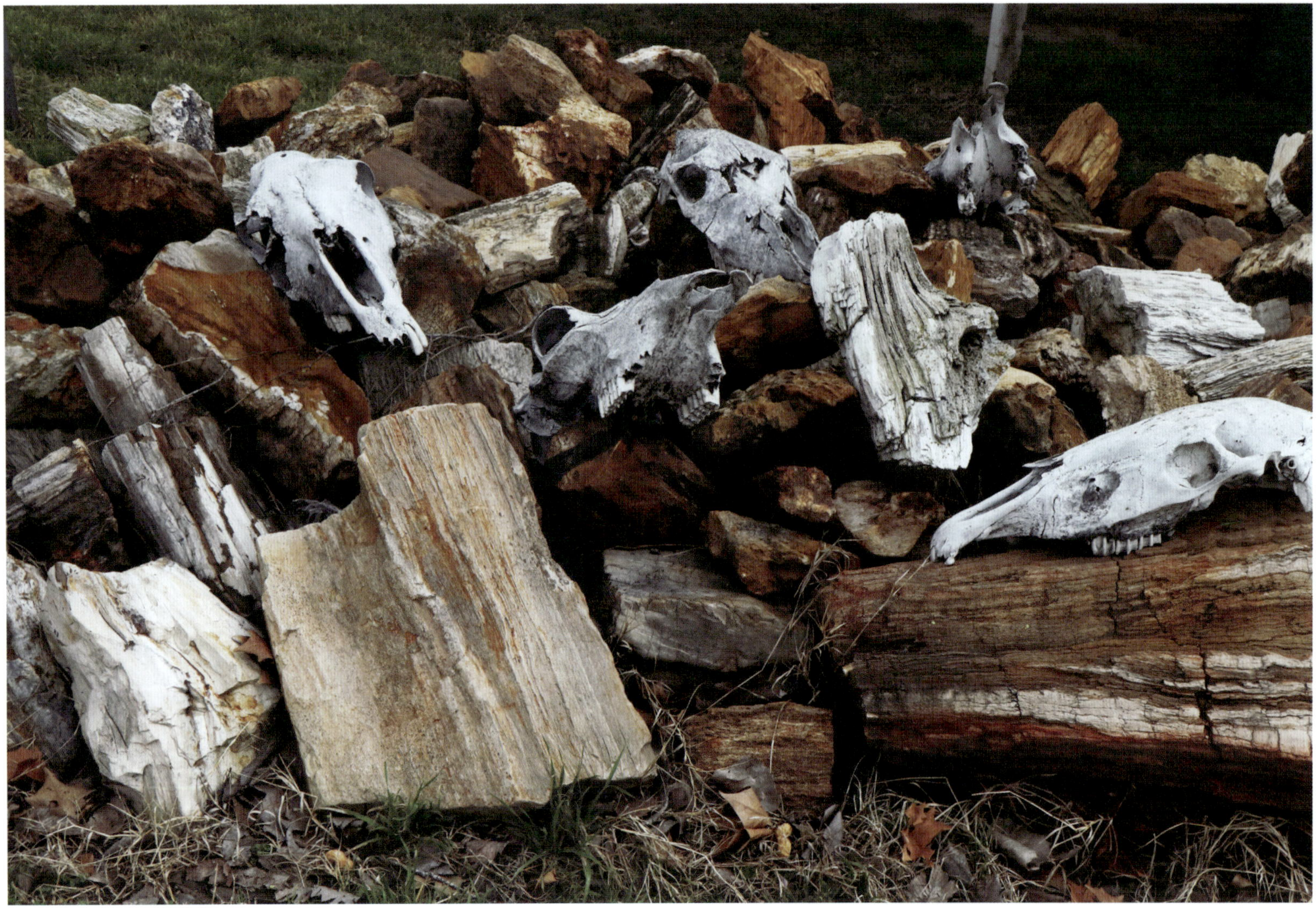

A pile of skulls and wood in Calvert. PHOTO BY DUSTIN RICE

The zoo evolved as it grew, adding fishponds, native bird exhibits, and even a large monkey cage. It was frequently forced to adapt, as animals seemed to die just as quickly as expansions were undertaken. They had a red deer stag that died early on, presumably because it was kept in dank conditions as the zoo was being constructed. There was also a bear that was rumored to have been donated by a Caddo woman after she had raised it from a sick, abandoned cub. It died a few years into its time on exhibit as well; whether out of a twisted sense of fun, out of boredom, or just to ruin things for everyone, someone snuck in at night and poisoned it. The bear's short stay at the zoo is documented with a picture in the 1927 Cisco High School yearbook. There was also an article in the local paper about a time it escaped and three teenage boys returned it, unaided, using only a forked stick, a rope securing its paws, and eventually a wheelbarrow. They simply walked the bear home.

I found a number of interesting anecdotes in old message boards during the course of my research. One post stands out in particular, from May 29, 2007. A man named Charles Porter inquired about the location of the zoo and shared his memories of a day he spent there as a six-year-old. Charles's aunt, Fannie Bess, took his brothers, a cousin, and him to the pool and the zoo for the day. While they were walking through the exhibits, "a very unhappy monkey escaped from its cage and began making threatening advances toward us. Aunt F. B. was kept quite busy trying to hide us all behind her and ward off the monkey with an umbrella at the same time." I have no idea what kind of staff the zoo had, but it must have been a chaotic scene getting that monkey back into its cage.

Like many of its animals, the zoo didn't last long, either. The Depression took away funding and, like so many places of its kind, the zoo went out of business in the late 1930s. It fell into disrepair and was soon taken over by overgrowth; in time, it simply disappeared into the hillside, becoming part of the scrub oak forest that covered the back of the dam. It was all but forgotten until 2021, when a group of locals called SAFE (Students, Athletics, Families, and Education) proposed a cleanup. With the help of the surrounding community, this group created a walking and hiking trail system that accesses the old zoo grounds.

That's how we found ourselves hiking there in the late fall of 2021. We weren't alone: the parking lot was half-filled in the late afternoon, as news of the new trails had spread. Evidence of the clearing was everywhere and freshly cut limbs on old oak trees revealed previously unseen graffiti. This was once a place where local teens gathered. I was amazed by all the old wrought iron the cages were curled, bent, and broken by trees that had fallen over the course of the last century, making them look like metal sculptures in some cases, like old bones in others.

Soon enough I found myself at the bear exhibit. I had never had the opportunity to see a zoo from an animal's perspective, which I then realized was why I had come. I had to be in that den, to shoot from the bear's point of view. I crawled in and began taking photographs. Once I reached the back, where the bear slept, I peered out and was suddenly very uncomfortable. I had the sensation of helplessness, of complete isolation. I took a picture in that instant, and it was easily the most striking moment of my day there.

Once a dump, forgotten and abandoned, the little zoo on the side of the hill has been given a second life and serves a function again, as a place for the public to hike, enjoy nature, and get a sense of a previous era. In a matter of a few minutes, the trails take you back a hundred years. It's interesting to find yourself staring into empty cages, looking down into dry ponds, gazing through gnarled bars at abandoned dens, and imagining it as it once was.

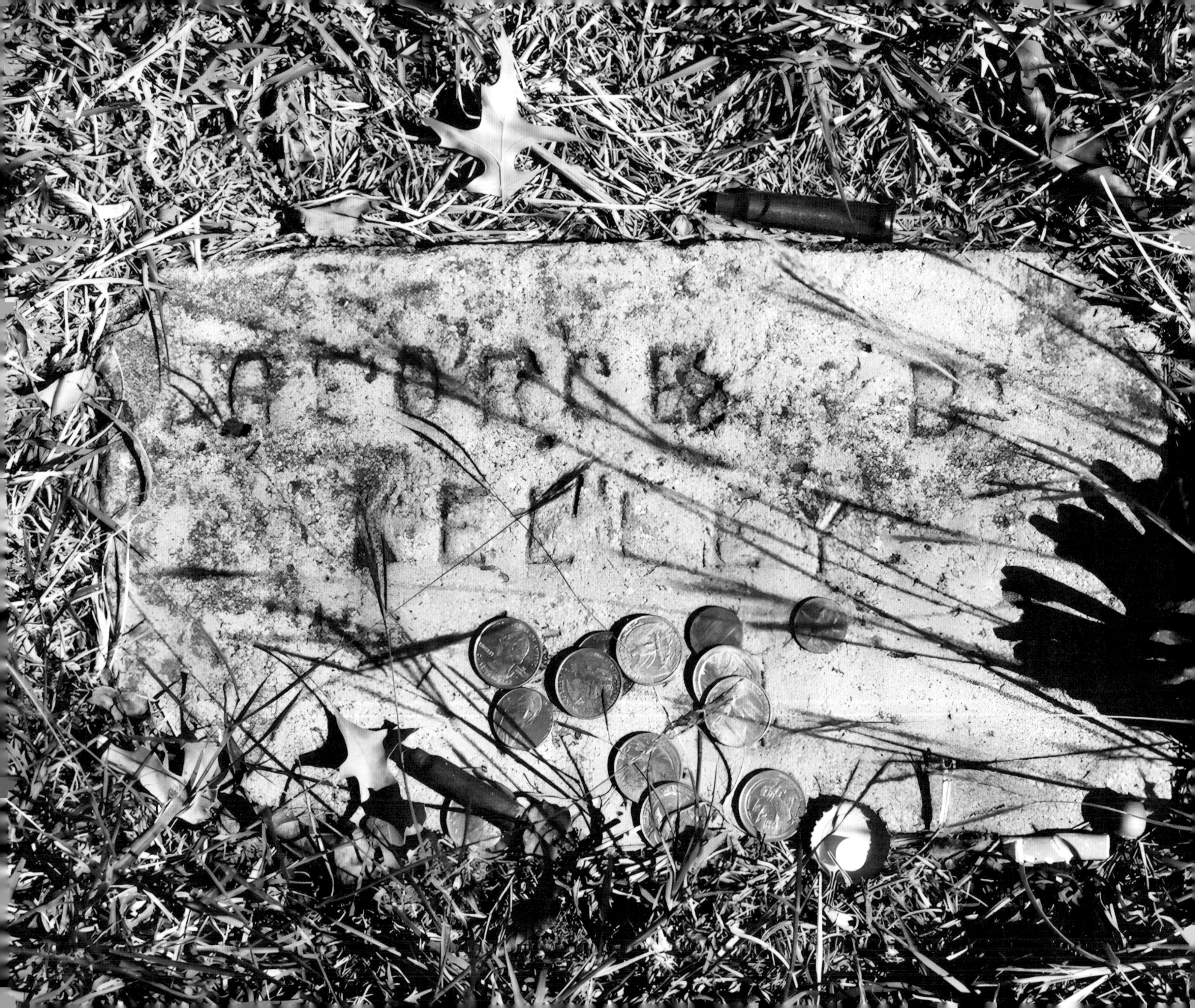

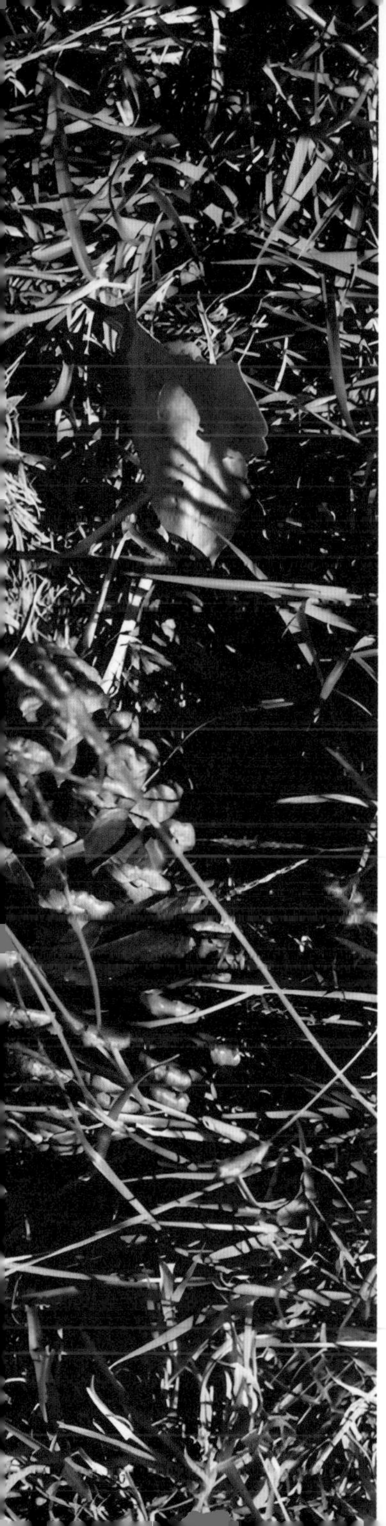

THE THORNE IN THE SIDE OF TEXAS (1930s)

DUSTIN RICE

In the pantheon of American gangsters, there is only a short list of those more famous than the man born George Francis Barnes Jr. It was a fairly ordinary name for a fairly ordinary bootlegger who seemed destined for obscurity. But everything changed in the fall of 1930, when Kathryn Thorne created Machine Gun Kelly.

Resting place of George "Machine Gun" Kelly at Cottondale Cemetery, Cottondale. Bullet shell and change were left by visitors before us. Kelly's name was intentionally misspelled in an effort to protect the grave. PHOTO BY MORGAN PAGE

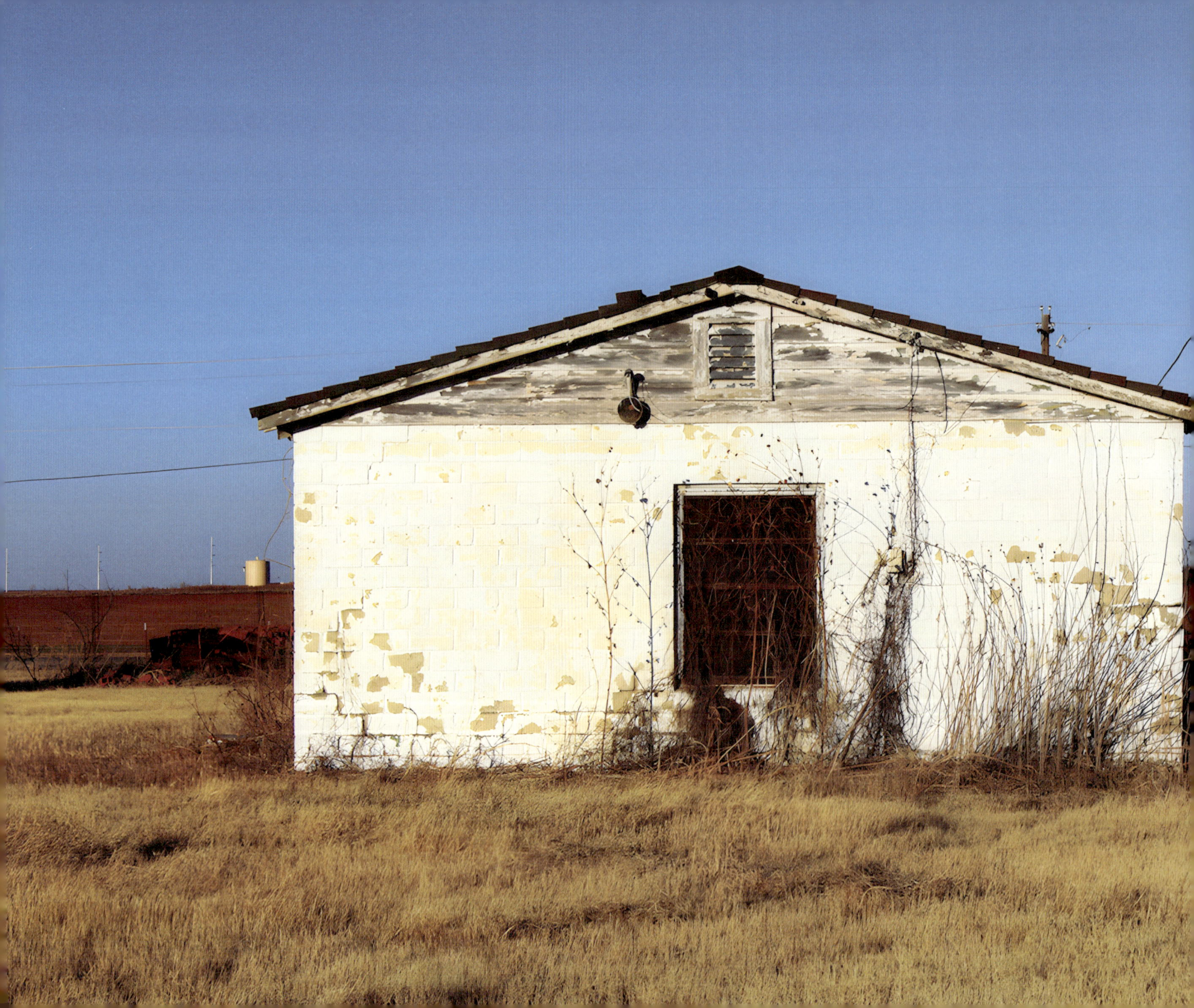

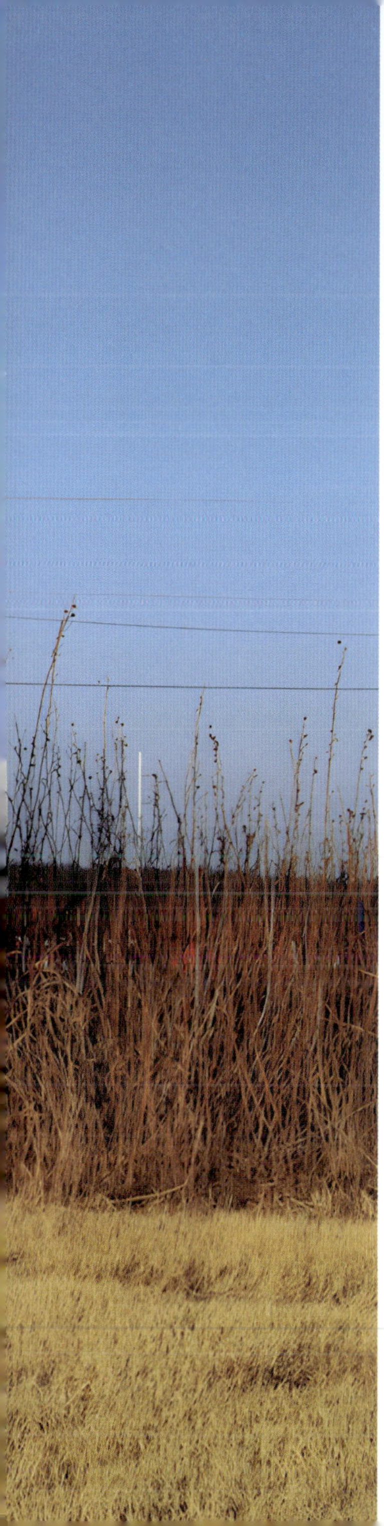

Kathryn Thorne, born Cleo Brooks, changed her name to match her personality. She left home at fifteen and married a man named Lonnie Frye, then had a child and divorced him. She quickly married again and just as quickly moved back home with Pauline, her daughter. It should be noted that home was her mother and stepfather's spread in Paradise, Texas. They ran liquor and were known to rent rooms to criminals in need of a hideout.

When Kathryn's third husband, Charlie Thorne, committed suicide, he left a note explaining all his problems and said goodbye. It was neatly typed and laid out beside him. This was suspicious because he was illiterate. The coroner's jury overlooked that detail, intentionally or not, and Kathryn went free. Charlie was, after all, a bootlegger and a friend to criminals.

By this time, the man named George Barnes was out of Leavenworth Federal Prison, having done three years for bootlegging. He met Thorne and was smitten. He had been married once before, but this was different. She saw him for what he was, a criminal with muscle and drive, and she appreciated that he was a bonehead. To throw the law off his trail, by this time Barnes had changed his last name to Kelly, but it was Kathryn who would come up with the name "Machine Gun" Kelly.

Kathryn bought him the Tommy gun he would become famous for at a Fort Worth pawn shop, Wolf & Klar. She insisted he practice with it daily at her family's farm in Paradise, shooting pecans and walnuts from fence posts. She also ran about Fort Worth giving away her husband's bullet casings, saying that they were souvenirs from Machine Gun Kelly and promising that "he was out robbing banks somewhere." Thus the legend was born. They did start robbing banks, though not every robbery said to have been committed by Kelly actually was; some were pinned on him by reputation. Bank robbing, though, was not what brought him and his family down.

Kelly and Thorne kidnapped millionaire oilman Charles F. Urschel from his sprawling mansion in Oklahoma City on July 22, 1933, and took him to the ranch in Paradise. The ransom of $200,000 set a new record when it was paid nine days later. Urschel was released safe and sound.

And that would have been the end of it, except Urschel had a photographic memory. His recollection of such details as the time spent driving, the noises of pump jacks and airplanes, and even the exact number of footsteps taken from the house to the car led the FBI right to the front door of Kathryn's mother, Ora, and stepfather, "Boss" Shannon. After some months on the run, Kelly and Kathryn were also captured, in Memphis, Tennessee.

All of them went to prison, the first individuals to be prosecuted under the "Lindbergh Law," so named because of the Lindbergh baby's

Home in Cottondale. PHOTO BY MORGAN PAGE

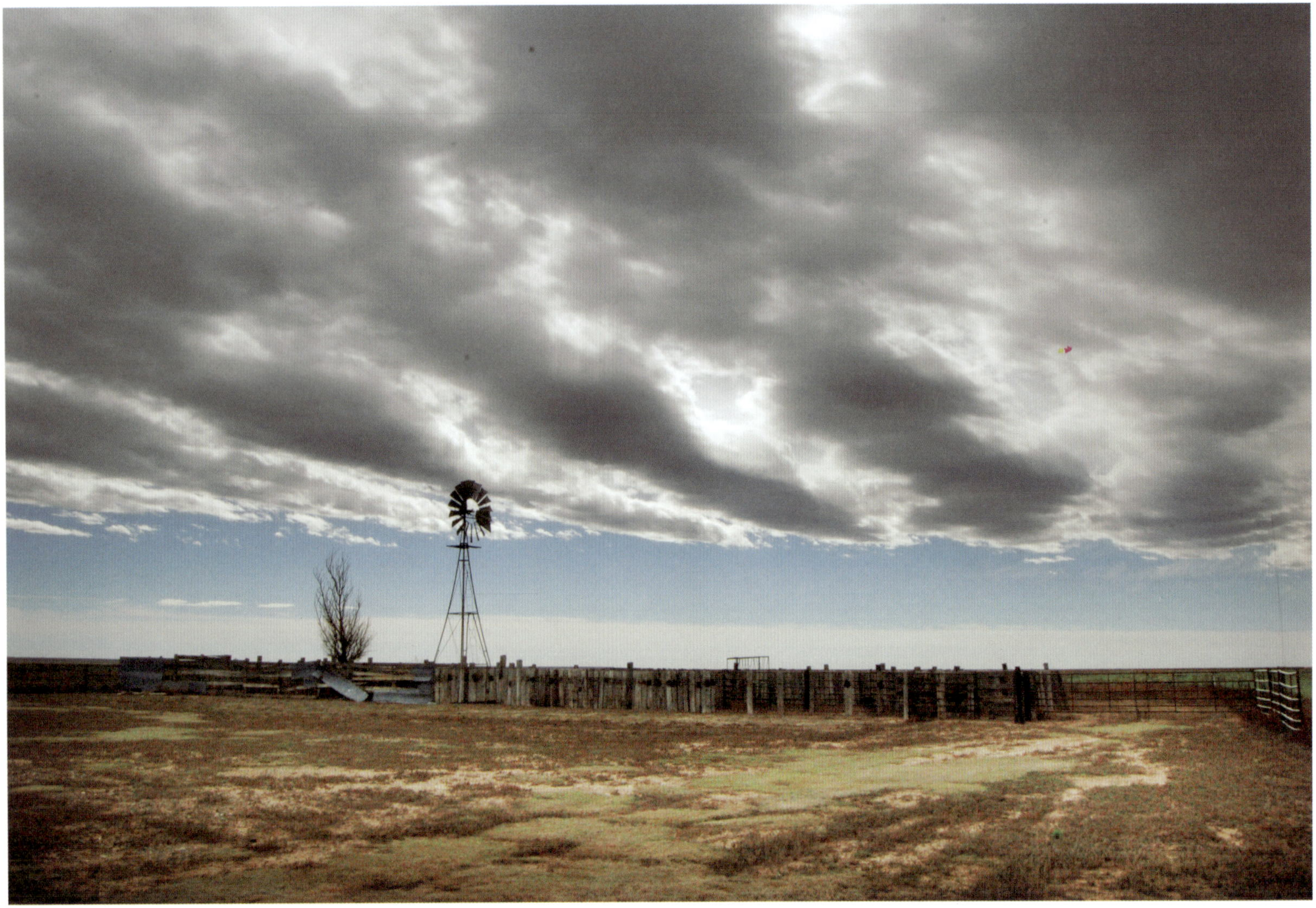

Stop along the way, Texas Panhandle. PHOTO BY DUSTIN RICE

kidnapping; it made kidnapping a federal crime. Boss got nine years, while Kathryn and her mother spent twenty-five years in a West Virginia correctional facility, going in and coming out together.

Machine Gun Kelly spent twenty-one years in prison before dying of a heart attack in Leavenworth, Kansas, in 1954, on his fifty-ninth birthday. Although he had spent seventeen years in Alcatraz, his life and sentence ended in the place that nurtured him as a young criminal. His body went unclaimed until Boss saw to it that he was laid to rest in one of the family plots. Kelly was buried less than five miles from where he held Charles Urschel hostage. The ransom he reaped from the crime may be nearby, too; Kelly buried the money in mason jars that he intended to dig up later. The FBI, to this day, has only recovered approximately half of the $200,000.

Kathryn died in relative obscurity in 1985, a clerk at the Oklahoma County Poor Farm. Forgotten in all the drama was perhaps the biggest victim of all: Pauline, Kathryn's daughter, was left alone after the bust at the farm when her whole family was taken to prison. She was fourteen years old. She jumped in Kathryn's car and drove more than two hundred miles to her great aunt's house in Asher, Oklahoma.

There, she was raised by H. T. and Pearl Hopkins. Thanks to an unlikely benefactor, Pauline made a different kind of life. She graduated as salutatorian of her high school at fifteen and applied for college, though she didn't have the money to pay for it. A judge informed her that funds had been donated. For the rest of her life, she believed it was the judge who had paid for her education, but instead, the anonymous benefactor was Charles F. Urschel. He saw past the crimes of her family and recognized the needs of a little girl. Pauline went on to have a long career educating special-needs children. She raised a family, promoting education amongst her family members, and two generations have since followed her into the field.

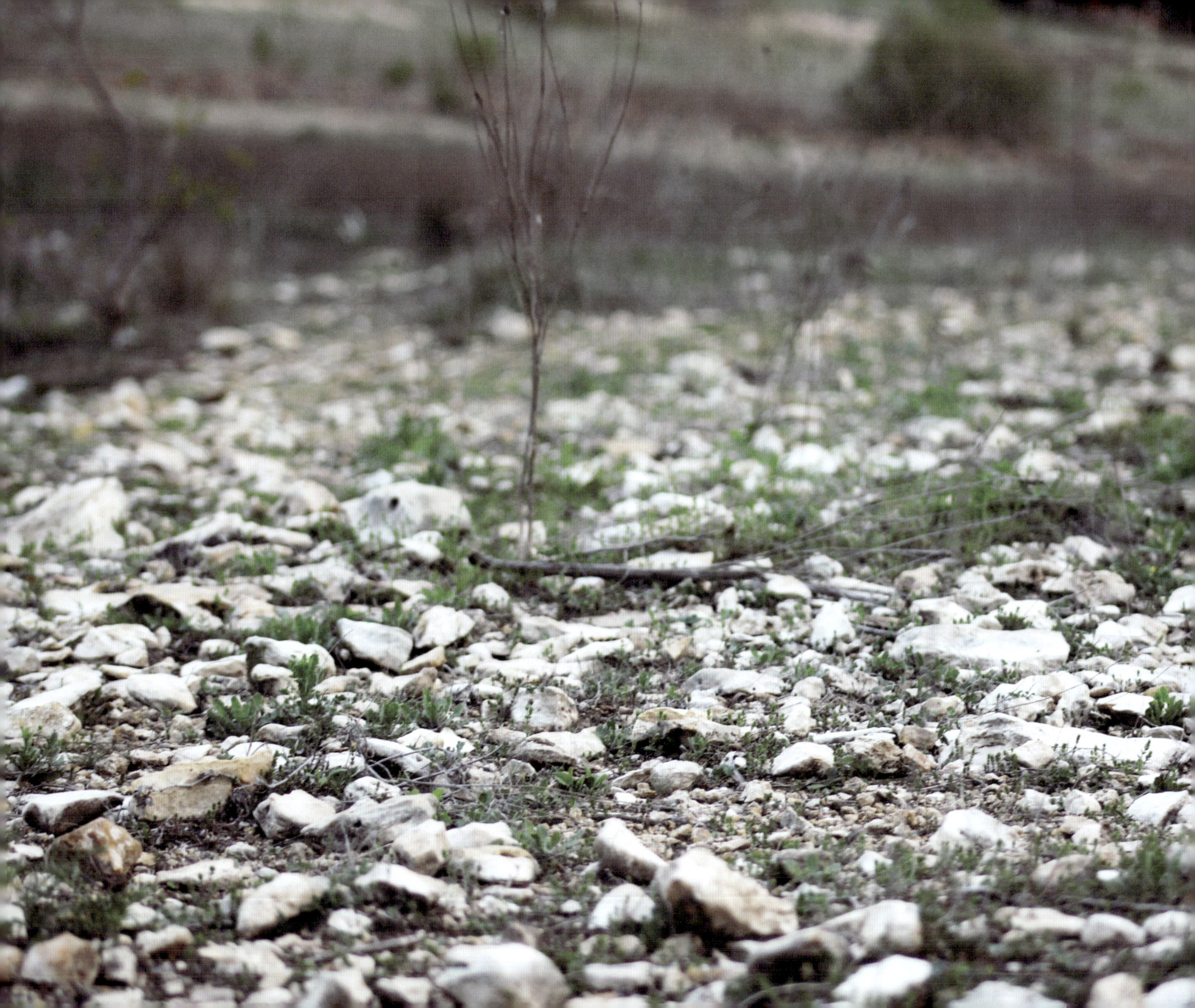

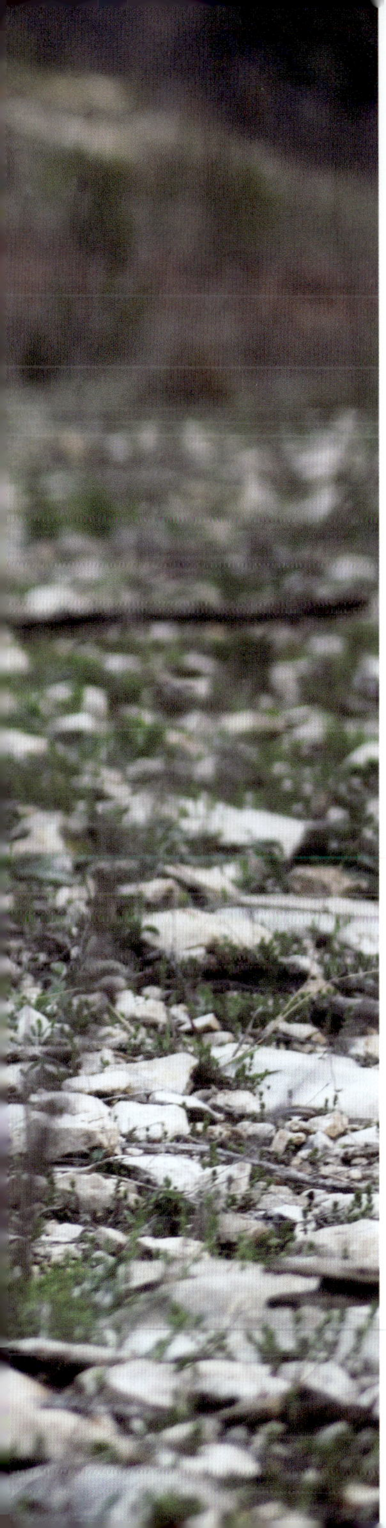

OCTAVIO MEDELLÍN (1930s)

MORGAN PAGE

Driving through Bandera reminds you how complex and diverse the history of Texas has been since its first inhabitants. For centuries, Bandera Pass has served as a passage for Native Americans, Spaniards, US Army units, Texas Rangers, and cattle drivers alike. And like much of the Hill Country, it has provided a tranquil setting for many important early settlers. Plentiful with rock quarries and places to fish, this land also appealed to the Mexican American sculptor Octavio Medellín, who decided to make it his home. He is most famous for his sculptures carved out of limestone from Central Texas and sandstone from West Texas.

Dried-up lake across from Medellín's property, presumably where he and his wife, Consuelo, went fishing. PHOTO BY MORGAN PAGE

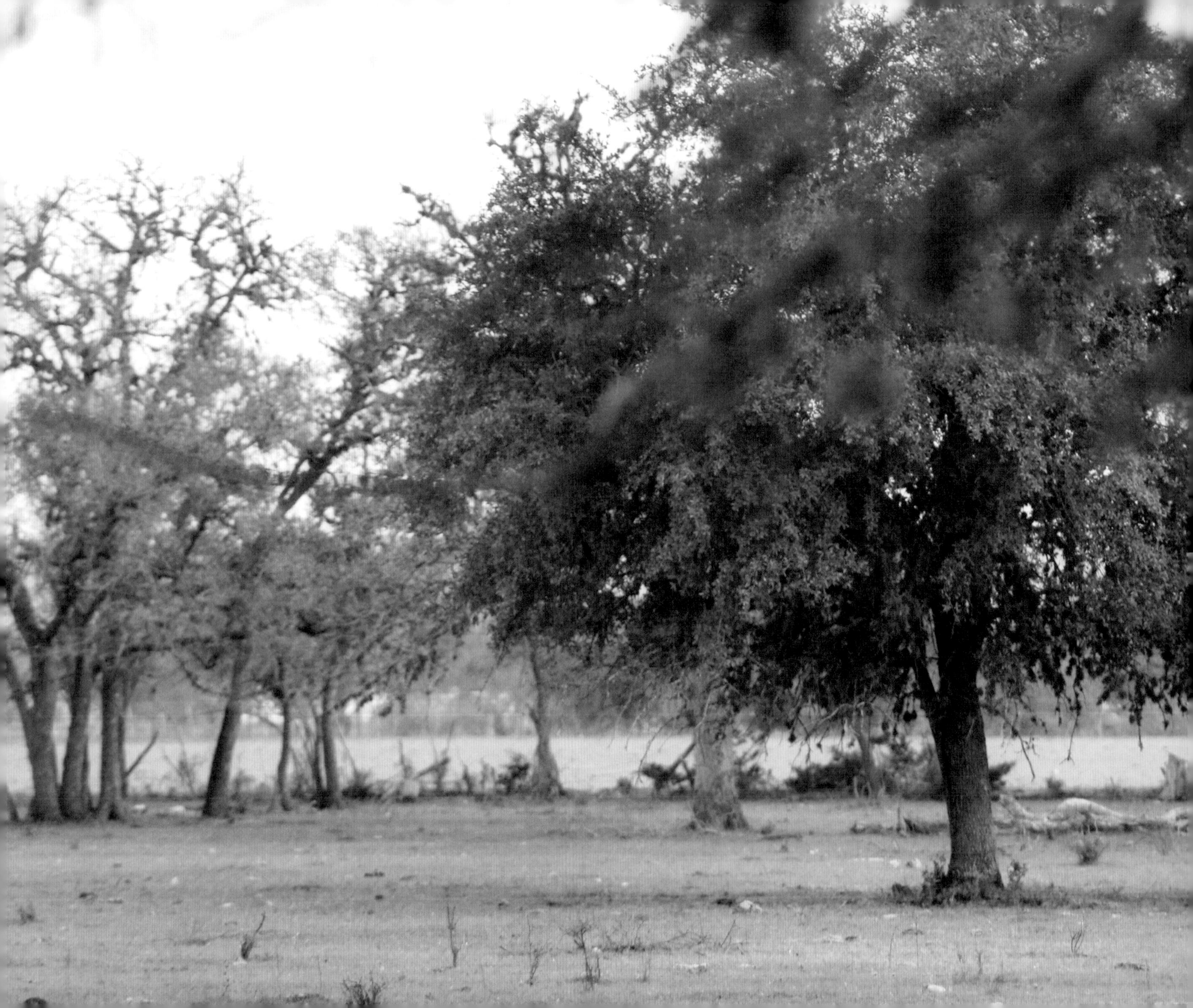

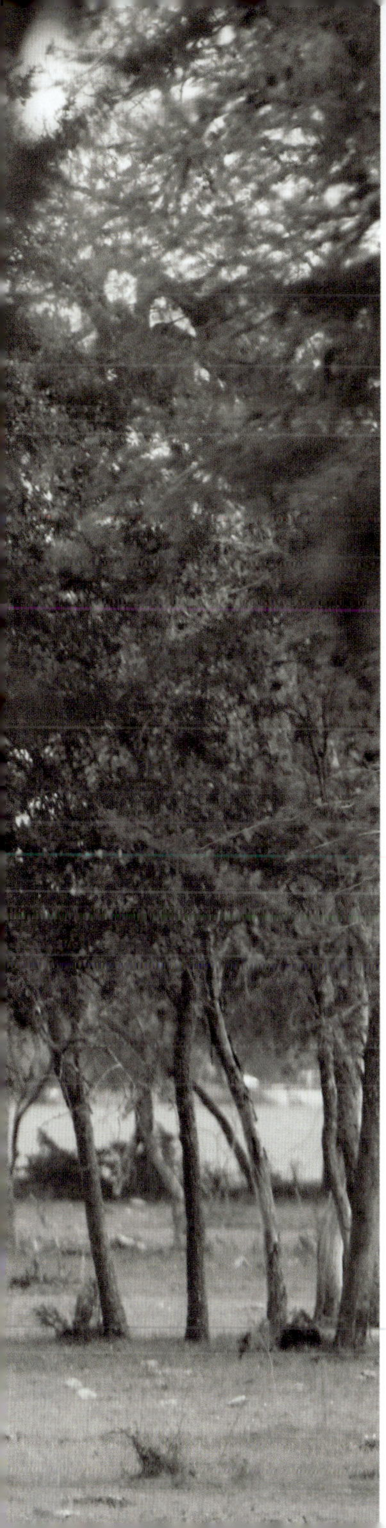

I had the opportunity to view a retrospective of Medellín's work at the Dallas Museum of Art in 2022, and many of his pieces have stayed with me. In particular, I often revisit photographs of *Father and Son*. Carved from red sandstone, a large male figure kneels to embrace a small child, their faces pressed together. The artist's own father, Manuel Medellín, was killed in combat during the Mexican Revolution, but before he died he instilled a love of art in Octavio.

Octavio came to Texas in 1920 at the age of thirteen, as the Revolution was coming to an end. Several years after emigrating, Medellín traveled back to Mexico with his family for an extended period to study Mayan and Aztec art and architecture, which became important influences on his body of work.

While Medellín took inspiration from Mayan and Toltec Indigenous cultures, he emphasized that his primary subject matter was common people and everyday life. In his art, he was able to bridge centuries of history and culture in Mexico and make his work relatable to a wide audience. Through incorporating many early Mayan and Toltec shapes and techniques into his own sculptures, Medellín brought to life contemporary figures who looked like they were from another time and place. The artist's grandson Brett has explained that Octavio believed the sculptures he made from Texas limestone and sandstone already existed in the material; he just needed to bring them out.

Octavio lived in different parts of Texas and eventually retired to Bandera in 1979. There, he spent long hours in his studio, up the hill from his home, where he would listen to Bach and Beethoven at high volume as he worked. His pet parrot, Pierre, was always close by, ready to yell, "Shut up!" in Spanish, which he learned from hearing Octavio mutter the words when he found someone bothersome. But Brett says Bandera was a place of peace for Octavio, where he could fish with his wife, Consuelo, while continuing to devote himself to his art.

In pondering Medellín's time in Bandera, it seems fitting to me that an artist who bridged centuries of cultural history, technique, and subject matter from Mexico, using Texas stone, would be pulled to live and create in the town of Bandera. It is a place that has been replete with cross-cultural intersections since the beginning of its recorded history. It is also a town touched by many historical figures in Texas's early settlements, and now by this timeless artist as well.

A view from the fence on the property where Octavio Medellín once lived with Consuelo, in Bandera. PHOTO BY MORGAN PAGE

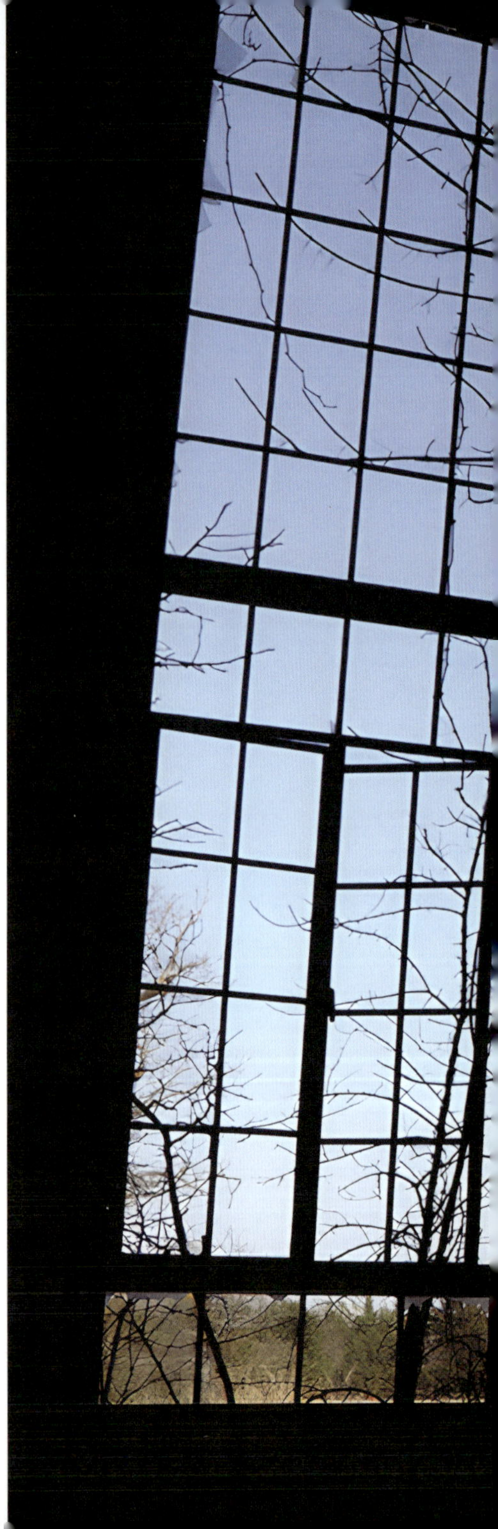

Built in the 1920s, the Woodmen's Circle Home, Sherman, was a shelter for orphans and widows. It was demolished in 2022. PHOTO BY DUSTIN RICE

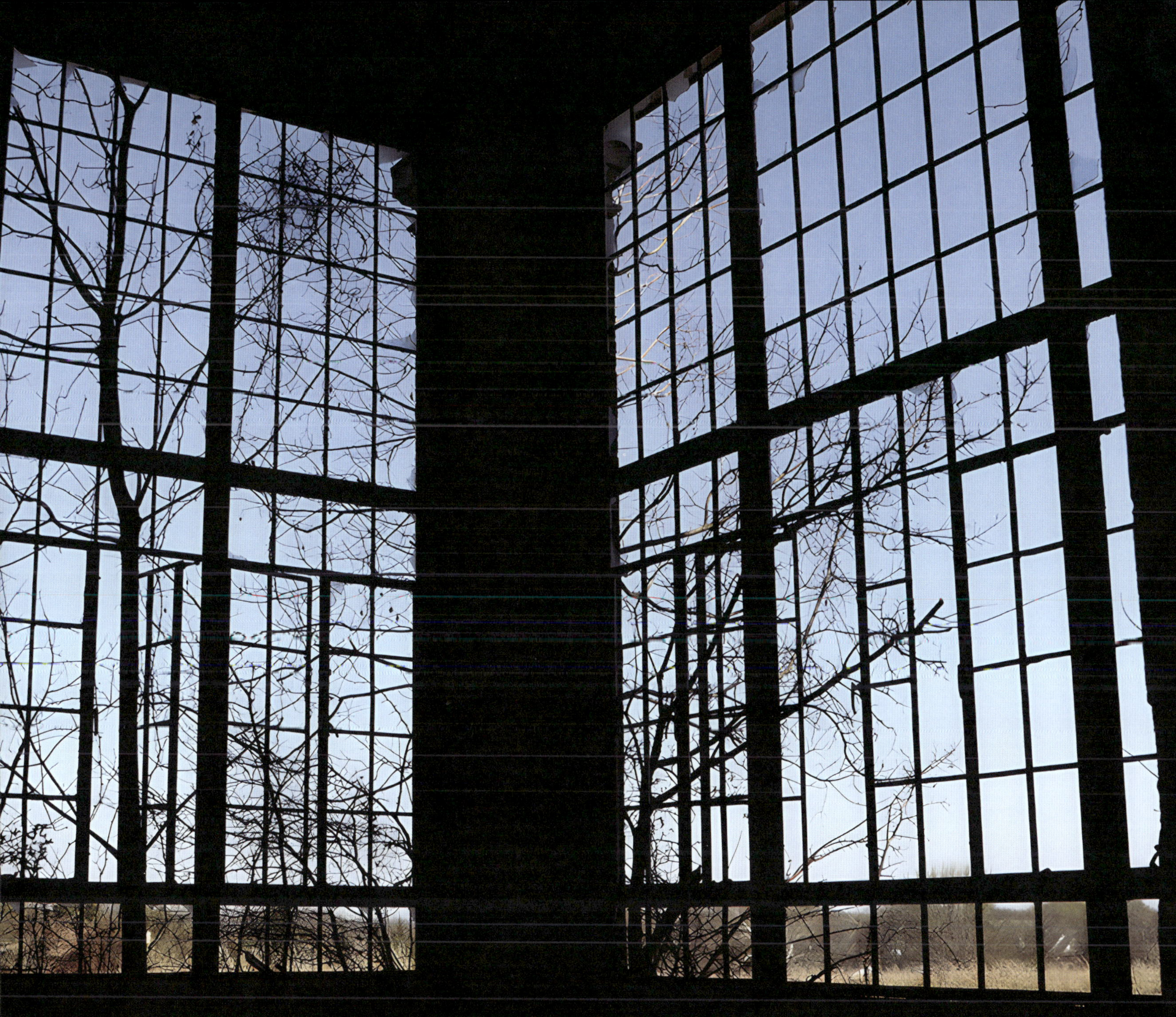

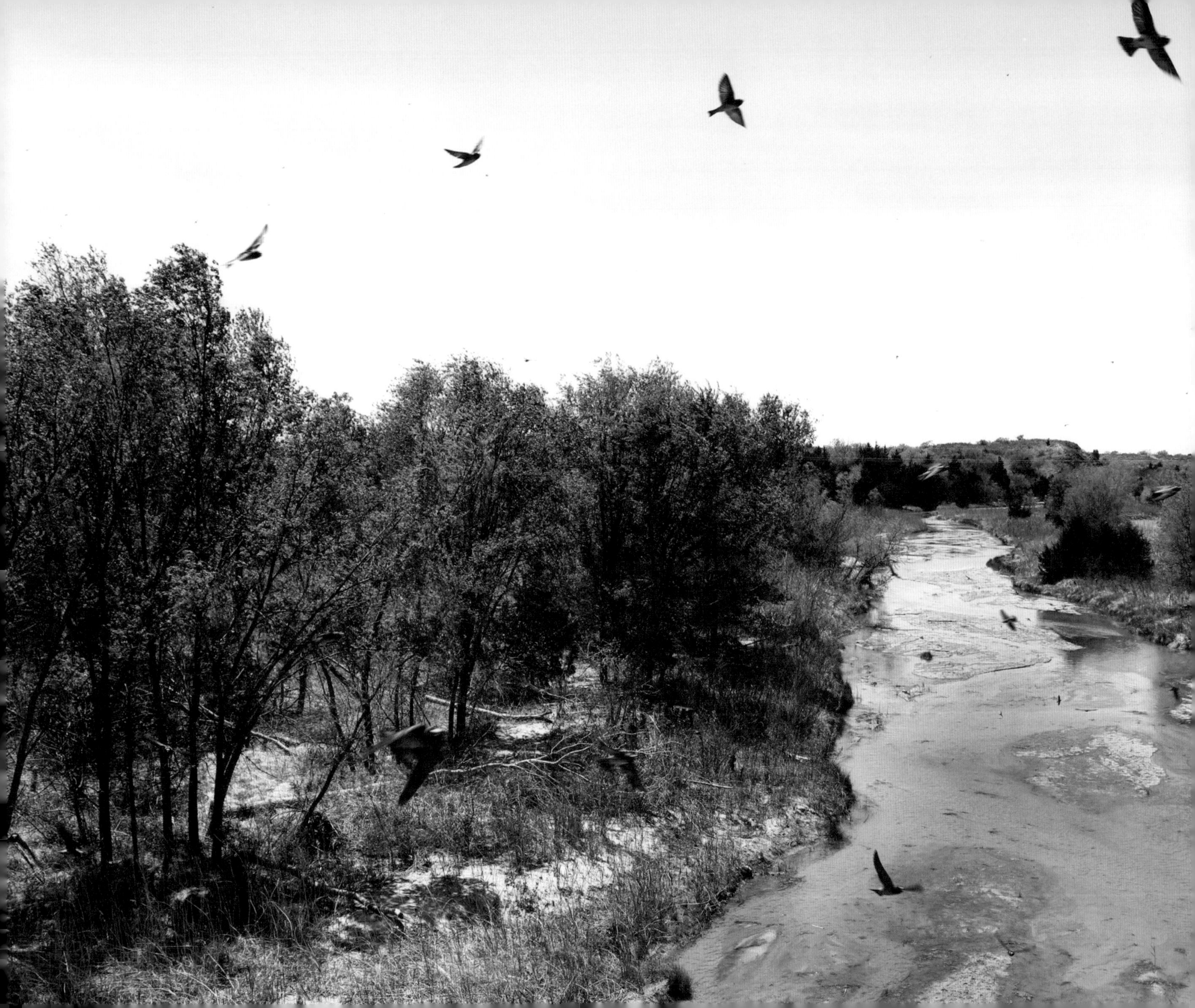

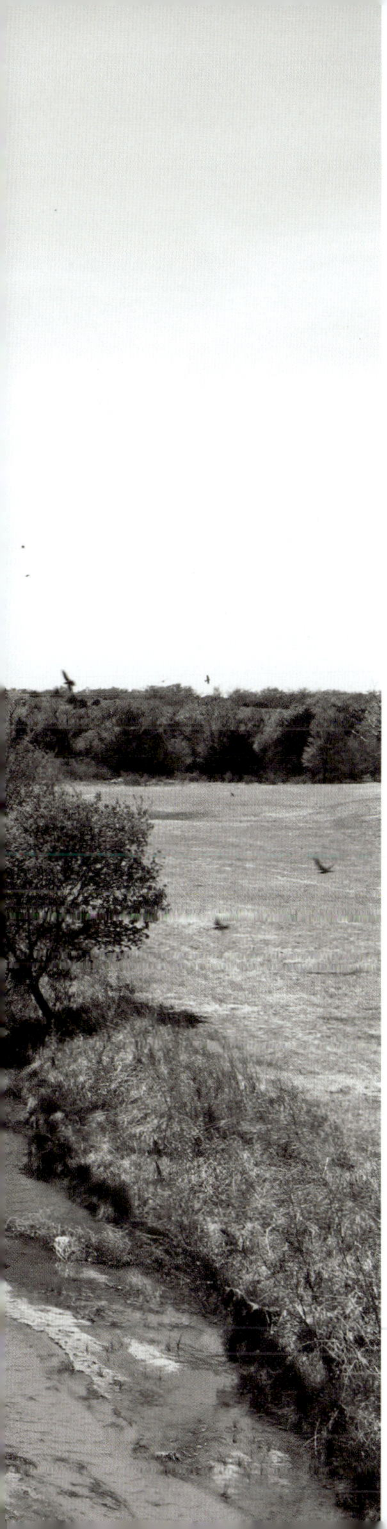

DARN FOOLS (1933)

DUSTIN RICE

The evening of June 10, 1933, was hot in Wellington, Texas. Jack and Sam Pritchard, along with Lonnie Cartwright, Sam's son-in-law, were just sitting down to homemade ice cream. It was their one treat those days, and they had all taken turns cranking the machine. Looking up, Jack saw a maroon car racing down the road that ran past their farmhouse. "Just look at that darn fool, if he don't slow down he'll run off in the river," said Jack, never one to interrupt but knowing this car was going way too fast.

About seven miles north of Wellington, the highway ran all the way to the river, but the bridge wasn't due to be completed for months. There were barricades, but this driver never saw them. A cloud of fine Panhandle dust rose, along with the unmistakable scream of a Ford V8. About ten seconds later came the sound of steel twisting and glass shattering. Launched from

Where outlaws took flight: This is where they landed in the middle of the river. They crossed again just out of view around the bend, near Wellington. PHOTO BY DUSTIN RICE twenty-five feet up the embankment, the car landed on its side, halfway across the shallow river.

The Pritchard family did not get to enjoy their ice cream. Sam, Jack, and Lonnie yelled out to their wives for help and ran. It was a hundred or so yards to the Salt Fork of the Red River. As they got there it seemed to be getting darker by the second. Working by lamp, they could see the car was smoking; the doors were jammed. They went around the front to the blown-out windshield and helped two men out. A woman was screaming somewhere inside. The men immediately went to the back, showing no concern for the woman, and began throwing objects that looked like sticks and boxes free of the wreck. Jack saw that the sticks were Browning automatic rifles and Tommy guns. Jack got hold of the woman and helped her wriggle free from the wreckage. She was the smallest woman he'd ever seen. Her leg was covered in battery acid that was burning her to the bone. The car caught fire just as they got her free, and they all scrambled to put the fire out mid-river.

The woman had passed out from the pain by the time they got her up the bank. Sam suggested that they come to the house. When they got into the light it dawned on the Pritchards how young these people were; they were kids. One had just turned seventeen. Lonnie offered to go to town for a doctor. "No, we're hot! If she dies, she'll just have to die," was the other's response. The Pritchards were confused, but they had been to town enough to hear of the Barrow Gang, who had been terrorizing the country for a year. They could tell these weren't tourists, and Jack swallowed the lump in his throat as he introduced himself to Bonnie Parker, Clyde Barrow, and W. D. Jones.

The next few hours were chaos. As Bonnie rested, Clyde and W. D. went to the back porch to figure out their next move. They were supposed to meet up with Buck and the rest of the gang in Sayre, Oklahoma, but now they were going to be late. Meanwhile, Lonnie snuck away and drove to town in the family Dodge. He talked to the sheriff and deputy, who dispatched an ambulance. Whether Lonnie failed to tell the two who they would be dealing with or they didn't believe him is unclear, but they went to the Pritchards' place only expecting to check on a car accident. Instead they found Bonnie, who quickly sprang to life and disarmed them as Clyde and W. D. appeared from the porch and fired a warning shot overhead.

It was obviously time to leave. As Clyde was loading Bonnie and the two lawmen into the sheriff's Chevrolet, W. D. thought he saw Lonnie's wife reaching for the door and he fired his shotgun. She was hit in the hand with five buckshot pellets as he dashed to the car. On his way, W. D. shot out the tires on the Pritchards' car. They crossed the river where they should have in the first place, at a shallow crossing a quarter mile west, and headed for Oklahoma.

According to the sheriff, sometime later Bonnie's pain became too great, and she was moved to the back seat where she lay across the laps of the lawmen. She wouldn't see a doctor for a week; that would be in Missouri. Traveling as they did, her leg didn't heal properly and she would have to be carried or walk with a limp for the rest of her short life. She and Clyde would be killed in Arcadia, Louisiana, almost a year later.

After some debate among the outlaws, the sheriff and deputy were rewarded for their cooperation and allowed to live. They were handcuffed and barbed-wired to a tree, but they managed to make their way back to Wellington the next day with the story of a lifetime.

The car sat in the river for a time. It had been stolen from a doctor in Madill, Oklahoma, and his insurance paid him out. A local mechanic eventually pulled the car from the river, and he could be seen for years driving around Wellington in that maroon Ford, a standout in a sea of black cars.

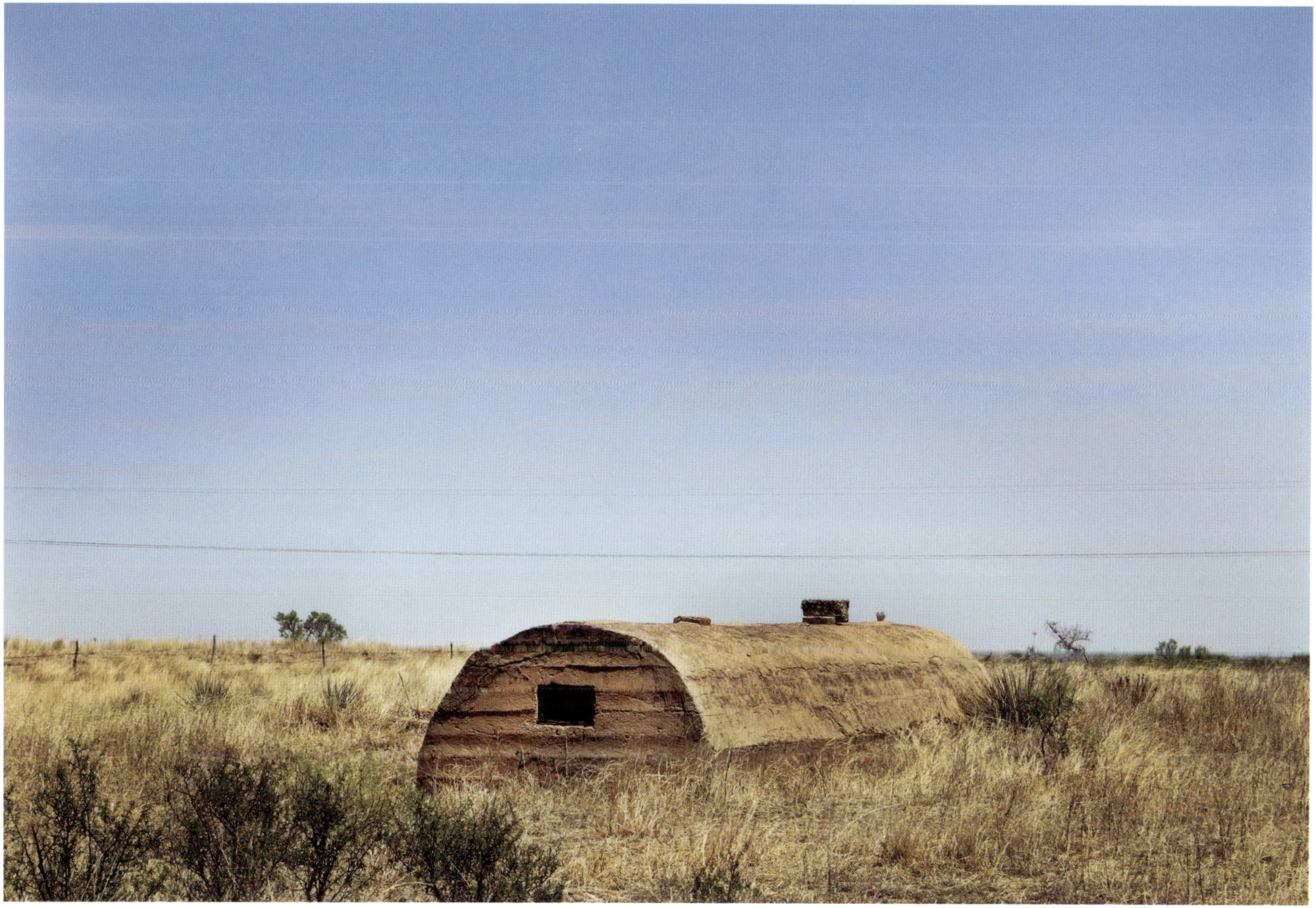

Storm shelter in Wellington. PHOTO BY MORGAN PAGE

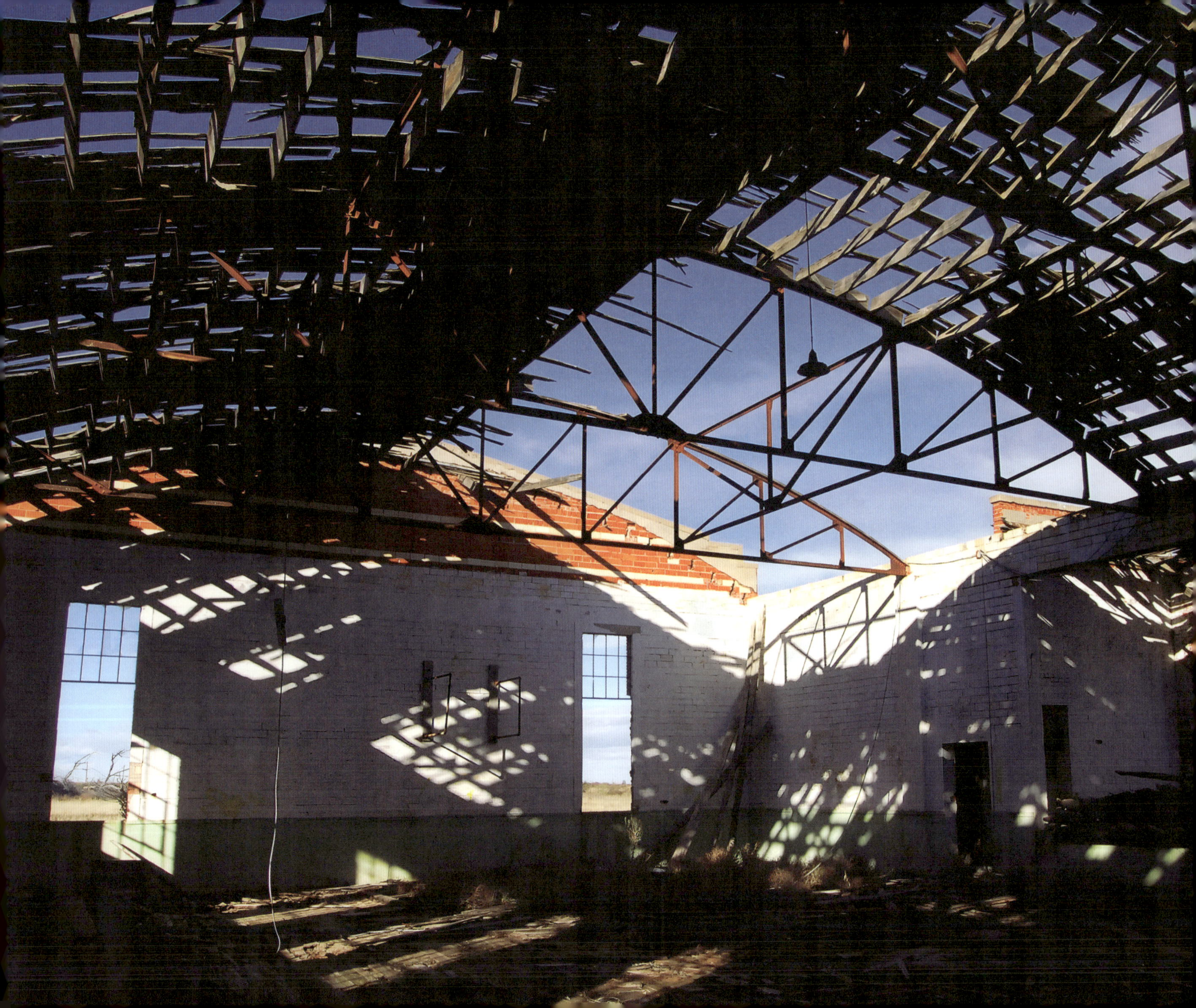

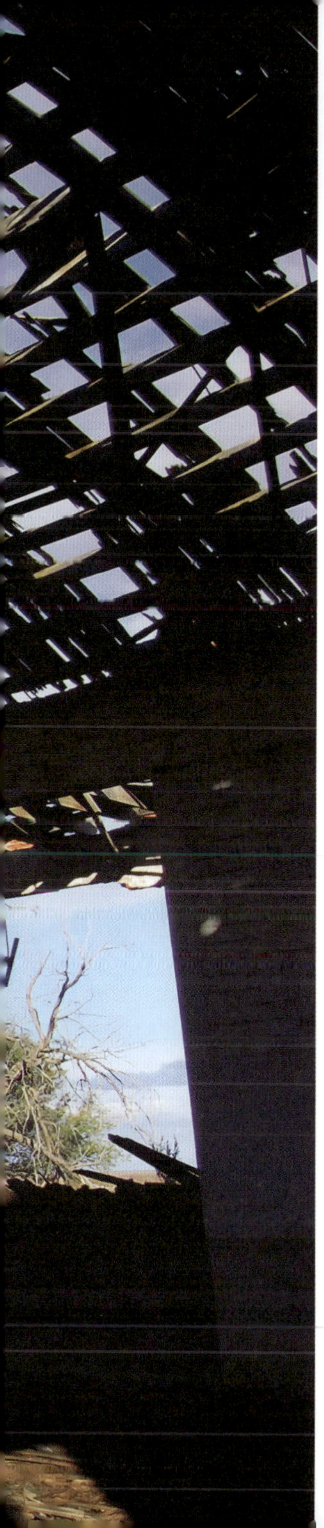

GUESTS FOR THE EVENING (1934)

DUSTIN RICE

Doing seventy-five miles per hour, we had nearly passed the gym when it caught the corner of my eye. Even though I was focused on the gas gauge and making it to a Texline filling station, I knew we had to turn around. We were the only ones on the highway when I pulled over, so there was no road noise or traffic. When there is no wind on the Panhandle prairie, no movement for miles, there's an uneasiness that is an experience unto itself. That was what I felt here.

The gym at Perico. PHOTO BY DUSTIN RICE

To get to the door, I crunched through waist-high dead grass covered in frost, which kept Morgan in the car. When I entered, I was immediately in awe at this cathedral of decay. Its maple floors rippled with rot, for the roof had long ago opened to the weather. Lights still hung from the trusses, unlit for generations. Wire-frame mattresses, worn by the elements, were strewn about beside the scoreboard, which had been dashed to the floor many years ago and was accompanied by, of all things, an old tricycle.

Photographing inside the Perico Gym was an experience I'll never forget. It felt like seeing through time. For me, the best part of this project is not knowing. You never know what is around the next corner, what lies behind the next door. As I've said, musing on the places we've visited, you can get a feeling when walking into abandoned places. Some have a certain gravity, a weight that can be felt. Others can seem uplifting, with a positive vibe. In the gym, as I experienced it, I clearly felt the presence of community. I could tell when I walked in that it had been a place of entertainment. Even through the grit and grime, there was joy. It sent my mind wandering about what had happened in this place before it became what I saw. I imagined dances in a 1930s small Panhandle town, homecoming games, Christmas raffles, and cake walks. But now the stands where the fans once cheered were buckled and broken, the crowds long since quiet.

When I got home, I started researching Perico. To say not much information is out there would be an understatement. There are some references to it online, some information about its beginning and peak, but very little about its end. Some pictures of the area are posted on social media, and luckily there are comments from those who used to live there to fill in some details. I found out that the school, and therefore the gym, closed in "probably 1959," according to a commenter's mother.

This lack of information led me to old newspaper articles in museum archives. One day, completely at random, I stumbled on a story that I had to read a few times to understand. I couldn't help but imagine myself climbing the stands, popcorn in hand, eyes adjusting to the light, then getting settled on the handmade bench just in time. Grab a seat yourself—what I found may be the most Texas story I've ever read:

In February 1947, two towns' citizenries gathered in a gymnasium in the far northwest corner of the Panhandle. There was excitement in the air for a high school basketball game but also a low murmur in the crowd. Instead of the usual conversations analyzing who would be the leading scorer or dissecting previous games in the season, the crowd was talking about when the trailers would arrive. Trailers?

Donkeys can be cantankerous beasts. Ranchers use them to guard herds of goats, sheep, cattle, and horses. They'll grab coyotes by the scruff of the neck, lift them above their heads, then slam them to the ground again and again until the herd is rid of the problem. Donkeys will dance on rattlesnakes like they're being scored by judges. They will charge into confrontations between 2,000-pound bulls to break up fights in breeding season. They are protective, the guard dogs of the pasture. After a hard day's work, some will even yodel for their dinner. Donkeys have personalities as varied as their owners'.

Tonight's game was going to be something different. Perico, the night's host, had released news of their starting five for the game: Frank Hudson, Glen McCarty, Jimmie Brewster, and the Stewart brothers, John D. and Delbert. This would be the most memorable night of these players' careers. Texline, their opponent, had taken a more guarded approach to the lineup, wisely "keeping them in the dark," as a local newspaper reported.

About a half hour before tip-off, trailers arrived, pulled by beat-up trucks. Local ranchers had brought with them an unusual addition to the game, and chuckles erupted from the crowd as the trailers were unloaded. The boys from Texline and Perico would be battling on the backs of jackasses, shod in rubber shoes to protect the gym's "prized maple floor."

A quarter for admission meant that people poured in from miles around. The novelty of the night wasn't how proficient the players would be atop four-legged animals. These boys were raised on horseback and had all been bringing in cattle since they were just out of diapers. Both communities were residents of the former XIT ranch, once the largest ranch in the world, and cattle and ranching were a way of life. What made this night exciting was the unpredictability of the jacks and jennys. To keep the animal outbursts to a minimum, the referee was equipped with a "hot shot." As the *Dalhart Texan* reported, "He will use this touching gadget not only in lieu of the regulation whistle but to keep the grass-eaters on the move as well as to ward off any 'kicks' on their part." It's safe to say that animal rights groups would not allow such a game today.

Modified rules were laid out about passing and shooting, since dribbling wasn't an option. If a ball was on the ground and a player dismounted, they had to pass or shoot. (No word on what constituted a foul when riding a 500-pound donkey.)

There are no reports on the game's results, just the excitement leading up to it. The score didn't matter. One can imagine a gym filled with the din of the crowd and smatterings of applause, warm greetings from neighbors, conversations to catch up, excited children happy to be out on a Wednesday night. Over everything, the unmistakable sound of a donkey braying rings out, and another in response: the sounds of the barnyard transported to the gym. The chorus of "hee-haws" fades, then laughter booms as the absurdity of it all sets in for the crowd. Everything from tip-off to final horn defies logic: uniformed basketball players on the backs of donkeys passing, steering, shooting, chasing, dismounting, mounting, passing again, and on and on.

It was surely a night to remember for everyone who was there, then a legend retold for generations. Nearly seventy-three years later, on a bitterly cold January afternoon, we found ourselves in front of this gymnasium. As I left it, I felt profoundly overjoyed on the one hand, having taken from that gym a once-in-a-lifetime experience, one that I still reflect on. But I was also sad: strewn about that gym were reminders of what would never be again, the tricycle in particular. How did it end up in a gym in the middle of nowhere?

Since our visit in 2020, the gym's roof has collapsed, presumably from one too many heavy snows. All too often we hear about the demise of places we've visited, and this reinforces the importance of documenting them. It reminds us of the inimitable opportunity we have, being allowed to bear witness to these venues of history. This stop also offered an additional lesson: doing research, even if you are frustrated by dead-ends, can lead to the most rewarding and obscure successes. By digging around we are able to bring to light stories from history that have been almost entirely forgotten, in this case small-town Texas history.

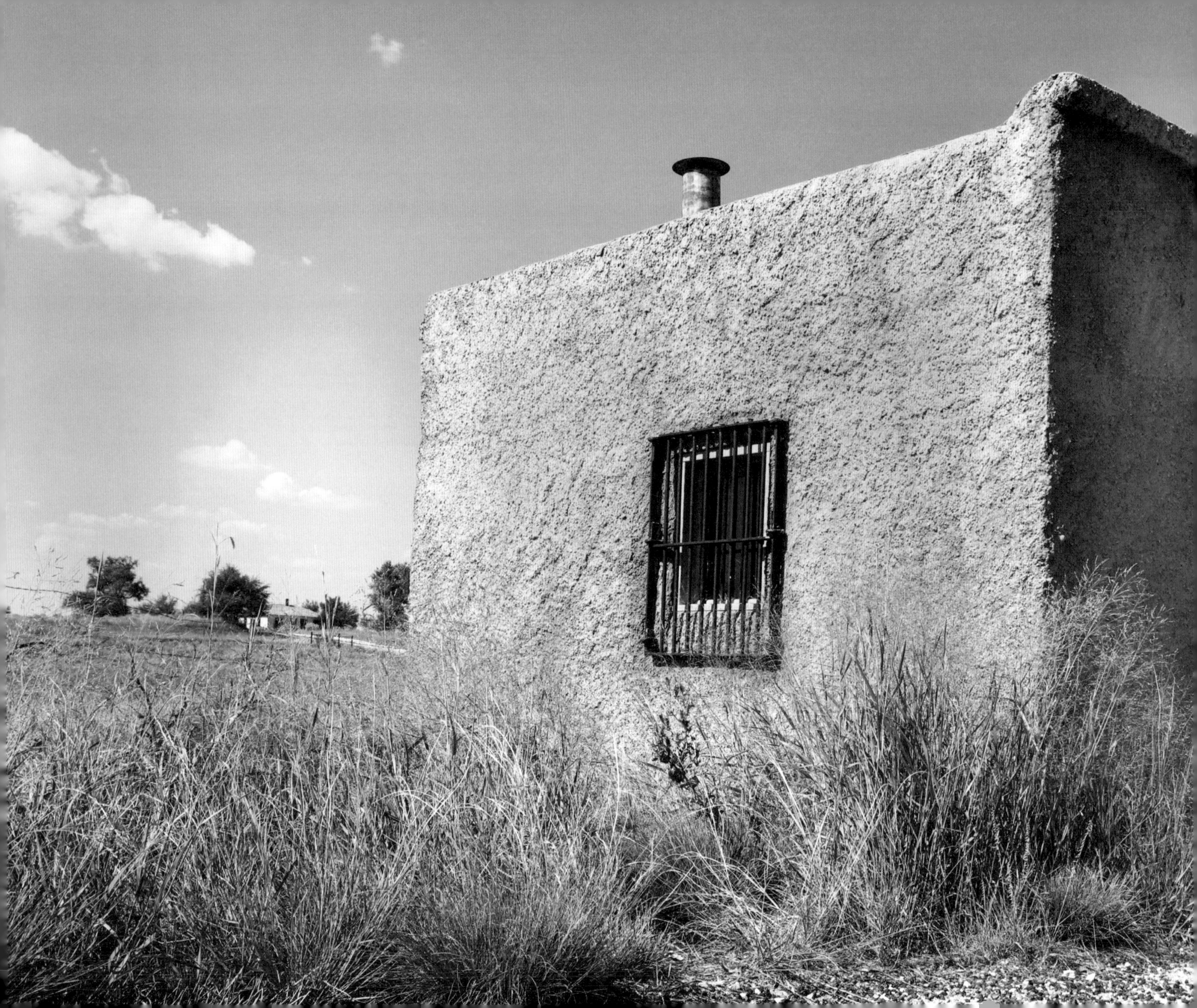

AN ANGRY SKY (1947)

DUSTIN RICE

A farmer was working in his field when he noticed a change in the wind direction. He smelled rain, and looked up to see a thunderhead rolling his way. Storms were common in late spring on the plains, but this storm was different. The man had spent his entire life in the fields, and he knew when a storm was going to be bad. As he pulled his tractor into the barn, the bottom fell out of the sky. Rain came down in sheets, and he couldn't see ten feet in front of him. He got to the house soaking wet and out of breath. His wife had tuned in the local AM radio report from Canadian, a small town nearby. The newsman was frantically reporting on a tornado they could see for themselves from the studio.

A concrete life raft, Glazier. Most of the survivors walked out of this door. PHOTO BY DUSTIN RICE

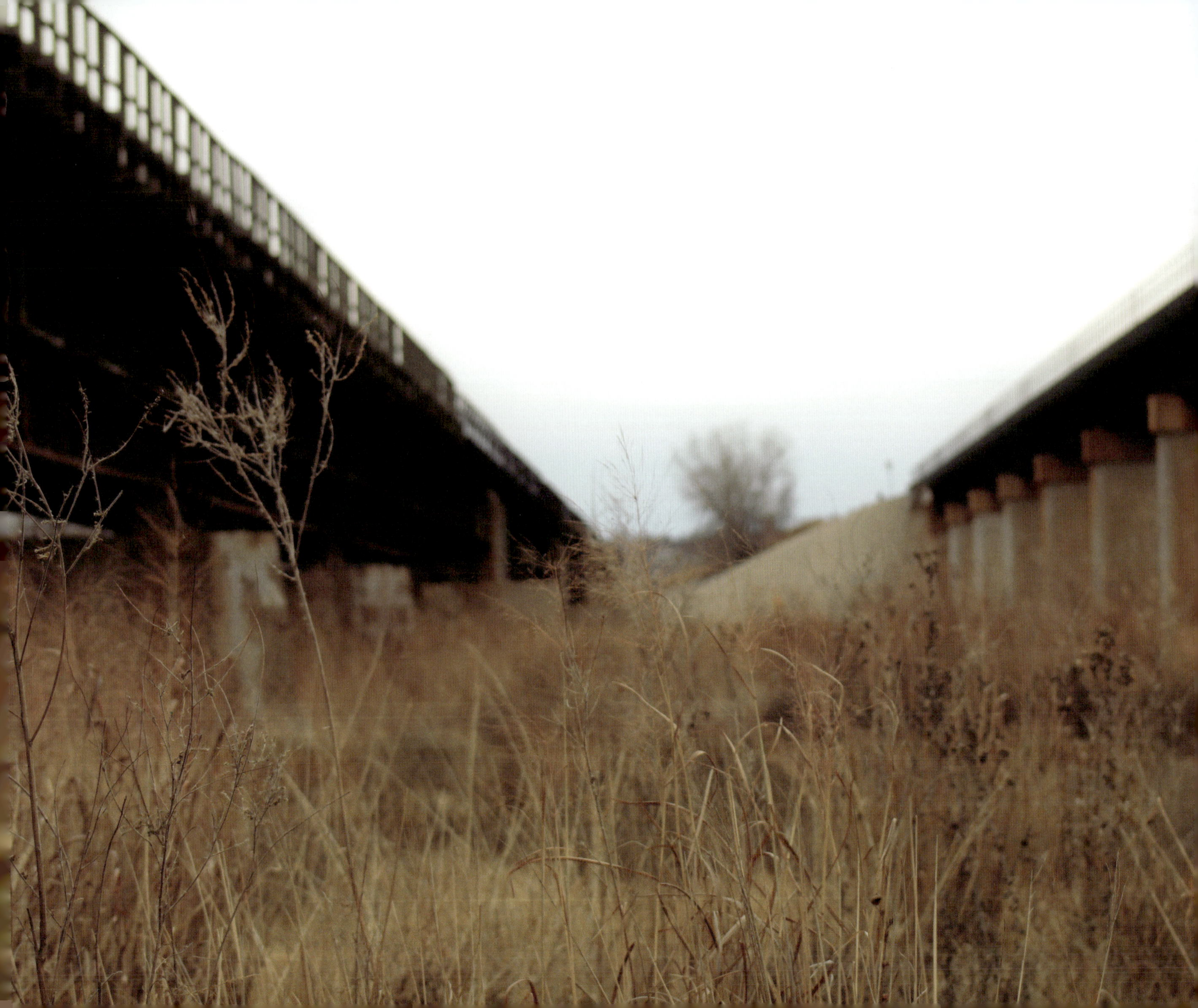

Hail started, and quickly the hailstones were the biggest either of them had ever seen. They jumped in the farm truck and headed for Glazier, a long three miles away. The man had survived the Great War and had heard stories of World War II, but April 9, 1947, would leave a path of destruction equal to anything he had ever seen or experienced.

They drove toward town, their little 1930 Ford truck sputtering; he pushed her for all she had. They were headed for the jail. That little calaboose was the most secure room for a hundred miles. He was driving by guess the last quarter mile. The wind was blowing sideways; their tires were skittering as the poor truck was pushed all over the road. He had the wheel turned right to go straight. Finally they could just make out the building.

The farmer and his wife clasped hands as they exited the truck and were about twenty feet from the jail, surrounded by the cars of those inside, when they were picked up by the tornado. At that point it was about two miles wide—and just gaining momentum.

The jail was packed that evening. An estimated twenty people were crammed into that concrete cube. What those people heard was an indescribable sound. They had broken the windows early on for fear they'd explode, and their screams were just barely audible over the cacophony of it all. They were the lucky ones.

The winds were estimated to have been in excess of 220 mph. Glazier was made up of clapboard houses. There was one brick building that was lifted off its foundation and set back down just a little way off. It and the jail were the only structures that survived in the whole town.

The man and his wife were found about three miles apart, alive but injured, both a mile and a half from town but in opposite directions. Their story was one of the few relatively good ones of the day. They were counted among the fifty-one injured. The remains of the less fortunate were in some cases mangled beyond recognition, and the earth itself was scarred for years.

A lone pilot from Canadian was able to land the next morning and found survivors hunkered down and sheltering under anything they could find. It was chaos. Neighbors had been up all night calling for each other and searching by flashlight. The town was wiped out. The plane had room for one person on a stretcher as well as room for one more in the back. All day and all night, for two days, the pilot ran first aid to Glazier. The wounded were taken, one by one, to Canadian. This included the farmer and his wife. The plane was the only way in or out due to downed power lines. Patients filled the small hospital in Canadian, as well as two church basements, and the school gym housed the survivors.

The tornado that wiped out Glazier that night also did severe damage in Higgins, Texas. Then it went on to level much of Woodward,

Canadian. PHOTO BY MORGAN PAGE

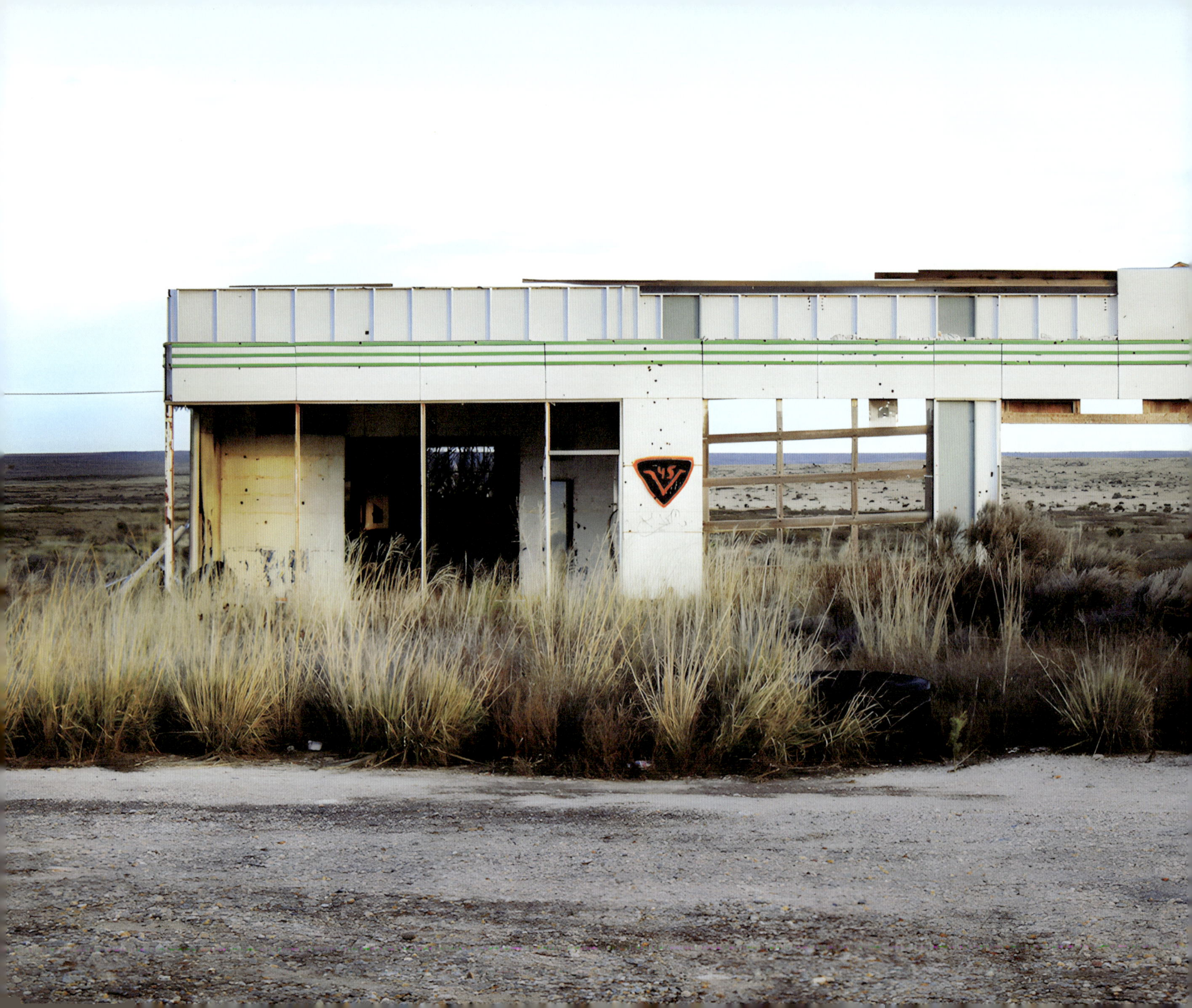
45

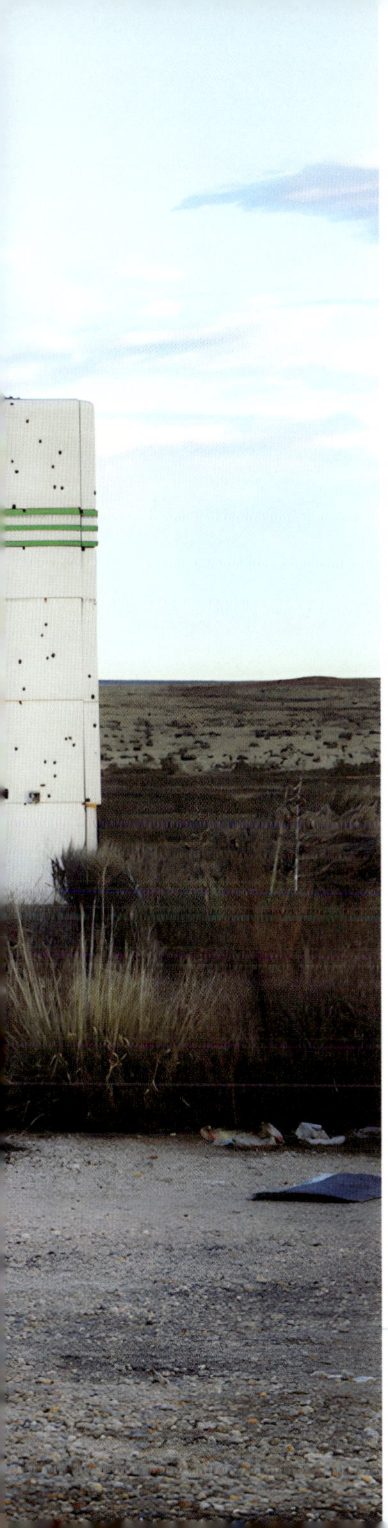

Oklahoma. It was one of the longest continuous F5 tornadoes in recorded history. Seventeen died in Glazier, fifty-one in Higgins, and 107 in Woodward, and the storm even continued into Kansas. It was part of a tristate supercell that produced between five and eight tornadoes and is one of the largest storm cells ever recorded.

We went to Glazier and the surrounding area one day while killing time during an overnight stay in Canadian. We had just set up a photo exhibit at a museum there, then set out on the backroads of the far northern Panhandle. We stopped to get gas and asked about the little jail on the side of the road. We were regaled with the story of the tornado and the people found miles apart. It was a good tale. The anecdote about the man with the plane was found in the comment section of *Texas Escapes*, a site I use frequently as a planning guide for our trips. I was never able to identify the farmer or his wife, something that gave me pause; I got part of the story from one source and an incomplete reference from another, not the multiple sources I would have preferred to have. But once my research showed the Glazier/Higgins tornado to be among the worst in recorded Texas history, I decided the story needed to be told.

Abandoned service station in Borger. PHOTO BY MORGAN PAGE

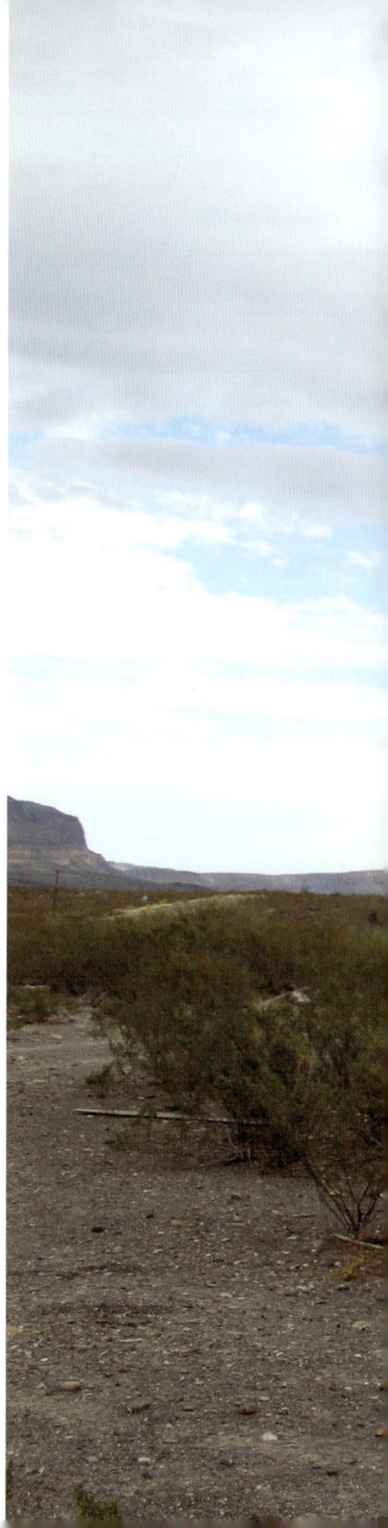

House in Adobes. PHOTO BY MORGAN PAGE

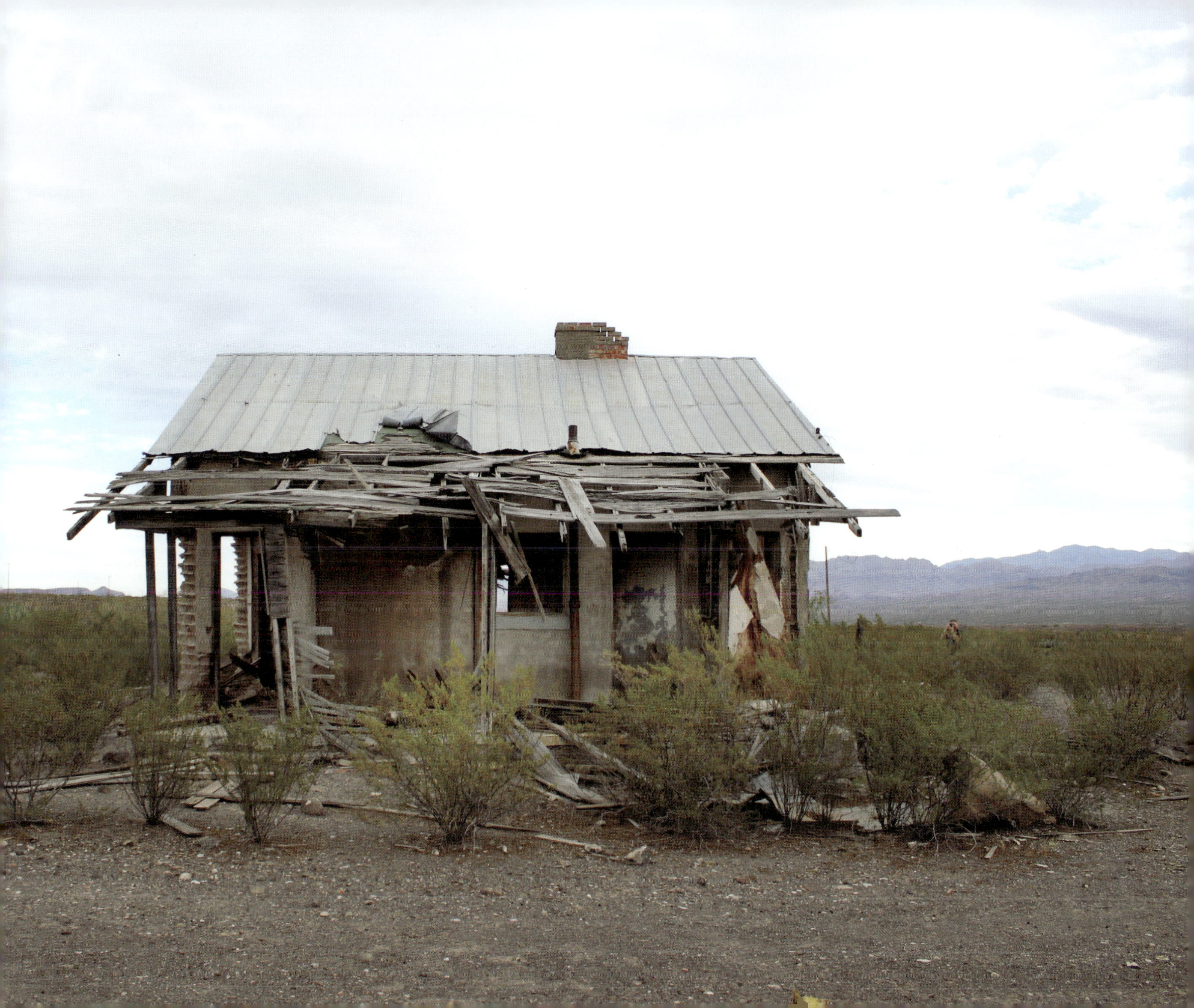

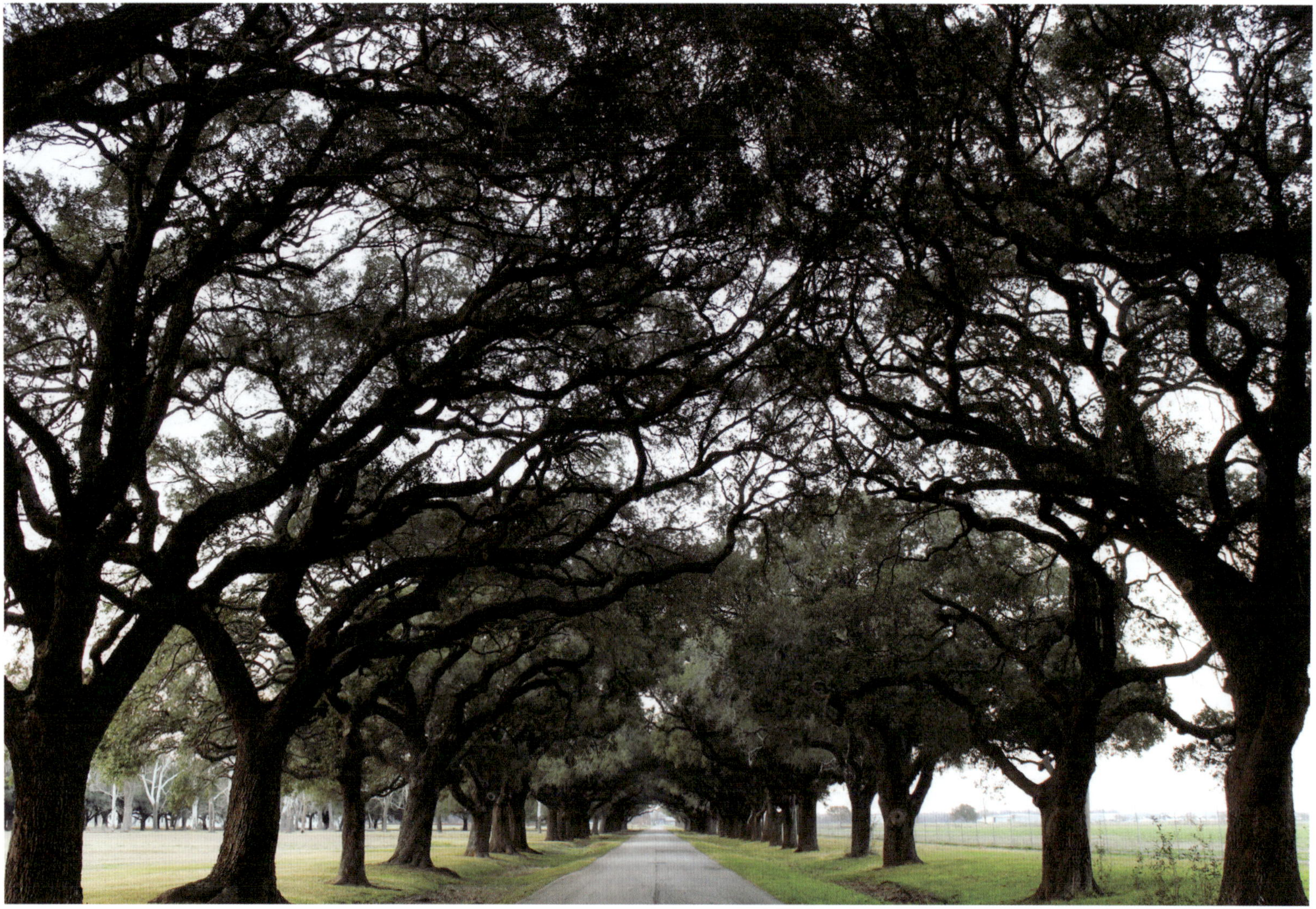

Entrance to the Central Unit at Imperial State Prison in Sugar Land, where Leadbelly wrote "The Midnight Special." PHOTO BY MORGAN PAGE

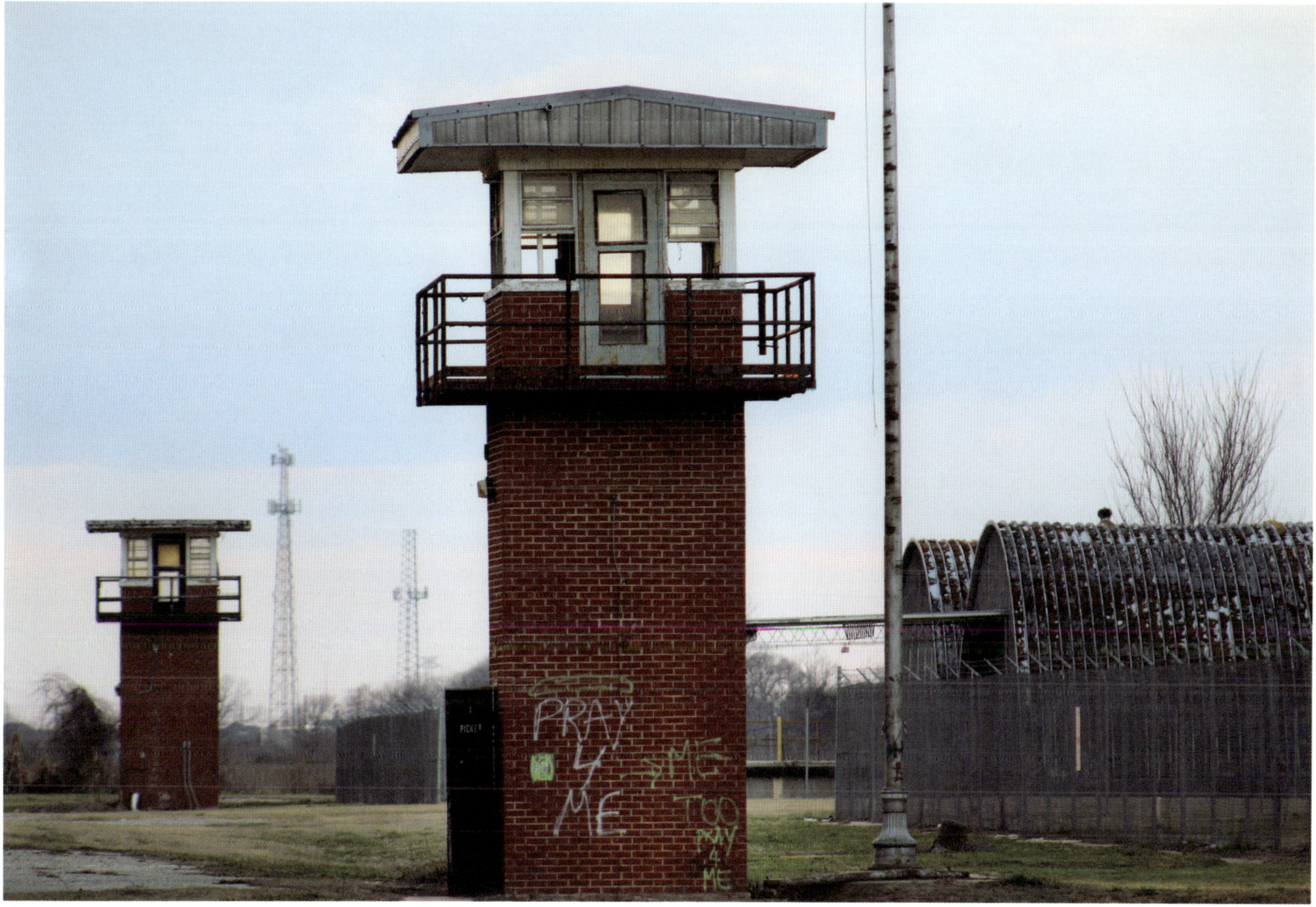

Central Unit at Imperial State Prison in Sugar Land. PHOTO BY MORGAN PAGE

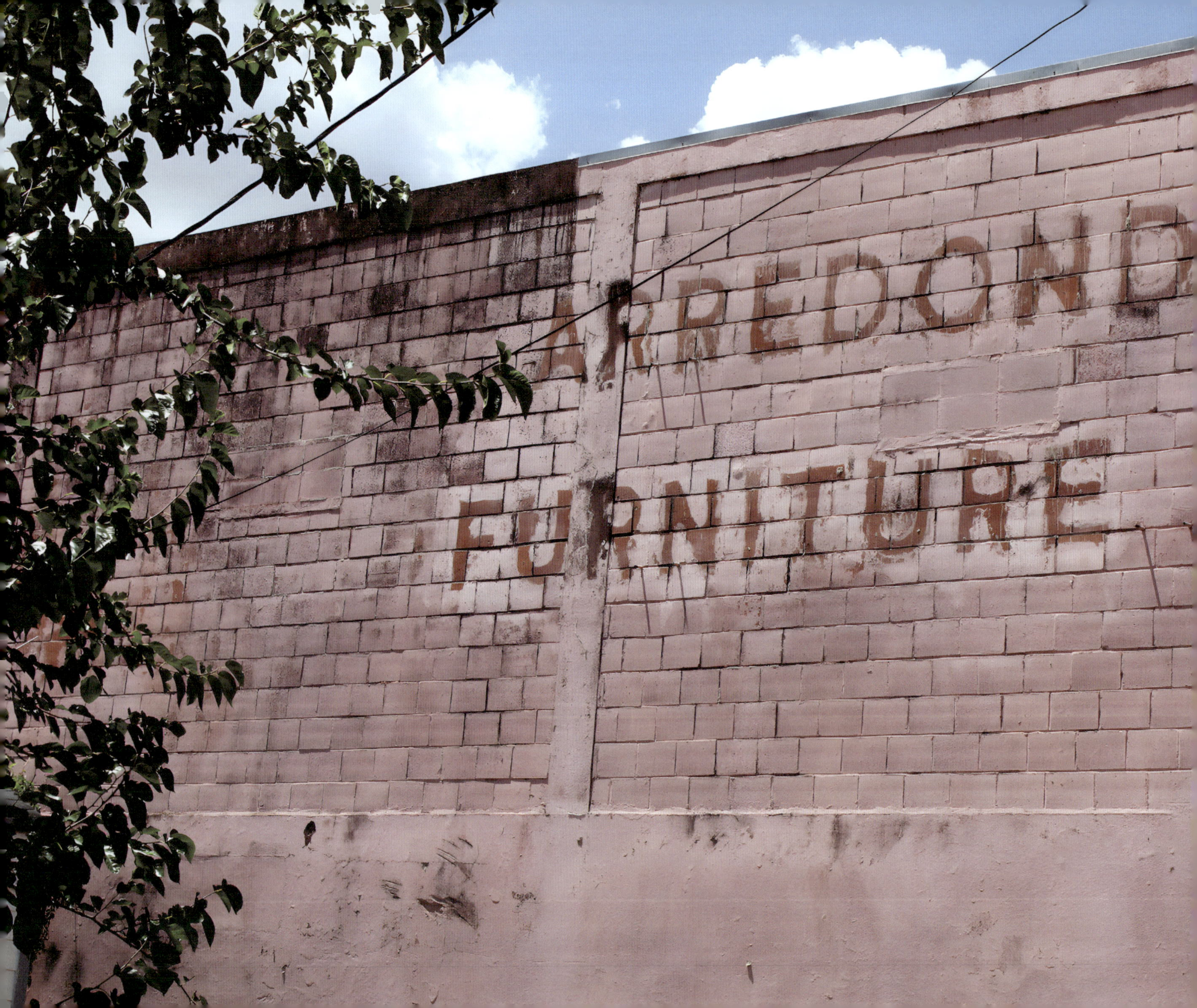
ARREDOND
FURNITURE

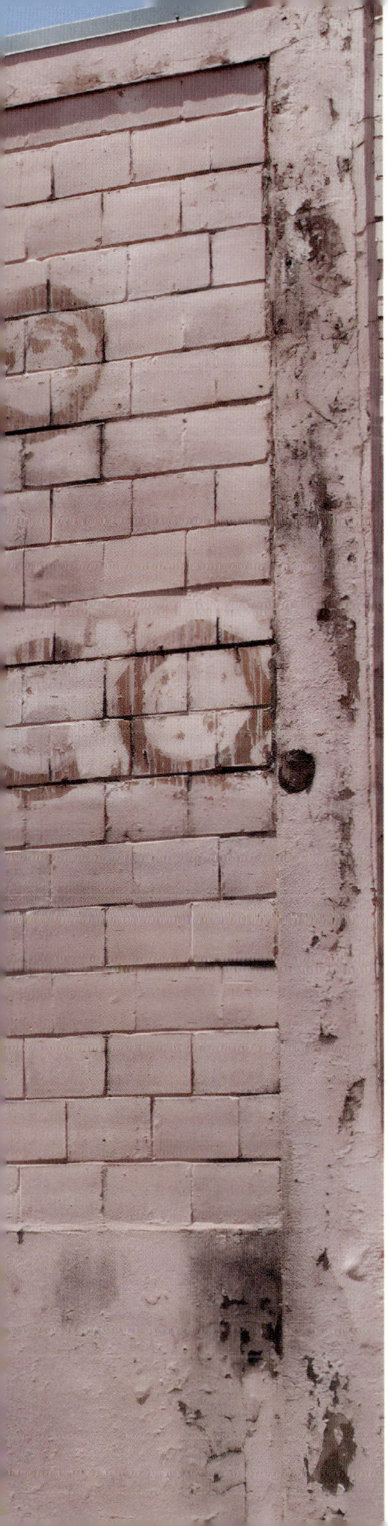

THE SIT-IN (1948)

MORGAN PAGE

Beatrice Cerda was born on July 29, 1936, and grew up in Rosenberg, Texas, a railroad city just southwest of Houston. The oldest of four children, Bea was as tough as nails, even to me, her granddaughter. Because Bea could speak English and her parents couldn't, she was asked to quit school and go to work at age thirteen. My Great-Aunt Esther would sometimes tell me how smart my grandma was, and how she pondered what might have become of her had she been able to finish school.

Former site of Arredondo Furniture Company, Rosenberg, the employer of Eutillo "Tilo" Cerda, father to Bea and Esther and great-grandfather to Morgan Page. PHOTO BY MORGAN PAGE

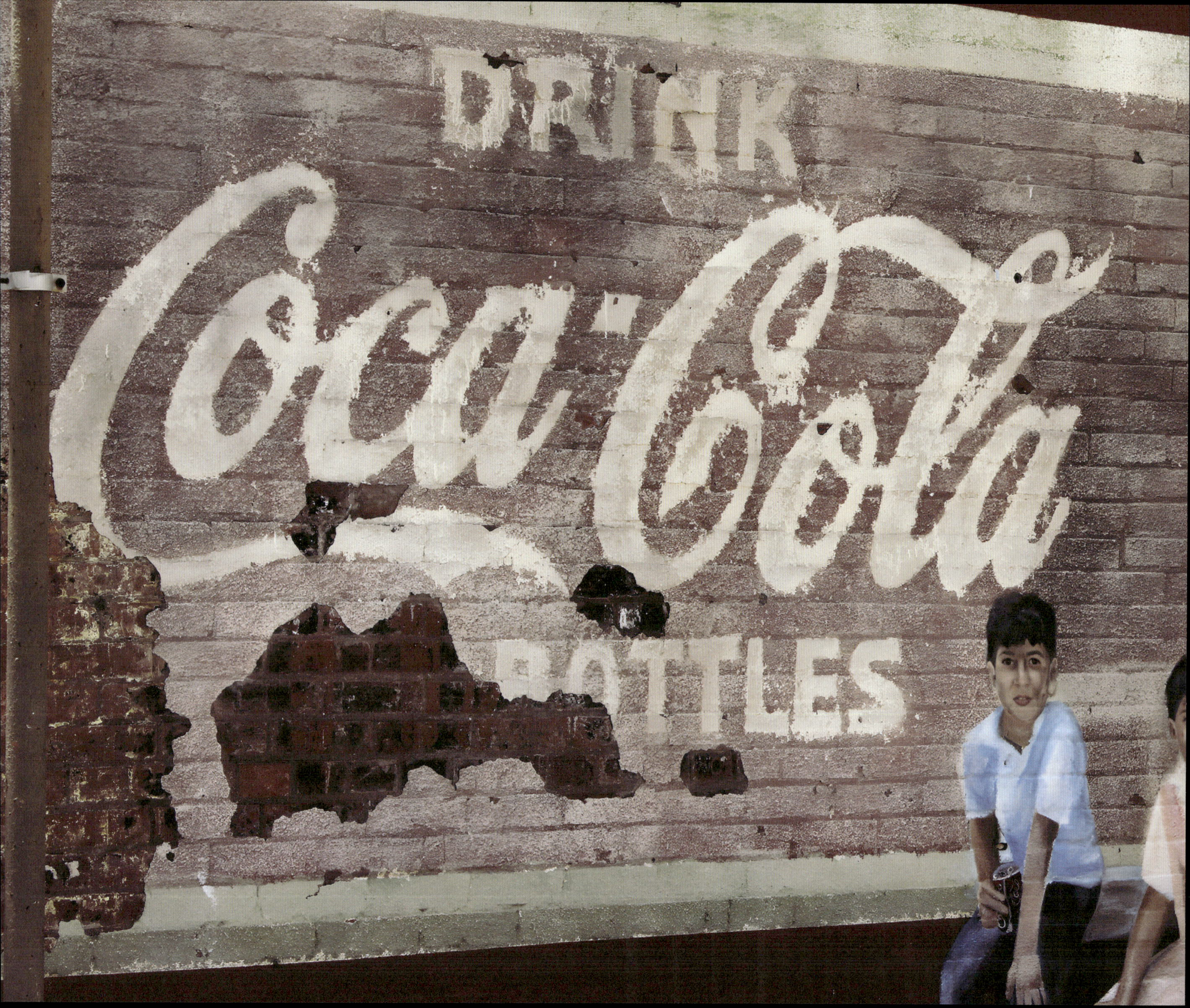
DRINK
Coca-Cola
BOTTLES

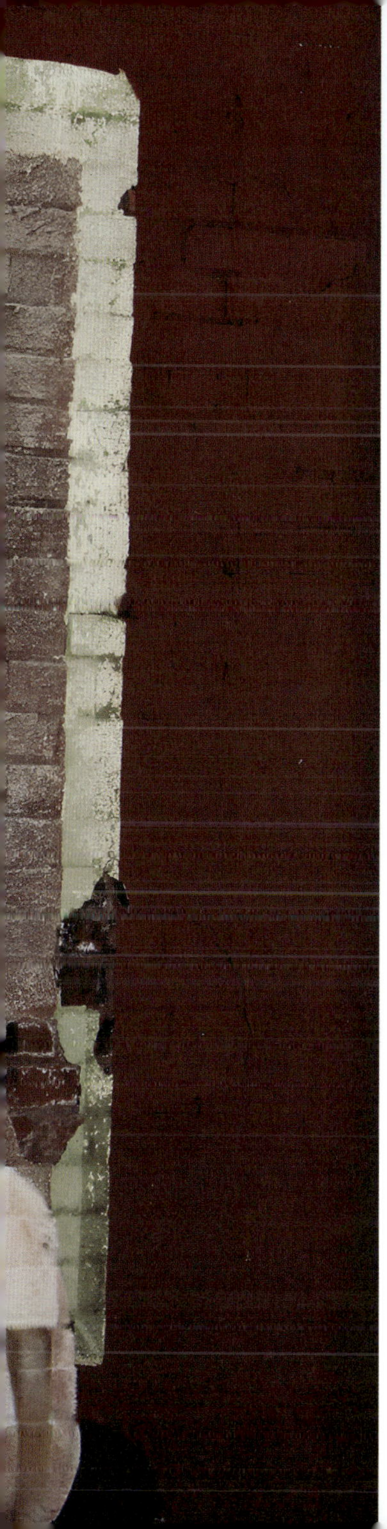

Growing up, I saw my Grandma Bea as demanding, excitable, and often callous. On the other hand, my Aunt Esther was always tender and warm. Honestly, I sometimes wished she were my grandmother instead of Bea. I had a lot to learn about my grandmother, though, especially after she passed away in 2003.

Aunt Esther loved to tell stories from her childhood. She spent so much time talking about Rosenberg that at some point we decided to visit the town. We walked the streets of Rosenberg, some still barely paved, the summer heat coming up but not quite suffocating just yet. As we wandered through a cemetery, streets the children once played on, and finally downtown, Esther began to tell me about a similarly hot day long ago when she had asked Bea to take her for ice cream.

When Beatrice was left in charge of her younger sister, the rules were simple: Don't go outside, and don't answer the door. Not everyone had these rules in 1948, but their father had been clear. Rosenberg was a rail hub, with a large station through which thousands of people passed every day, and their father recognized that it could be dangerous.

That afternoon was like any other. Bea and Esther were playing and talking, as girls will do, when Esther casually mentioned ice cream. Bea, whether she was bored or, more likely, feeling rebellious, said, "Get your shoes on." Esther knew this was a bad idea, but went along with her older sister.

As they made their way downtown, Esther grew more uneasy the further they got from home. Cars sped past them, and though they were on the sidewalk, she didn't like what she and her sister were doing. She knew they were going to be in trouble when their parents got home.

Eventually they came to a café downtown, one that is no longer standing. There was a sign on the door. It read "No Mexicans Allowed." Even a child knows when hatred is aimed their way. Esther knew they weren't welcome. When she looked at her older sister, she saw that Bea had a look on her face that she only got when she was really mad. Bea had a temper, a bad one. As they went in and sat at a table, she could tell her sister was agitated.

A woman came to their table and asked if they could read. What a strange question, Esther thought. Without thinking, she said yes, and the woman clapped back with "Then I guess you read the sign!" Without acknowledging the woman, Bea asked for two ice cream cones. The woman walked away.

Esther wanted to run and hide, or scream, or be anywhere but where they were. People were looking, shaking their heads, and wagging their fingers. One woman kept telling them to leave, and that's all Esther wanted to do, but Bea kept saying no. She refused to go. Faced with no good outcome, nine-year-old Esther decided

Mural in downtown Rosenberg. PHOTO BY MORGAN PAGE

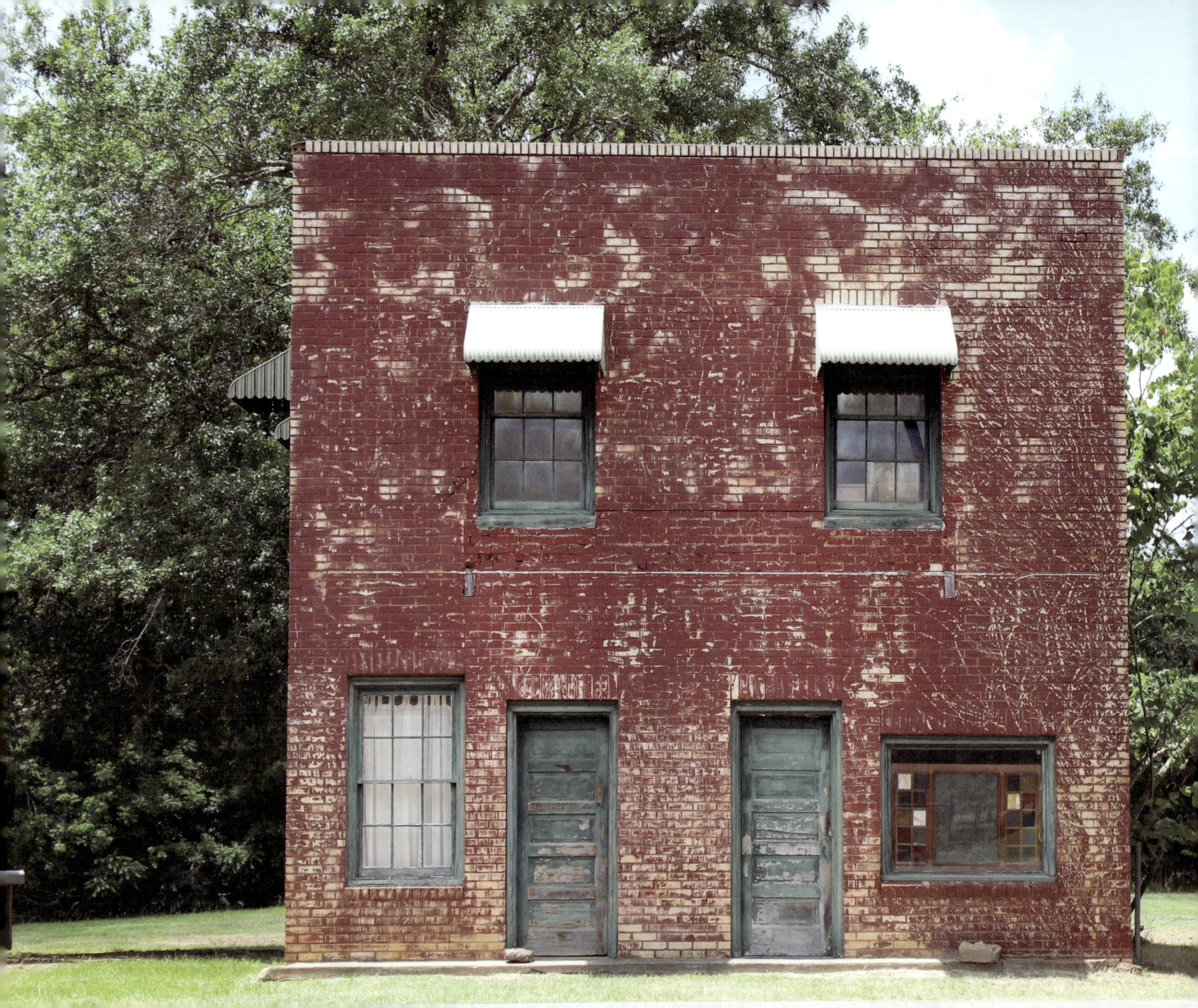

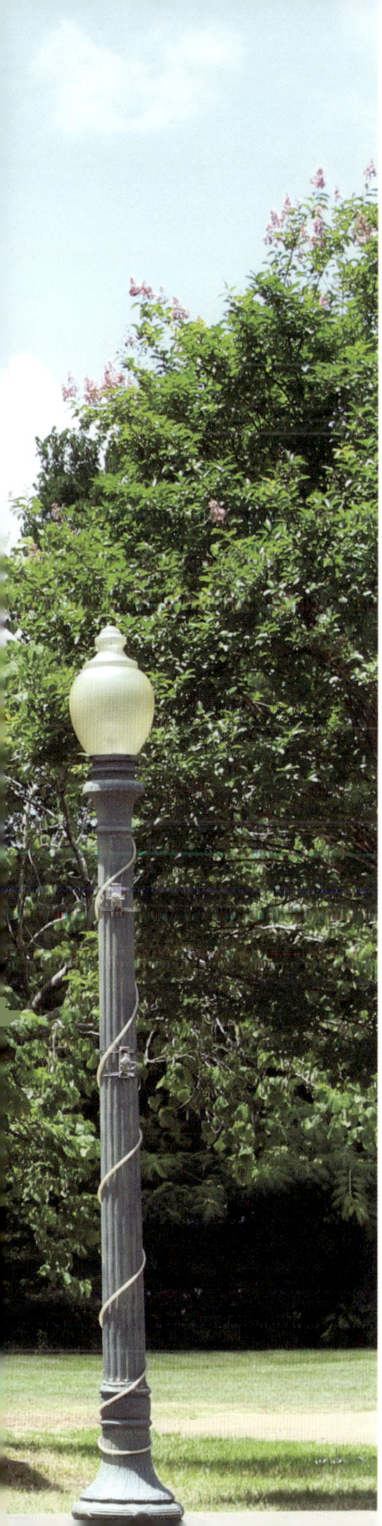

to leave her sister and walk home alone, over a mile. When she had told her sister she wanted ice cream, she didn't know what the consequences would be. So, she left her sister sitting in a booth and began the long walk home.

It seemed to take twice as long going home as it did to get to the café. Esther was crying and scared and utterly alone until she arrived at her street and started running to her house. She was out of breath when she burst through the door and was greeted suspiciously by her father. A feeling of dread and despair came over her that she had only felt in her nightmares. That's what this was to her—a waking nightmare.

Esther explained where her sister was. Her father, Tilo, spoke little English, but as Esther told her dad about the sign on the door of the café where Bea sat demanding to be treated like any other paying customer, he knew that sign was for him.

Tilo immediately marched to the café, with Esther following. All the anger in Bea turned to fear when she saw her father through the café window. She hadn't planned what she was doing; she had just done it. The look on her father's face was one she had never seen. He looked scared. He went around to the back and asked, with the help of his youngest daughter, about his oldest, and they told him to go get her. The only time he ever went in that café was to snatch up his daughter and sweep her out the front door in a flash. He never stopped scolding her on the way home, and she never said a word.

Bea was a character all her days; her temper never faded. She punched her brother's fiancée upon their introduction, leaping over a counter to do so. But she fought for the underdog, too. She took in women and children who were down on their luck and often provided for those who couldn't provide for themselves, keeping a dry goods pantry on the second floor of her house. In many ways, she stayed that fiery little girl. In the years that followed her "sit-in," she never walked past that café without a smile—and the woman inside always knew who she was, though they never spoke again

Avinger. PHOTO BY MORGAN PAGE

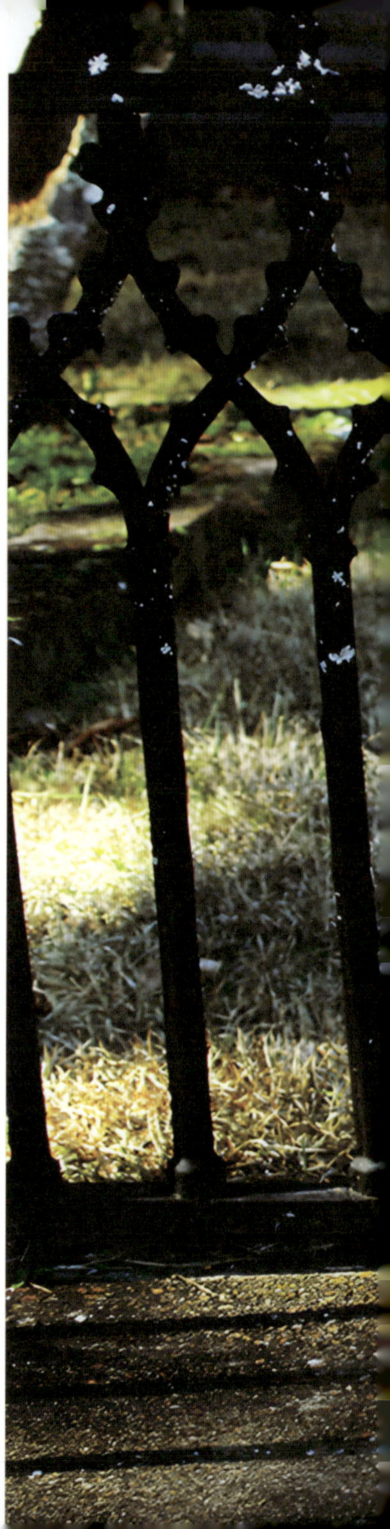

Gravesite of Bessie Moore, also known as "Diamond" Bessie. Bessie was murdered by the man who accompanied her, Abraham Rothschild. Bessie got off the train covered in diamonds but none were found on her body. The people of Jefferson raised $150 for her burial. PHOTO BY DUSTIN RICE

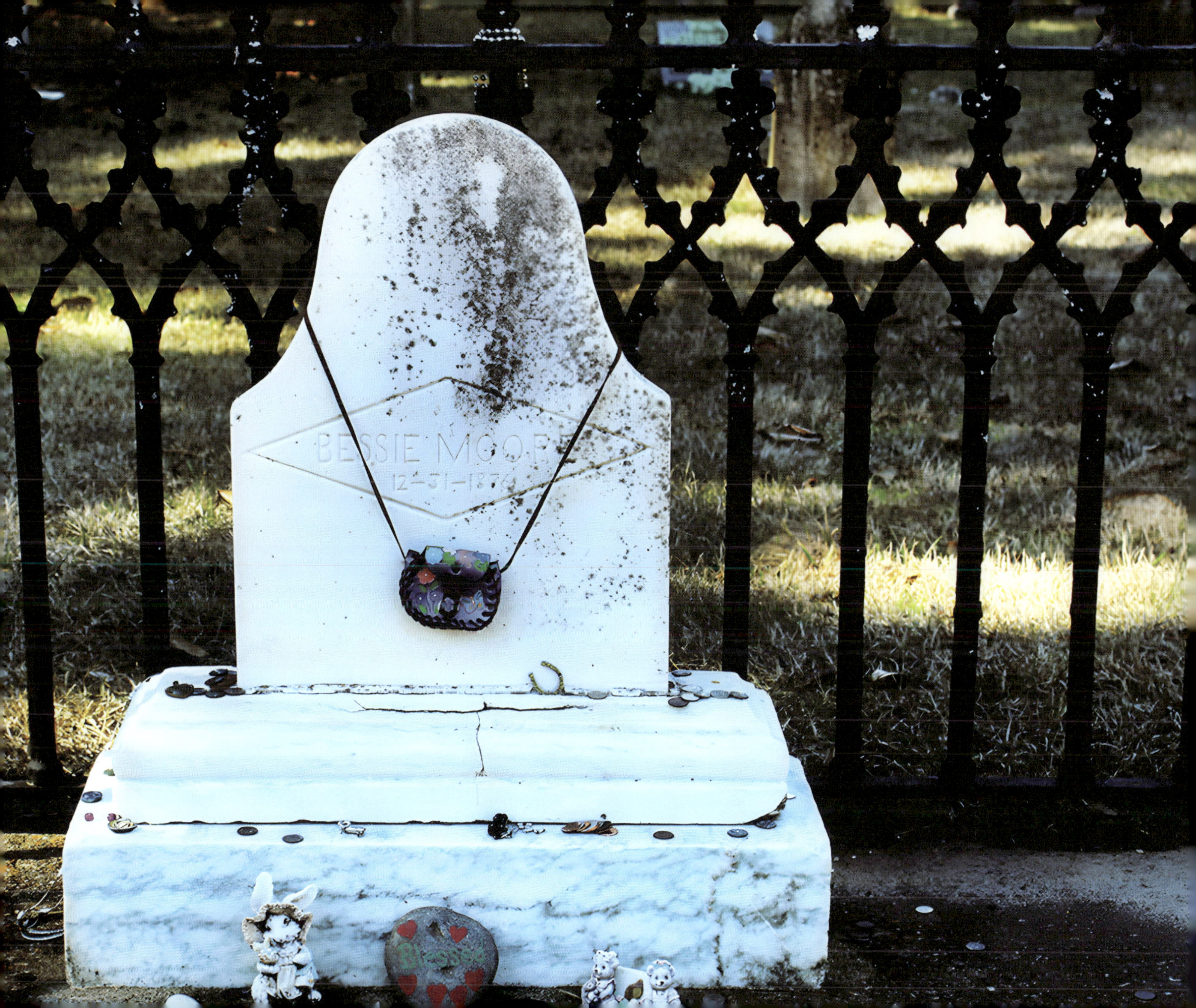
BESSIE MOOR
12-31-1876
Blessed

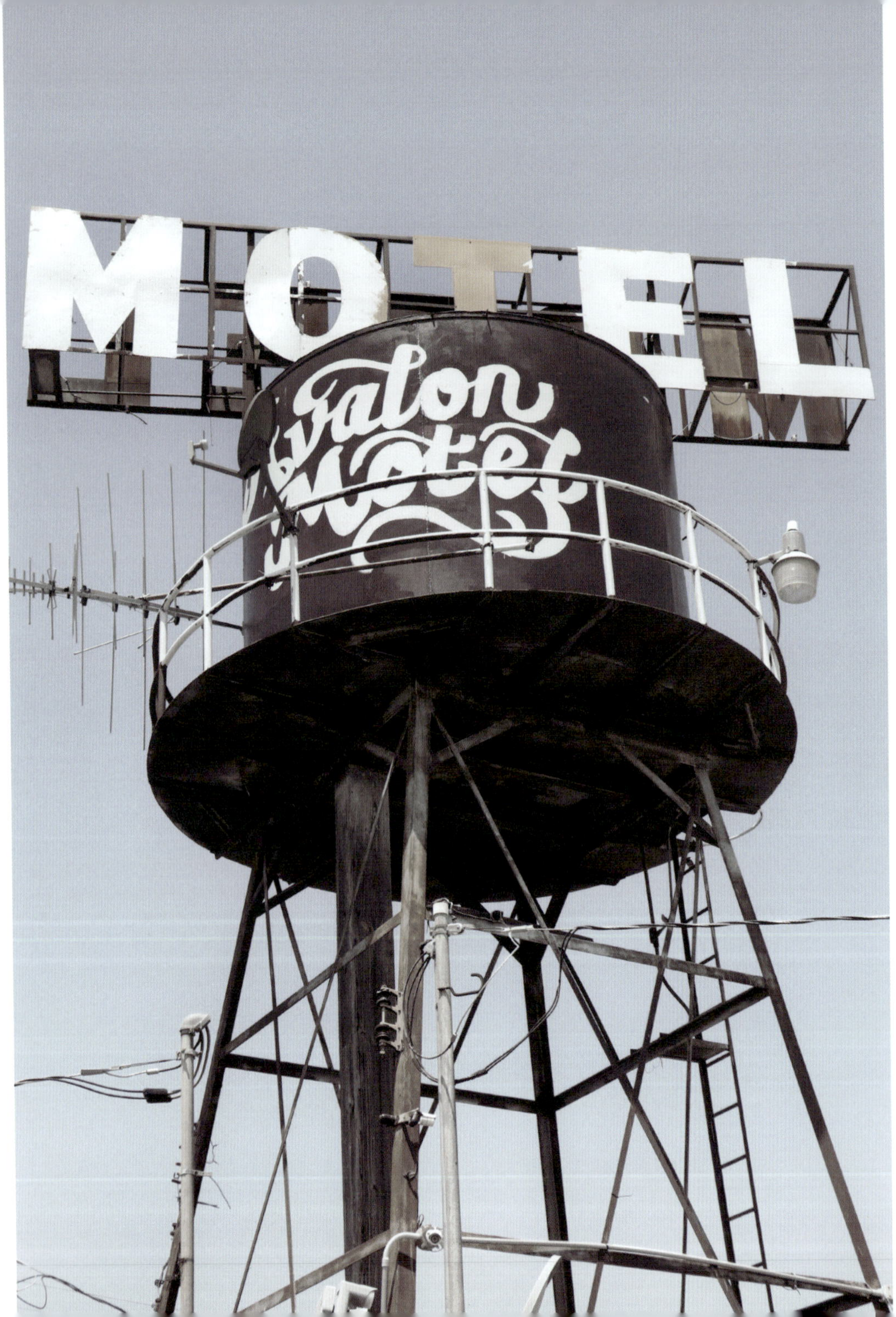
MOTEL
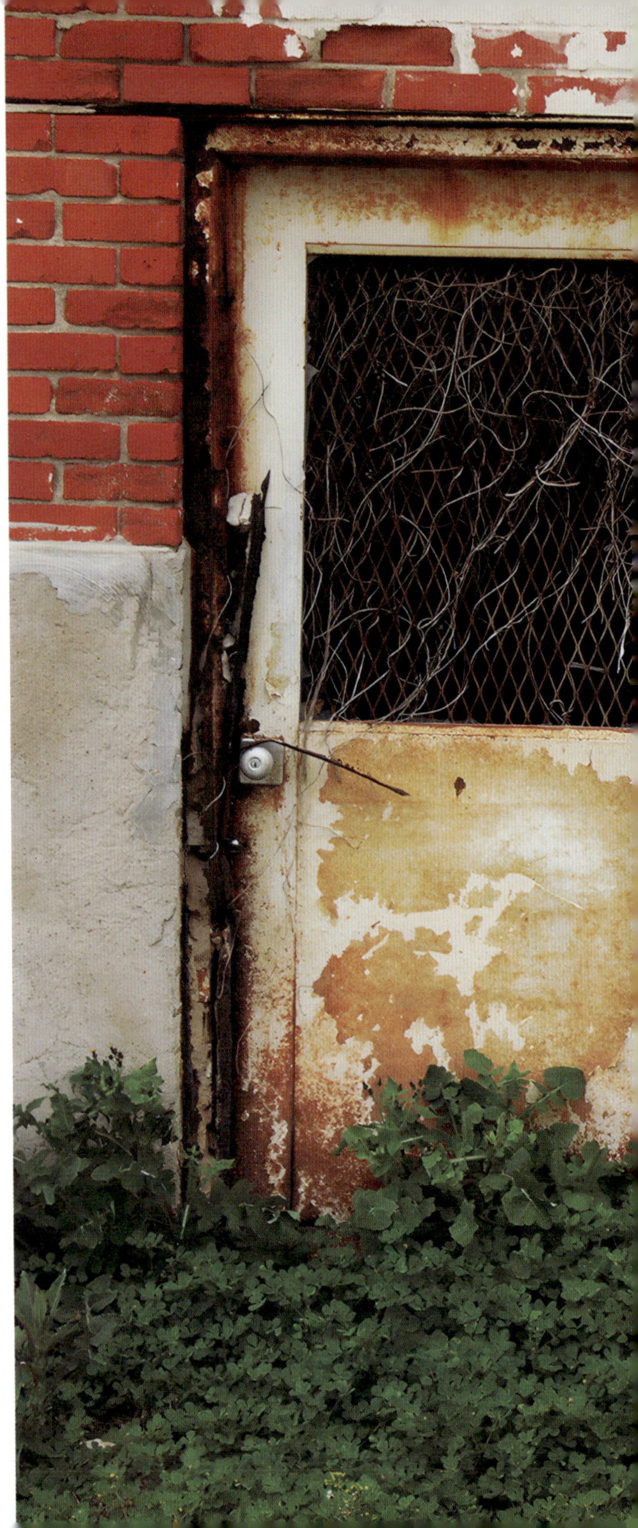

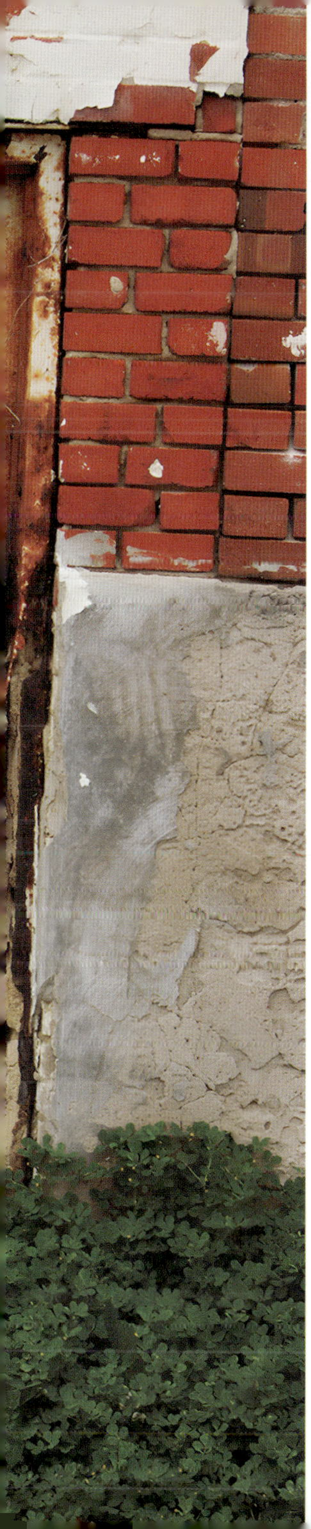

THUNDER ROAD (1951)

DUSTIN RICE

Herbert Noble didn't notice the details on his last day. Even though he usually had an almost clairvoyant sense of self-preservation, no hairs stood up on his neck. Noble hadn't slept past sunrise in years; he had poured his usual morning cup of coffee at 4:15 a.m. He smelled juniper in front of the house, freshly cut the previous day, as he got in the car, planning to head down his long driveway and check his mailbox.

The previous year, when his wife and unborn child had died in a bombing intended for him, Noble had hired extra security. He had gotten dogs and retreated to his ranch, but he couldn't escape Benny Binion. The weariness of years of paranoia finally wore him down, making him careless. He didn't

FAR LEFT: *The Avalon Motel is one of the last from the gambling era still standing on Jacksboro Highway.* PHOTO BY DUSTIN RICE

LEFT: *Door in Rosebud.* PHOTO BY DUSTIN RICE

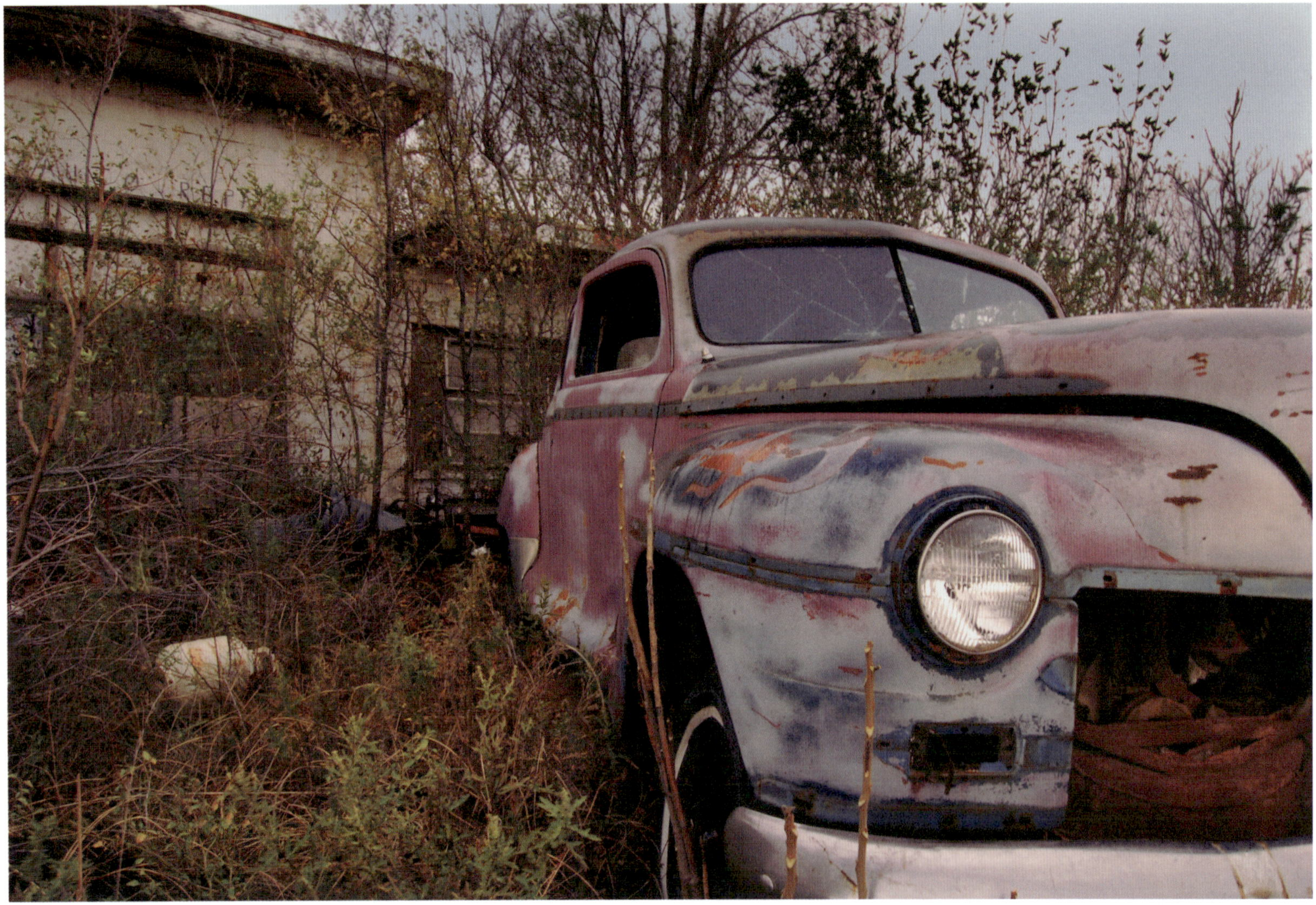

Mercury hot rod with original flame paint job in Borger. PHOTO BY DUSTIN RICE see the small things, like the tire tracks, which were hard to spot in the early morning light. He had not had his guys walk the grounds. As he turned the ignition, nothing happened, and he breathed a sigh of relief. He made his way to the end of the drive, planning his day. As he neared the mailbox, maybe thinking of an outstanding check or two, he drove over the trigger to a pipe bomb. The blast, aimed perfectly at his door, killed him immediately, leaving a four-foot-deep hole in the ground. The investigation, such as it was, led to no arrests. No trials were held, just as it was for his wife and child.

Noble and Binion's rivalry began at the end of a legendary era. During Prohibition, there was a righteous frenzy in Ft Worth. Drinking and gambling were outlawed, and Hell's Half Acre, the neighborhood where law enforcement had previously allowed unsavory activities, was cleared out. But those places, that lifestyle, still had to have a place. By the end of World War II, the issue had sorted itself out: gambling in Ft. Worth retreated to a hilltop, and Jacksboro Highway became Thunder Road.

Benny Binion was a ruthless visionary who saw clearly the shift that was happening, what he stood to gain, and which threats could cause him to lose it. But Binion wasn't going to let that happen. He had run gaming in Dallas for years and had expanded into Ft. Worth during the war. He had dozens of hitmen who were a phone call away, and he had earned the nickname "The Cowboy," though not for his horse skills. He drew down on someone "cowboy style," shooting from the hip over a rivalry in booze or gambling, and the name stuck. Binion was never a great gambler himself, but he made millions running games. Dice and cards were the lifeblood of the full-throttle, cut-loose nightlife that had made the area famous throughout the 1920s and '30s. Binion couldn't manage every single game being played in two counties, but if they got big enough, they demanded his attention. The proprietor of such a game had a very simple choice: pay a cut or have the gun pointed at your head go off. The going rate had always been a 25 percent cut to Binion.

Noble had earned his own nickname, "The Cat." He'd had eleven attempts made on his life before that fateful morning in August 1951. By then, Noble knew he was not long for this world, even though he was only forty. He had been drinking heavily of late and taking too many pills. He already looked like an old man. And the bullets, slugs, and buckshot from years of battling with Binion made him walk like one, too.

Noble's games were big, and the 25 percent Binion demanded had been fine. But when Binion increased his demand to 40 percent, Noble saw it as a slap in the face. When he refused, he got a slap back. This set off a back-and-forth of hits and bombs and carnage that lit up both cities. There were gunfights through county roads at high speed, flipped cars, and hideouts in the dark, and "The Cat" lost more men than he could count.

Binion moved on to Las Vegas, but rumor had it that he had a hit out on Noble for years. The price had gone up to $50,000 in response to Noble's audacious, but thwarted, plan to bomb Binion's house from the air using surplus war bombs. When Noble was finally eliminated, things calmed down, and Binion's place in history was cemented. He established a multimillion-dollar hotel in Las Vegas, the Horseshoe, as well as the World Series of Poker, and his empire continues to this day.

Herbert "The Cat" Noble's legacy is all but lost. Two bombs—one that ended his family, and another that killed him—will do that. The hilltop he and Benny Binion helped make into a destination is all but gone now. All that remains atop the hill are a water tower and a motor inn, whose rooms gamblers and outlaws once occupied as they slept in after long nights at the tables.

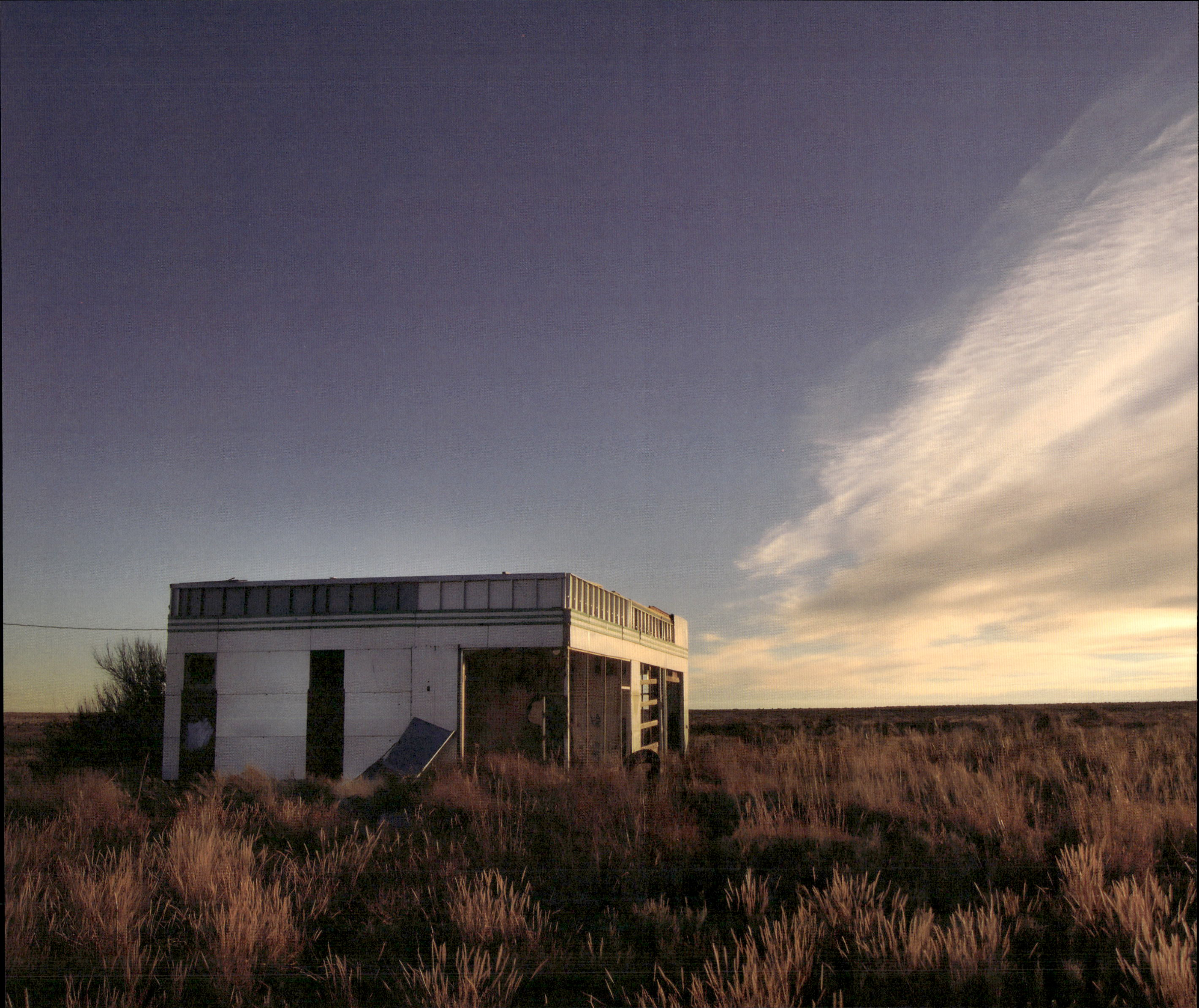

JOHN THE BUS DRIVER (1956)

DUSTIN RICE

Heroes come in many forms. Soldiers, police officers, EMTs, firefighters: all regularly do uncommon things, brave things, acts of service in the name of their fellow human beings. In February 1956, a bus driver proved himself an unlikely hero by doing the impossible.

Abandoned gas station on the north side of I-40 in Glenrio. PHOTO BY DUSTIN RICE

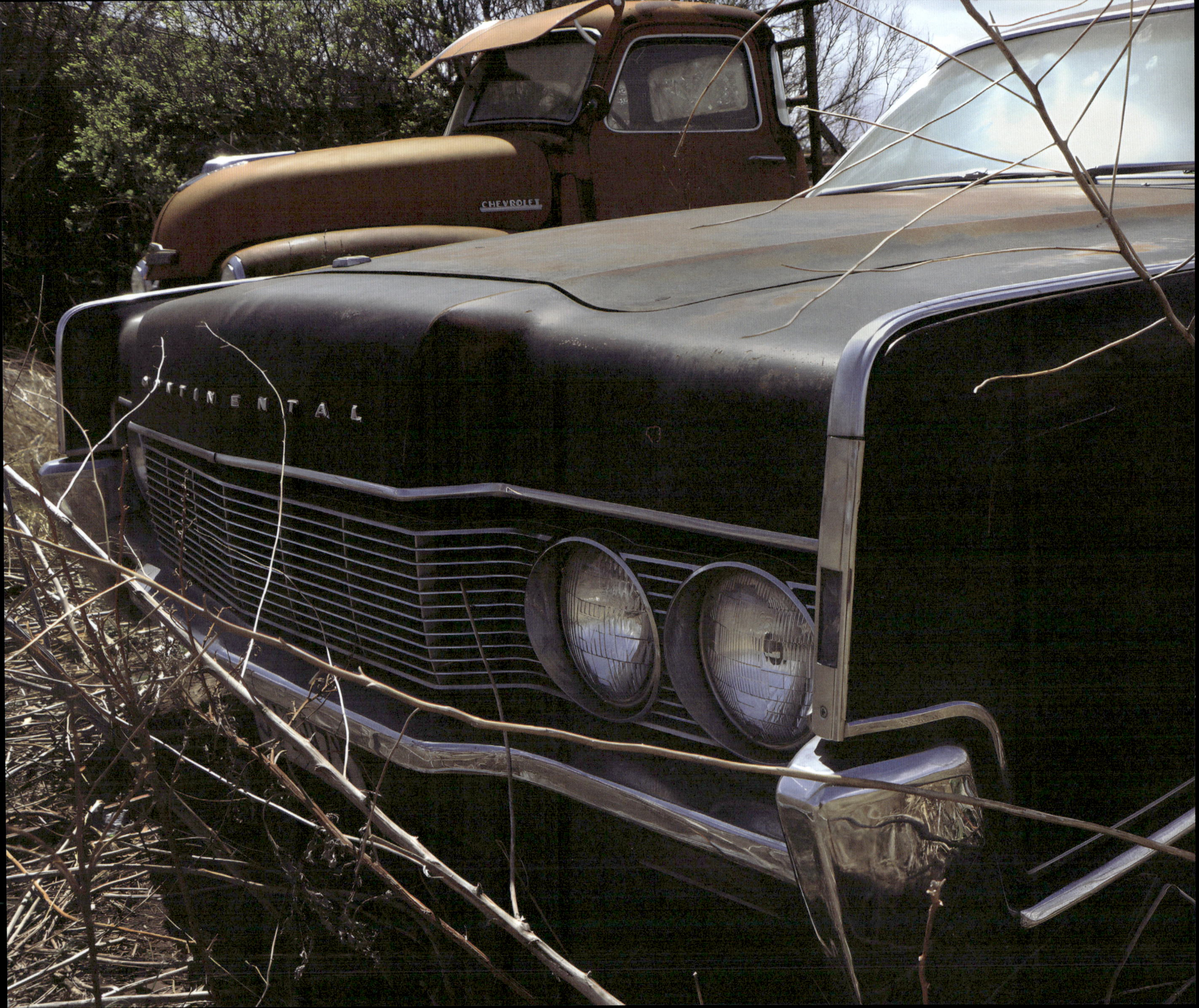
CHEVROLET

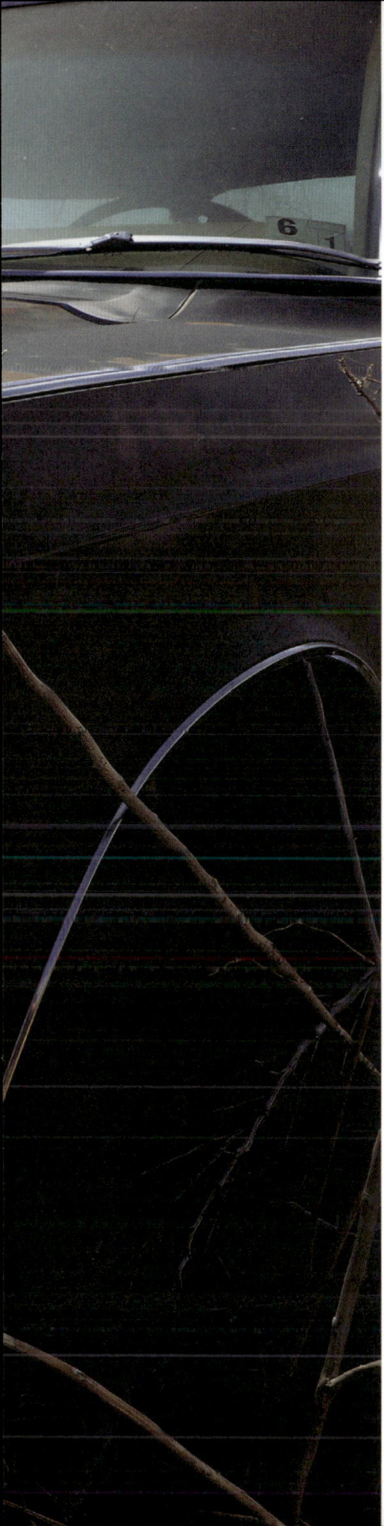

Depending on whom you ask, the number of lives John Hearon saved varies, ranging from fifteen to thirty-five. Probably around twenty-one people were on the Continental Trailways Vista-Liner Bus as it left Amarillo at 5:30 a.m. one morning for Tucumcari, New Mexico. The bus was already two hours behind schedule because of the snow. Snow in the Texas Panhandle is anything but abnormal in February, but no one knew how bad this particular weather event would be. At 9 a.m., the bus plowed headfirst into a chest-deep snowdrift and stayed there. None of the passengers really showed concern as John reassured them that they could just wait for someone to drive by and flag them down for help. The problem was that they were the last vehicle to enter Route 66 from the east before the highway was shut down entirely.

After five hours, John knew something was very wrong. The snow continued to pile up in the worst blizzard any of them had ever witnessed. With only two sandwiches to be found among the entire busload of people and half a tank of diesel to keep the heater going, the clock was ticking. Adrian was the closest town to them, a few miles east as the crow flies, but uphill and into the wind. John knew that the trek would be harder than setting out for Glenrio to the west. He made his mind up: he was walking to Glenrio.

John had to turn back once because of snow blindness, so he fashioned a headband with slits to see through the storm. Using the telephone poles that ran along the now-vanished highway as guides, John walked almost fourteen miles, fighting frostbite and hypothermia. He had fixed his thoughts on the hot coffee at the diner next to Joe Brownlee's service station.

And that's exactly where John collapsed. Outside the café, he whistled with everything he had. It had been nine hours since he left the bus. John told those who came to his rescue where to find the bus, and the diner's owner, with the help of several other men from Glenrio, loaded up his Dodge Power Wagon with blankets and set out. It took him four hours to get to the bus, even with chains on his tires and four-wheel drive. After several trips, all the passengers made it safely to Glenrio; each one owed their life to John.

By the time John got out of the hospital four days later, sixty-one inches of snow had fallen in the triangle formed by Tulia, Vega, and Glenrio. That's five feet in four days, a record that still stands.

Hamlin. PHOTO BY DUSTIN RICE

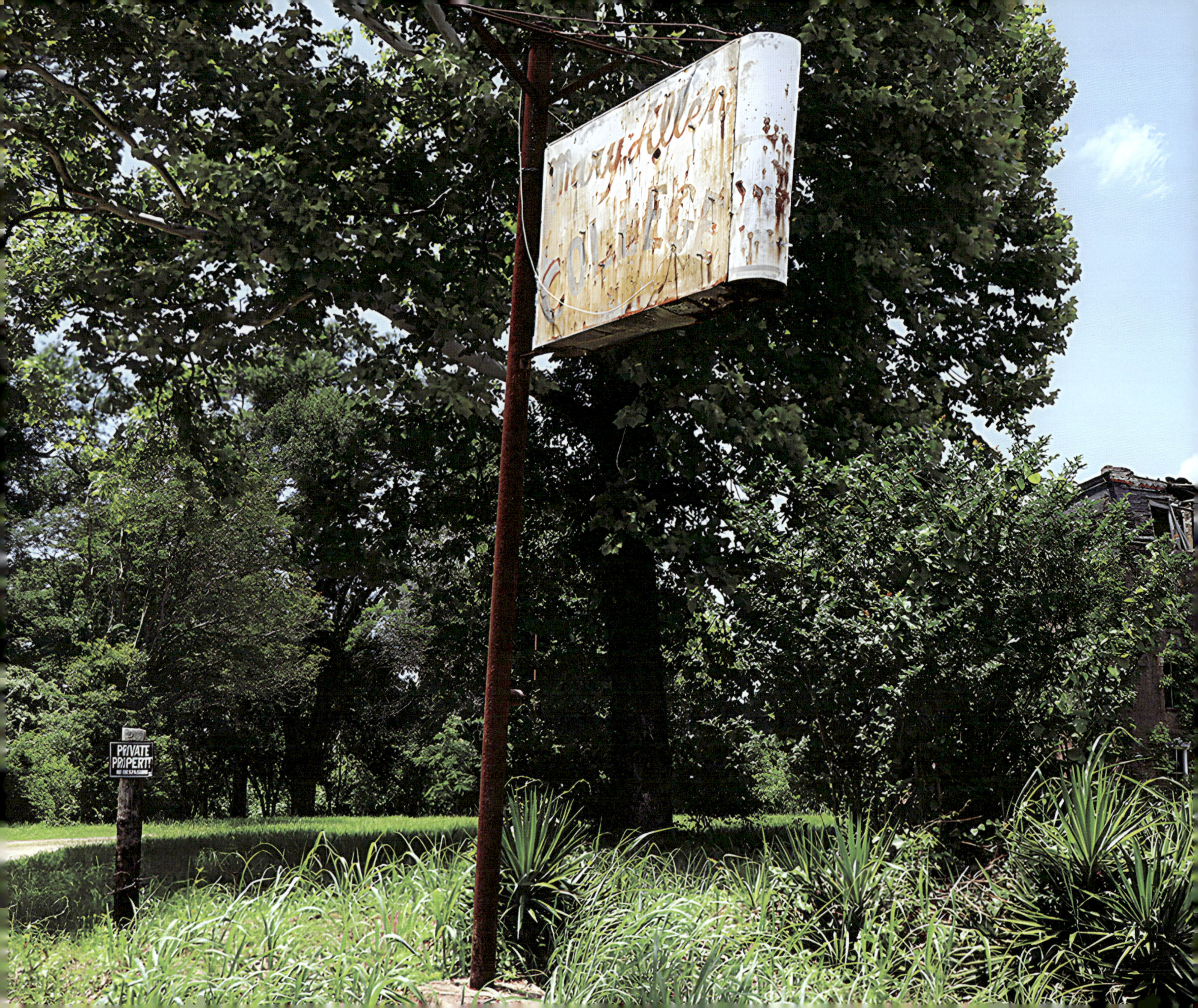
Mary Allen
COLLEGE
PRIVATE

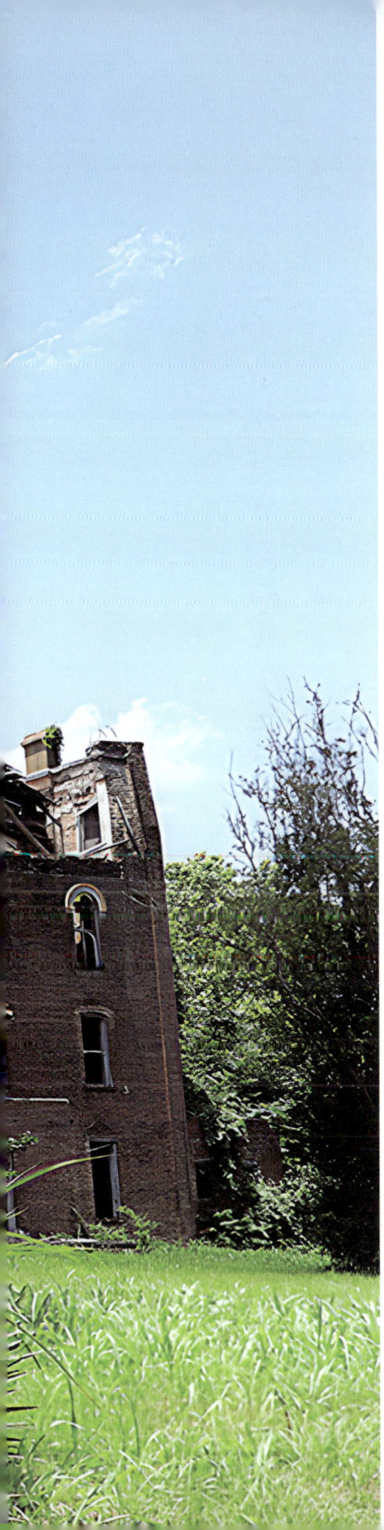

A CHANCE ENCOUNTER (1970)

MORGAN PAGE

Darris Dwayne Page, better known as DD, was born March 24, 1937, in a tiny town inside the Highland Rim region of Tennessee called Bumpus Mills. (Today it has a population of approximately 700 and is about ninety minutes outside of Nashville.) By the time DD was a teenager, he was sure his destiny awaited him in Texas. He left home around 1954 and told his sisters he was going to get a job working in construction on the new highways in Dallas and Houston. He first landed in Dallas, where he met my grandmother, Beatrice Cerda. Fast-forward fifteen years, and they had settled together in Humble, just north of Houston, where my father and three uncles were raised.

Mary Allen Seminary (exterior), the first Black women's college in Texas, est. 1886, Crockett. PHOTO BY DUSTIN RICE

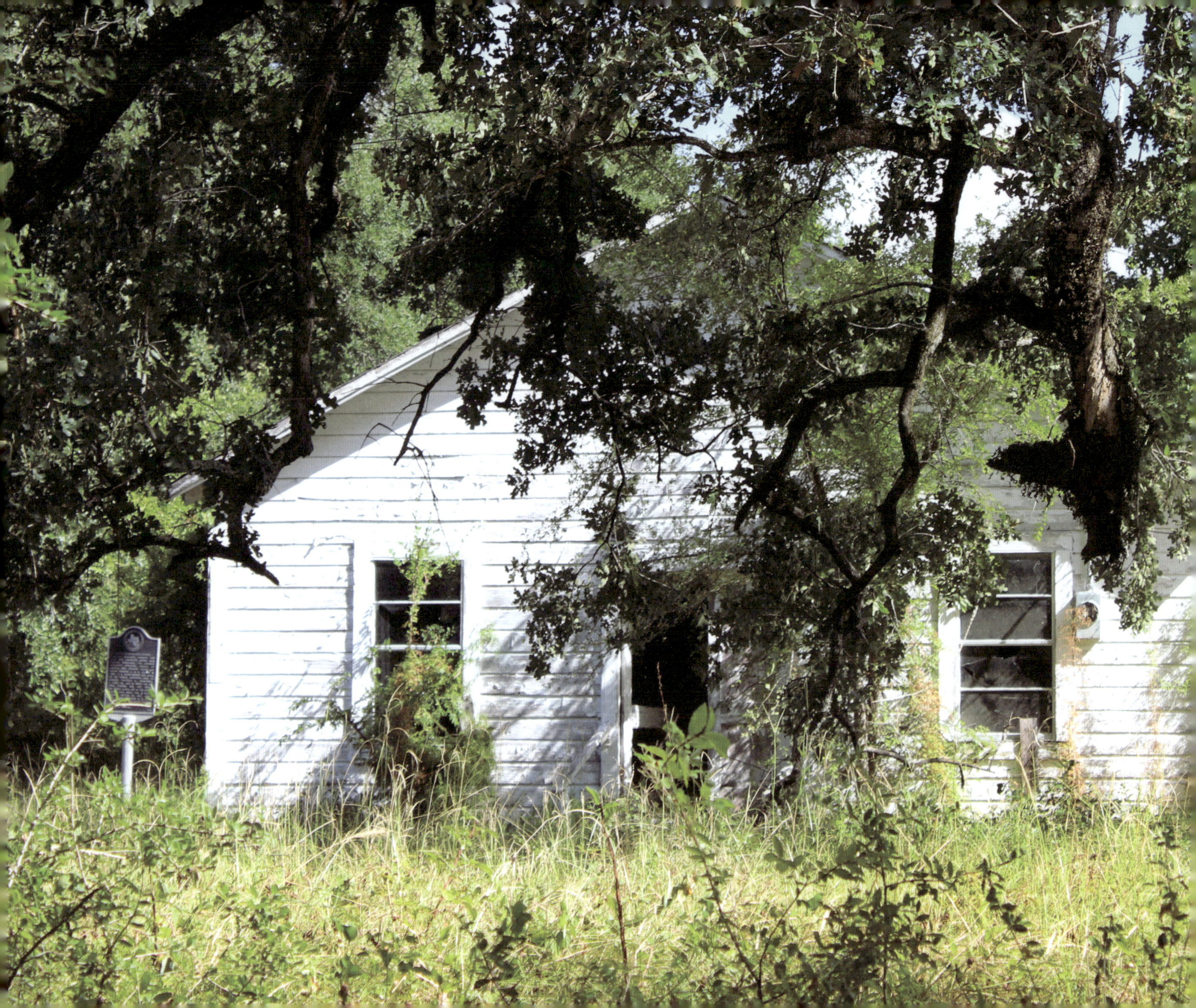

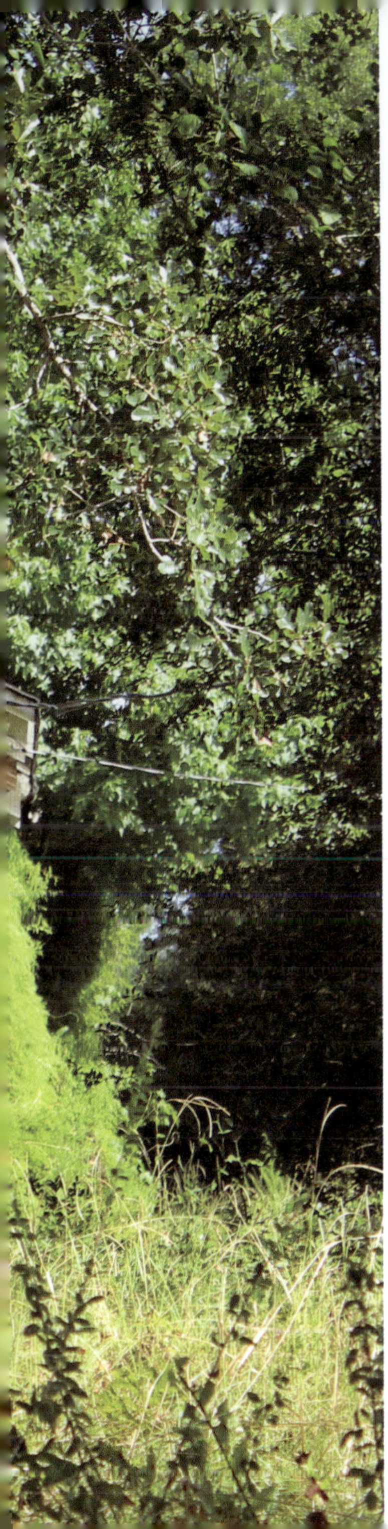

My earliest memory of my grandpa is of me walking through his garden and finding a fat green snake slithering up and down the rows. I ran to him, yelling, "Grandpa, kill the snake!" He scooped me up and walked me back to the garden, where he explained that the snake was our friend, and he was doing us a favor by eating all the bugs that were attacking his vegetables.

My grandpa nicknamed each of us by the time we were six months old. I was Bocephus; others were Little Mama, Butterball, Cricket, Peanut, and Shamu. He was soft-spoken and gentle, and always tried to make his grandchildren laugh, which is why one particular event is etched sharply in my memory.

In the fall, during deer season, my grandpa would come to my parents' house to pick up my dad for hunting trips. On one such occasion, a new neighbor of ours walked over and struck up a conversation with my dad. I don't remember the context of the exchange, but I will never forget my grandpa turning to the neighbor and saying in his quiet but stern voice, "You use the N-word in front of my granddaughter one more time and I won't hesitate to shoot you right between the eyes, boy." I didn't know this for a fact, but perhaps in his youth in Tennessee, he had seen the kind of injustices that can open someone's eyes to the inhumanity of racism. I do know, now, that this day wasn't the first time he had shielded someone from it.

As a driver leaves Lovelady, heading east on FM 1280, they will pass the setting for a community that is now long gone. Its remains—a cemetery, school, and church—are a few miles off the road in a thicket of piney woods. Fodice, Texas, was once a self-sustaining Black community. One of hundreds of communities of its kind, it was home to many successful families with large spreads of land, generations of college graduates, and a history of military service that included a Tuskegee Airman.

Fodice was founded in 1869 by John O'Neil, a formerly enslaved man who made his way to Texas from Georgia. O'Neil married into one of the many Black families in the surrounding area, and as these families grew in number, they acquired significant stretches of land on the map. By the time the second generation matured into a third, their success was undeniable. Fodice residents served their country proudly in noncombat roles during World War I. Following the war, several of the men who returned went to college, received degrees, and came home to prosper.

Colored Methodist Episcopal Church in the Fodice Community of Lovelady, est. 1885 after T. H. Nelms deeded two acres of his former plantation land to church trustees S. Quantrell, J. Oneil Sr., and A. Berry. The Rev. Peter Steward was the first pastor. PHOTO BY MORGAN PAGE

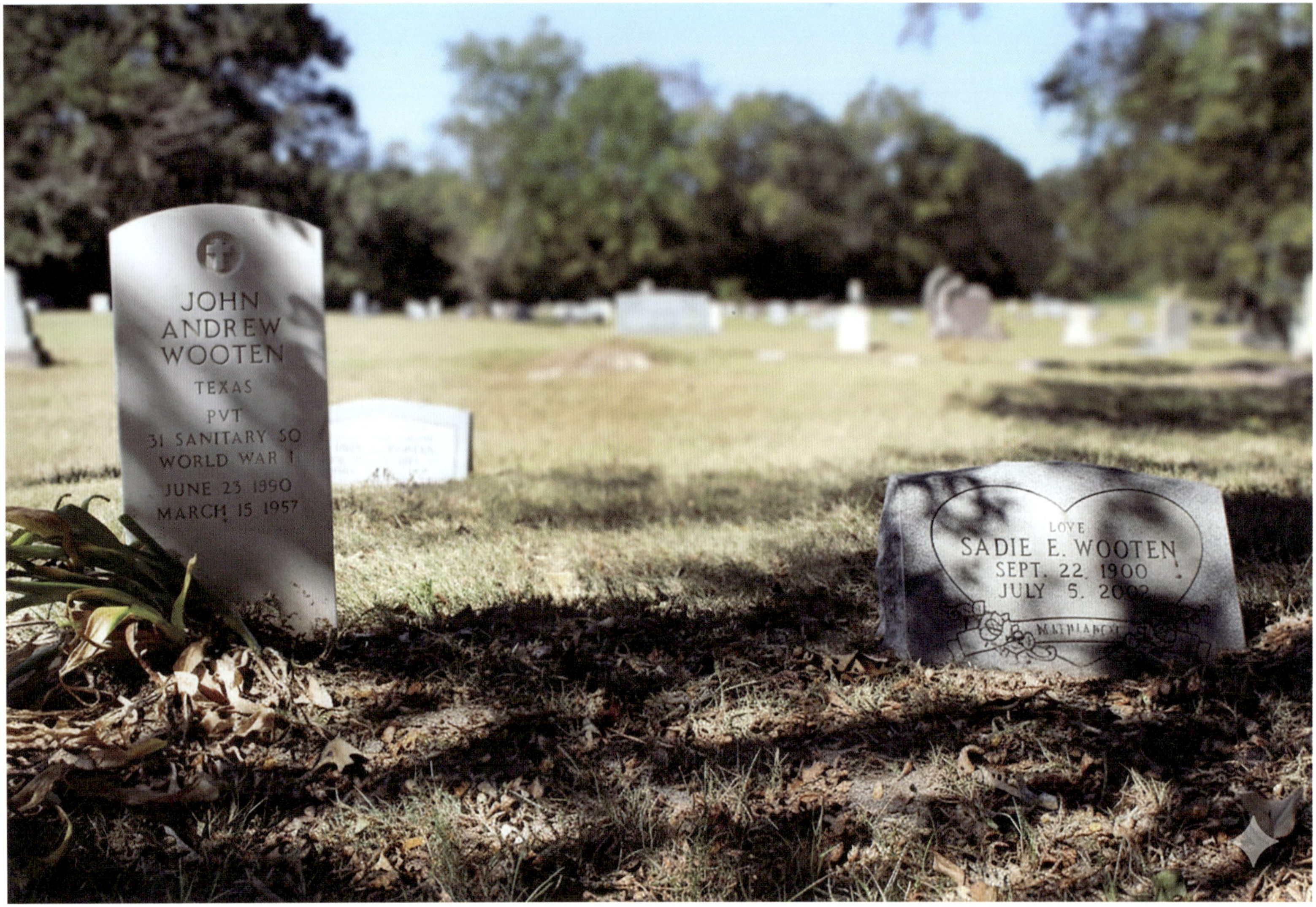

Resting place of John and Sadie Wooten in Lovelady. PHOTO BY MORGAN PAGE

John Wooten was a private in sanitation who returned home and immediately enrolled at Prairie View College. Upon graduating, he married Sadie Berry, and the couple set about making their own place in the world. By the time John passed away in 1957, they had over a thousand acres. John and Sadie's nephew, Howard, became a staff sergeant in the Army artillery, and then in 1944 started training as a pilot with the famed Tuskegee Airmen. Though he did not see combat, he was among the best pilots in his class. After his service, he moved northwest to escape the Jim Crow South, but died at twenty-eight in a fall while working on a bridge. Years later, his picture was selected from the many who served to become the face of the Tuskegee Airmen Foundation in advertising and remembrances.

Despite their prosperity and generations of national service, the Wootens knew that even in 1970—when Sadie Wooten's car slid into a ditch coming home from Crockett, the town where residents of Fodice went to shop—violent racism remained prevalent in East Texas. She hoped a friendly face would arrive before an unkind one. When DD Page, my grandpa, pulled over, she thought she was in trouble. Instead, he drove her home. Then he went back for her car, never asking for anything in return. His kindness struck Ms. Sadie. She welcomed him back to her home whenever he wanted to come. He took her up on the invitation and, over time, they became close friends. He brought her vegetables from his garden and checked on her when he came to hunt on the lease she asked him to manage. She allowed his family to hunt on the property for free. Sadie's grandchildren spent many fall nights with DD's children: generations of friendship resulting from one chance meeting.

Many years later, in 1992, DD was diagnosed with stomach cancer and passed away within six months. It was my first experience with death; I had just turned eleven years old. I don't remember much of that time, but I have one memory of the gathering at my grandparents' house following the funeral. I hadn't cried yet, but while wandering around their house, the sadness hit me and I erupted in tears. Ms. Sadie was sitting on the couch in their living room, and she told me, "Come here, Morgan, sit on my lap." She rocked me back and forth and whispered in my ear, "Your grandpa will always be with you. Don't you worry about that. I miss him too, but I know he's around us and he still loves us." She let me cry in her arms for a few minutes, and then she hugged me very tightly. It was the greatest comfort I got from anyone that day.

Born in 1900, Ms. Sadie undoubtedly witnessed hatred, but she was full of love. She would spoil me with a table full of sweets, all homemade, every time we visited. She would spoil me with attention, too. I believe my grandpa also saw his share of racial hatred. Whatever their previous entanglements with prejudice may have been, DD and Sadie's friendship was an inspiration for their families. As a result of a chance encounter, the Page family and the Wooten family are friends to this day. Ms. Sadie died at the age of 101. She is still dearly missed.

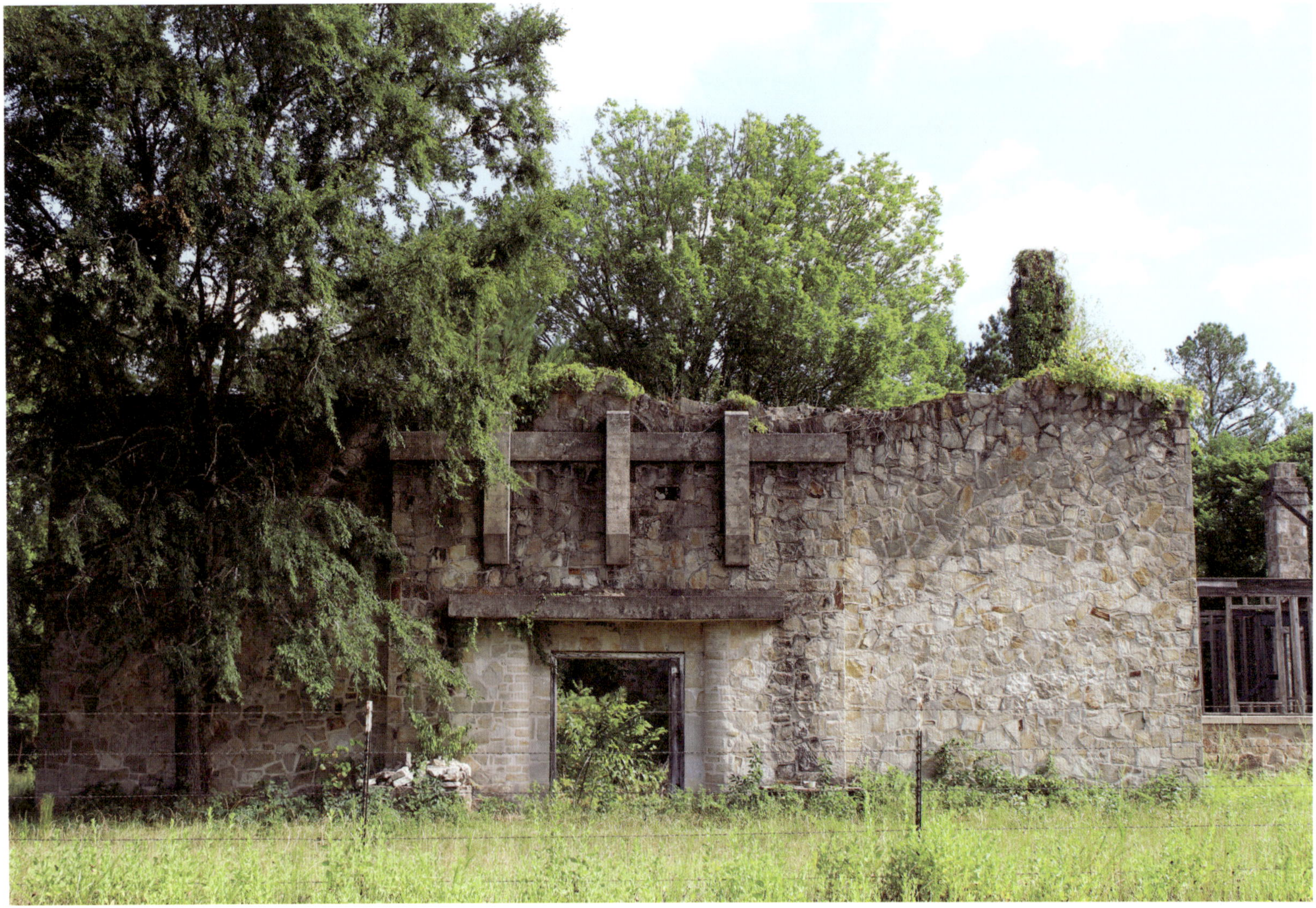

Original construction for the Fodice Community School, Lovelady, began in the 1880s. It is currently abandoned but there have been recent efforts to restore it.
PHOTO BY MORGAN PAGE

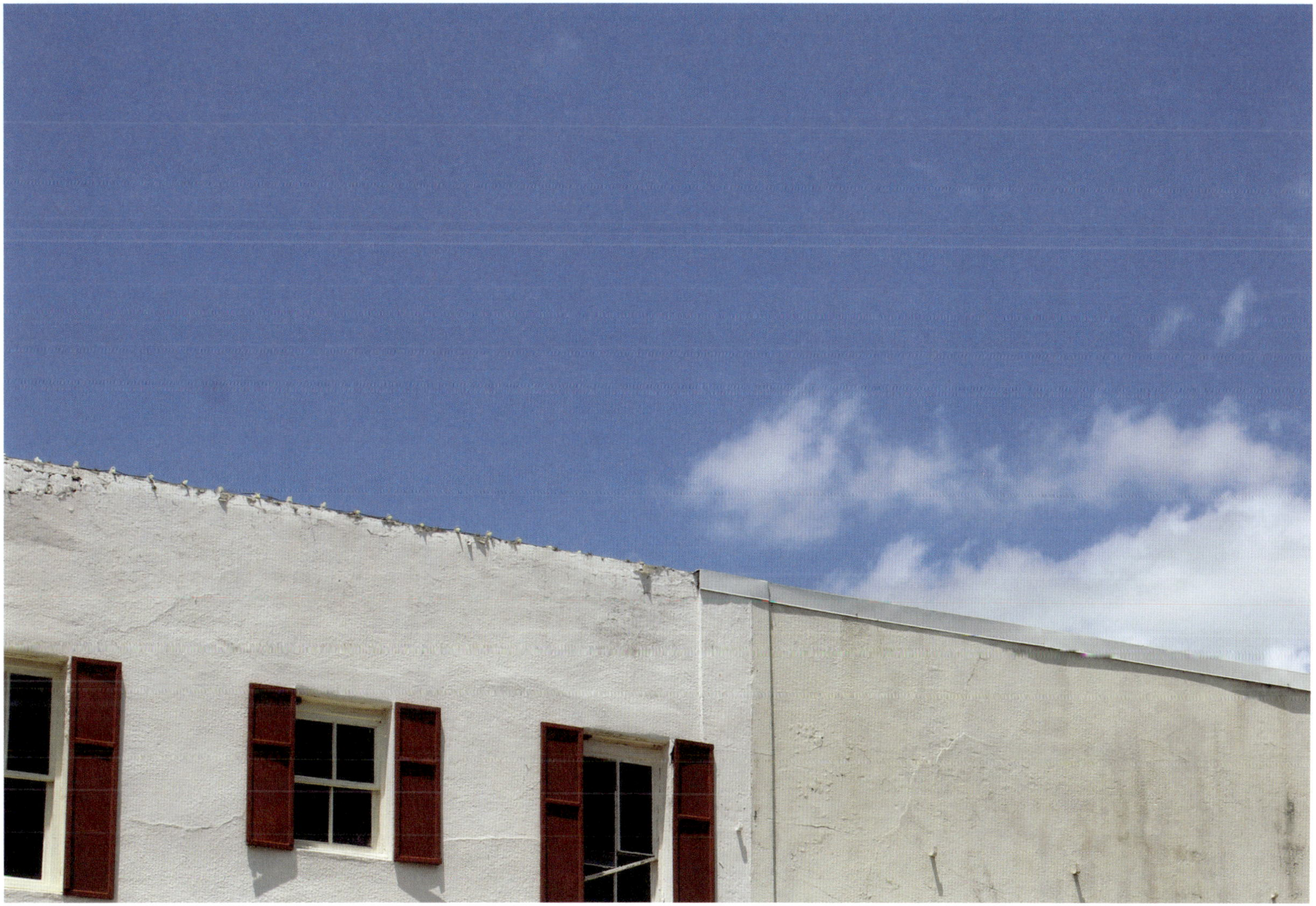

Rusk. PHOTO BY MORGAN PAGE

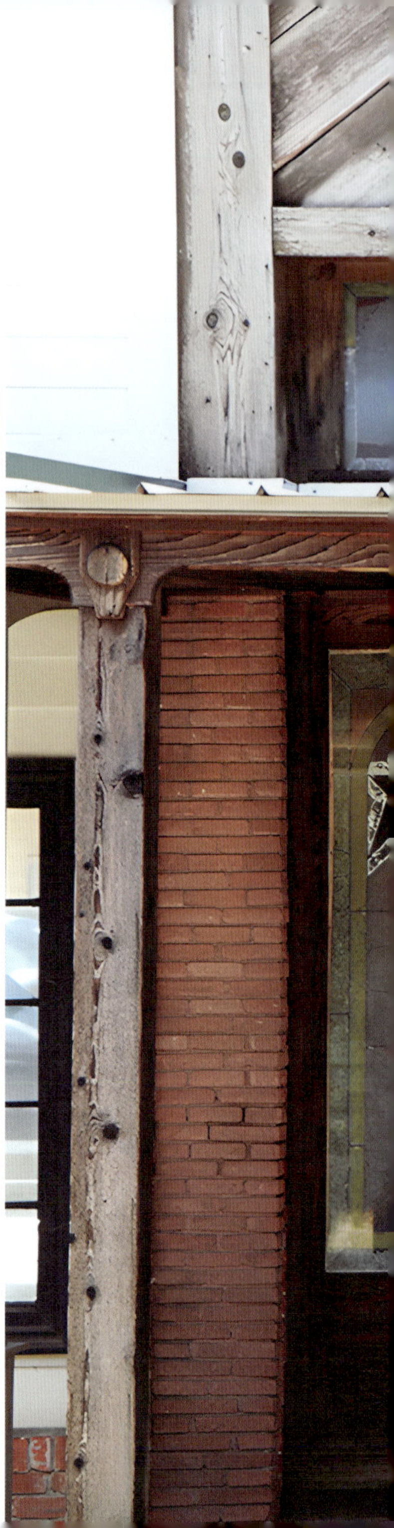

Crockett. PHOTO BY DUSTIN RICE

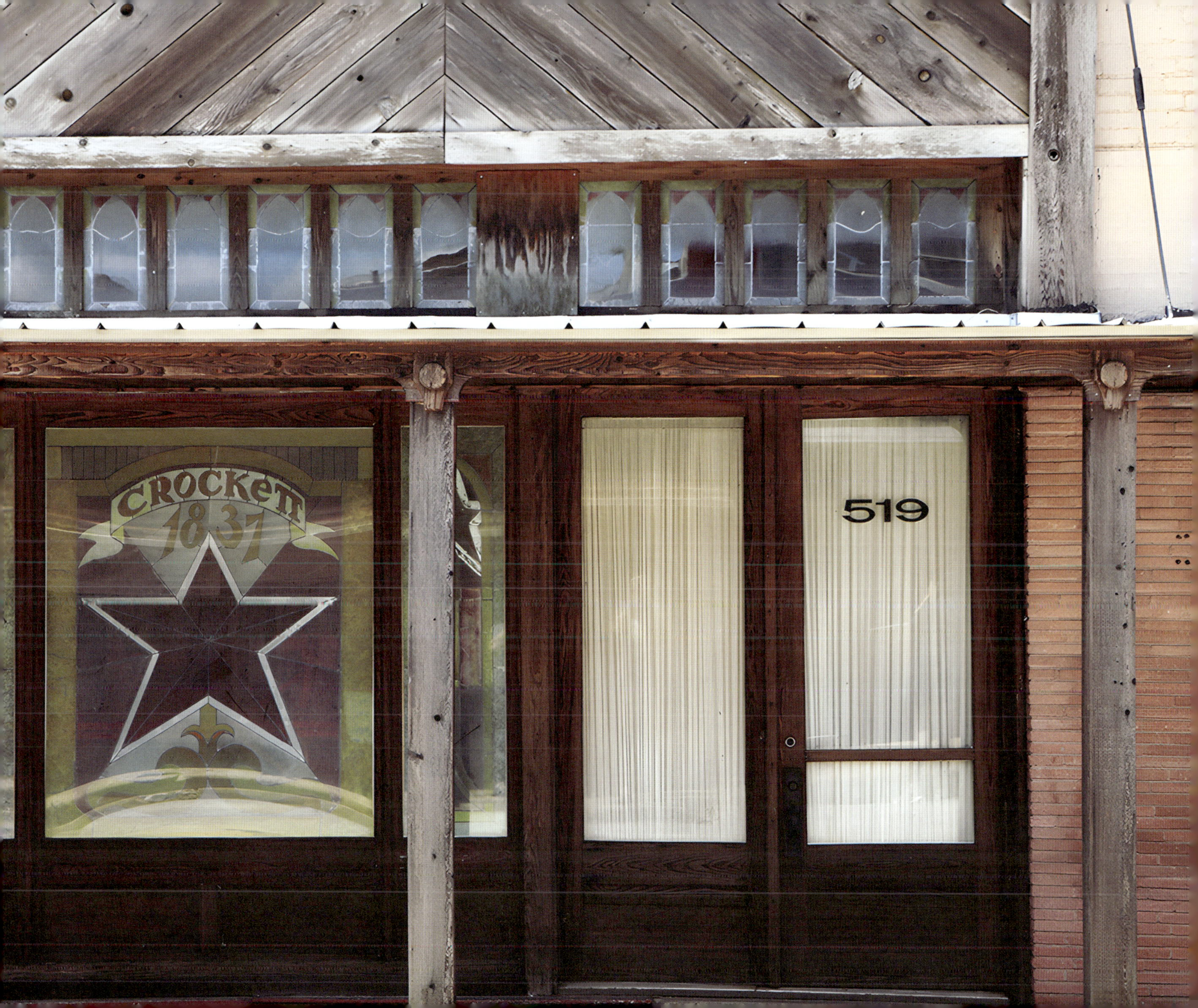
CROCKETT
1837
519

ACKNOWLEDGMENTS

We would like to thank:

Our parents and all of our family, friends, and coworkers who have been supportive of this project and book.

The Dallas Public Library.

The Museum of North Texas, especially former curator Madeleine Calcote-Garcia and her staff.

Former curator Wendy Wright of the River Valley Pioneer Museum, as well as the town of Canadian.

The Red River Valley Museum and curator Sherry Yoakum, as well as Cooper Alexander and their board members.

The Dallas Center for Photography.

Ellen Noël Art Museum.

Sam Houston Memorial Museum.

Fort Bend Museum.

The Houston Public Library.

Texas Parks and Wildlife.

Texas Department of Transportation.

The West Texas Historical Society.

Dr. Holle Humphries, Comanche scholar.

Lance Tahmahkera, great-great-grandson of Quanah Parker, for being open with us about his family and tribal history, for being willing to help us whenever we asked, and for allowing us to tell a small part of a much larger story.

Cheryl Lewis of Hamlin, Texas.

Oliver "Obbie" Loving IV of Loving, Texas.

Midwestern State University in Wichita Falls, Texas.

Texas Monthly.

Texas Highways.

Laura Rice of the Texas Standard.

Melissa Beck of KCCU.

Chris Samples of KXDJ.

Hasan Elahi and Anderson Wrangle, for their mentorship.

Casey Kittrell, editor in chief, University of Texas Press.

FOR FURTHER READING

We often started our research at Texas Escapes, a detailed online database for information on traveling the state, which has entries for counties, many small towns, and even uninhabited communities from the past. We also spent time at Traces of Texas, a historically-minded forum for sharing photos about local stories across Texas. What follows are specific sources for individual essays. If no source is listed, the information came from general knowledge and our own experiences.

Sources for Specific Stories

Introduction

Goldberg, Vicki. *Light Matters*. Aperture, 2005.

The Mounds (Precivilization)

Interviews with Quanah Parker's great-great-grandson Lance Tahmahkera and Medicine Mounds caretaker Joshua Smith by Dustin Rice, August 1, 2022, to January 1, 2024.

The First Sheriff of Bandera County (1860)

Hunter, J. Marvin. Essay. In *Pioneer History of Bandera County: Seventy-Five Years of Intrepid History*, 246–266. Bandera, TX: Hunters Printing House, 1922.

The Spark (Post–Civil War to World War II)

Holley, Joe. "Fort McKavett, Menard County, Texas, 1936." *Houston Chronicle*, August 9, 2019, sec. Native Texan.

Double Jimmy (1860s)

Gibson, Barclay. "Gooseneck, Texas." Gooseneck, Texas, Young County ghost town, and Gooseneck Cemetery, May 1, 2017. https://www.texasescapes.com/TexasGhostTowns/Gooseneck-Texas.htm#google_vignette.

"Obituaries: Young County." *Weatherford Times: Young County*, December 31, 1878.

Mother of the Panhandle (1870s)

Bok, Edward William, ed. "The Picturesque Home of the Goodnight Herd of Buffaloes." *Ladies' Home Journal*, 1901, 101.

McComb, David. "Texas, a Modern History." University of Texas Press, 1989.

"Goodnight Ranch History." Goodnight Ranch History | Texas Historical Commission, May 29, 2008. https://thc.texas.gov/state-historic-sites/goodnight-ranch/goodnight-ranch-history.

Queen of the Flats (1874)

Eckhardt, Charley F. *Tales of Badmen, Bad Women, and Bad Places: Four Centuries of Texas Outlawry*. Lubbock, TX: Texas Tech University Press, 1999.

Goldthwaite, Carmen. *Texas Dames: Sassy and Savvy Women Throughout Lone Star History*. Charleston, SC: The History Press, 2012.
Melzer, Richard. *Buried Treasures: Famous and Unusual Gravesites in New Mexico History*. Santa Fe, NM: Sunstone Press, 2007.
Rose, Cynthia. *Lottie Deno: Gambling Queen of Hearts*. Santa Fe, NM: Clear Light Publishers, 1994.

Bad Hand at Dead Horse (1874)

Interviews with Comanche Elder Carney Saupitty, Dr. Hollie Humphries, and Lance Tahmahkera by Dustin Rice, August 1, 2022, to September 1, 2023.

Field of Glass (1876)

Carlson, Paul. "Caprock Chronicles: Bison Hunters Worked South Plains in 1870s." *Lubbock Avalanche Journal*, September 22, 2017.
Interview with Cheryl Lewis, local Hamlin historian and owner of the Book Nook in Hamlin, by Dustin Rice, January 1, 2023.

Legends and Mythos (1872)

Horton, Thomas F. *History of Jack County*. Jacksboro, TX: Gazette Print, 1933.
Interview with Oliver Loving IV, great-great-grandson of Oliver Loving Sr., March 28, 2022.

Juice and Apple (1886)

Genealogy Trails History. "Oldham County, Texas Boot Hill Cemetery." Boot Hill Cemetery of Oldham County, Texas. Accessed February 1, 2019. https://genealogytrails.com/tex/panhandle/oldham/cem_boothill.html.
"List of the Dead." *Houston Post*, September 11, 1900.
Robertson, R. L. *Panhandle Pilgrimage: Illustrated Tales Tracing History in the Texas Panhandle*. Amarillo, TX: Paramount Publishing Company, 1978.
"Story of Old Tascosa, Once Famous Panhandle Cowtown." *Dallas Morning News*, April 11, 1942.

Good Intentions (1899)

"The Fate of Galveston." *Houston Post*, September 10, 1900.
Hegarty, Mary Loyola. *Serving with Gladness: The Origin and History of the Congregation of the Sisters of Charity of the Incarnate Word, Houston, Texas*. Milwaukee: Bruce Publishing Company, 1967.
Rhor, Monica. "Great Storm of 1900 Brought Winds of Change." *Houston Chronicle*, May 19, 2016.

Grace from Amarillo (1907)

Interview with Collingsworth County Museum staff about the Dust Bowl, March 1, 2022.
Interview with Russell Rice about Callie Grace, July 1, 2022.

Devil in the Mine (Early twentieth century)

Blumenthal, Ralph. "Quicksilver Memories of Hard Times in Texas." *New York Times*, October 29, 2007.
Ragsdale, Kenneth Baxter, and Joe B. Frantz. *Quicksilver: Terlingua and the Chisos Mining Company*. Texas A&M University Press, 2008.

The Express Manager (1912)

"Express Messenger Balks Train Robbers." *The Daily Herald*. March 13, 1912, 13 edition, sec. 51.

The Dark Halls of the T&P (1920s)

Grant, Chris. "Aldridge Sawmill." *East Texas History*. boarhttps://easttexashistory.org/items/show/83, accessed September 23, 2025.

Moyer, Lauren. "What the Heck Is This Creepy Abandoned Building in Marshall, Texas?" KNUE, May 6, 2021. https://knue.com/creepy-abandoned-building-in-marshall-texas.

The Road Between Mankins and Dundee (1925)

"Details—the D. S. Dudley Show—Atlas Number 5009005319—Atlas: Texas Historical Commission." Texas Historic Sites Atlas. https://atlas.thc.texas.gov/Details/5009005319, accessed September 1, 2019.

Gillette, Shannon. "The D. S. Dudley Show of Mankins." North Texas Farm and Ranch, August 14, 2017. https://ntfronline.com/2017/09/the-d-s-dudley-show-of-mankins.

"Historical Marker Dedication Sunday." *Archer County News*, October 24, 1974.

Booger Town (1926)

Pirtle, Caleb, and J. Ron Hardin. *Borger: Last Dance at Sundown: The True Story of the Wickedest Town in Texas*. Independently published, 2022.

Texas State Historical Association. "The Tragic Death of Asa Borger: A Historical Overview," January 5, 2022. https://www.tshaonline.org/handbook/entries/borger-asa-phillip.

The Little Zoo up the Hill (1927)

"Cisco Boys Capture Escaped Bear with Forked Stick; Returned to Zoo." *The Abilene Reporter*, December 5, 1928.

"Cisco Zoo Moved to Fort Worth." *The Abilene Reporter*, June 13, 1938.

McKinney, Noah. "Cisco Zoo Ruins to Be Converted into Hiking Trails | KTAB—Bigcountryhomepage.com." Big Country, June 11, 2021. https://www.bigcountryhomepage.com/news/cisco-zoo-ruins-to-be-converted-into-hiking-trails.

The Thorne in the Side of Texas (1930s)

Drummond, Dana Schuler. "Machine Gun Kelly on Camera: The First and Last Federal Criminal Trials on Film," 2005.

Interview with Kathryn Elaine Horn and her granddaughter, Dana Schuler Drummond, by Morgan Page, January 26, 2024.

Octavio Medellin (1930s)

Castro, Mark A. *Octavio Medellín: Spirit and Form*. Dallas: Dallas Museum of Art, 2022.

Interview with Octavio Medellin and his grandson, Brett Medellin, by Morgan Page, December 2023.

Darn Fools (1933)

Pritchard, Jack. Letter to Collingsworth County Museum. Wellington, TX: Collingsworth County Museum, 2011.

Guests for the Evening (1934)

"Donkey Basketball Game Is at Perico Tonight." *The Dalhart Texan*, February 19, 1947.

An Angry Sky (1947)

"Death Toll Reaches 53; Reconstruction Begins." *The Canadian Record*, April 17, 1947.

McCurdy, Otto W. "Glazier and Higgins Tornado of 1947." Texas Escapes, May 14, 2007. https://www.texasescapes.com/TexasGhostTowns/Glazier-Texas.htm.

The Sit-In (1949)

Interviews with her Great-Aunt Esther and cousin Veronica Lynne by Morgan Page, 2015 to 2024.

Thunder Road (1951)

"TEXAS: The Last Days of The Cat." *Time*, August 20, 1951.

John the Bus Driver (1956)

Haile, Bartee. "Bartee Haile: Record Blizzard Buries Panhandle and South Plains." *The Courier of Montgomery County*, February 1, 2023. https://www.yourconroenews.com/neighborhood/moco/opinion/article/bartee-haile-record-blizzard-buries-panhandle-17756581.php.

Maca, Kathleen. "A Hero On Route 66." Kathleen Maca: Tales From Texas, July 25, 2019. http://kathleenmaca.com/index.php/2019/07/25/a-hero-on-route-66.

A Chance Encounter (1970)

Holley, Mary Austin. "Austin Papers: Series II, Part II, 1818–1847." Portal to Texas History, n.d. https://texashistory.unt.edu/ark:/67531/metapth216301.

Interviews with her father about her grandfather by Morgan Page, 2001 to 2024.

Texas State Publications. *Bar A Ranch*, Vol. 20. Texas Department of Agriculture, 2005.

Wooten, Andre. "Howard A. Wooten (1920–1948)." Black Past, July 26, 2013. https://blackpast.org/african american history/wooten-howard-1920-1948.